Exu
and the Quimbanda of Night and Fire

NICHOLAJ DE MATTOS FRISVOLD

and the Quimbanda
of Night and Fire

SCARLET IMPRINT · MMXII

Published by Scarlet Imprint
© Nicholaj de Mattos Frisvold, 2012
Edited by Peter Grey & Troy Chambers
Design & *pontos riscados* by Alkistis Dimech
Illustrations of Exu by Enoque Zedro

ISBN 978-0-9574492-0-6

All rights reserved: no part of this book may be reproduced in any form, by print, or any other means, without prior permission being obtained from the publisher.

SCARLETIMPRINT.COM

CONTENTS

Benediction · Malediction · ix
Preface · xi

I *Black Sun Rising · 1*
II *The King of the City of Dust · 28*
III *Wardens at the Gates of Night · 42*
IV *The Fig of Fire · 68*
V *The Shadows at the Graveyard · 86*
VI *Nocturnal Mercury · 103*
VII *The Legions of Hell · 129*

Despacho · 325
Glossary · 327
Bibliography · 331
Index of Exus · 333

Illustrations

I   *Exu Meia Noite* · 7
II *Exu Morcego* · 13
III *Exu Lucifer* · 49
IV *Assentamento* · 111
V   *Maioral* · 137
VI *Exu Tranca Ruas* · 166
VII *Exu Veludo* · 182
VIII *Exu Caveira* · 249
IX *Exu Capa Preta* · 259
X   *Exu Asa Negra* · 266

DISCLAIMER

This book contains herbal formulæ of spellcraft that must be viewed as being of interest only for the anthropologist, ethnobotanist and researchers in general. Neither the author nor the publisher endorse the use of these herbal substances in any way, juvenile or cunning as they may be. We refrain from taking any responsibility placed upon us by anyone who has, in a learned or immature way, attempted to apply potentially poisonous and dangerous formulæ in their life upon reading this book. As such, those parts of the book should be viewed as curiosities of the cult.

Benediction · Malediction

EXU AND THE QUIMBANDA OF NIGHT AND FIRE is dedicated to true men of honour and dignity, to those Saints and savages walking amongst us even today, bearing the light of ascent whilst burning with the fire of Seven Hells. This book is a gospel of Saturn set aflame in the hearts of men, be they blazing in the blood of Asclepius, Dionysus, Vulcan or Hephaestus. This book I give forth to the King, the Queen, their Court and their Ruler. This testament I give to the world in the hope it will serve the world well and in this I give praise to my Elders, be they Ogboni, Imule, Bizango or Sanpwel and give praise to my support and nourishment in this our world of Mystery, Iya Osunkole Eyebonmi Adetutu Iyamisse.

By the virtue and grace of Exu Mor, his prophet and the dragon at his root, I will give grace and honour to fine exemplars of the male strain, be they living, dead, immortal or un-dead, men who are divine and brutal in their honesty. May you realise that you are blessed and allow the blessed station of your being to radiate upon the worlds. Now and forever more.

I wish to heap disgrace by the virtue of all crossroads of night on those men who are overly aggressive, consumed by egotism, cowards and those overcome by hubris, who are covetous, rude and generally blind to what lies outside their world as they are filled with erroneous justice, ill will and hatred in their self-loathing world of enmity – you know who you are – may you also be blessed in your ignorance as I offer up the prayer that the Mothers will embrace you – completely. Now and forever more.

As always gratitude and love is due to Peter Grey and Alkistis Dimech, beautiful exemplars of human dignity, may you two walk from strength to strength, from abundance to abundance. Now and forever more.

Preface

THERE IS MUCH TO BE SAID about Quimbanda; in this book I will reveal as much as I am permitted to, and, in doing so, border upon the forbidden. I do this because this tome is my testament to Quimbanda and is also revelatory of the measure which spirit has allowed. It is my firm belief that a tradition is only living when it paves the way for a genuine connection with source and spirit. This connection should be so strong and so vivid that the tradition tears itself away from the book and the connection with spirit opens up the truthful and ever living Book of Nature to the pilgrim. When someone insists on a particular expression of Quimbanda being more *true* or *real* or *genuine* than any other, the test rests in the connection made with spirit.

This book is my stone in the shoes of many. It is the sweet scent of herbs opening the gates to all quarters of the world. This book is given to you as the vapours of truth, breath, falsity and deception, and in this whips your attention to see the truth as it stretches as a nail from the Pole to Hell. So, I state clearly that this is my vision, but I also claim to have been provoked by spirit in the birth of this text and hence I am simply the scribe of the legions of Quimbanda. They express the powers of the left hand side, what is pale in its darkening and what is both bone and decay.

Over the years, both as scholar and practitioner, I have been presented with many differences in opinion concerning Quimbanda and its origin and content. There is such a great variety that at some point you need to accept the variety as its nerve and fire; as its truth. Over the years I have come to see Quimbanda as nests and clusters of serpents, dragons and scorpions all of them spawned by the fire of passion and the sulphuric earth of memory and temporal life. I have come to accept the varieties of the cult as symptomatic of its dynamic, copulative inner essence. It is as if Quimbanda replicates the apocryphal legend of Lilith's banishment to the Red Sea where she daily spawned hundreds of offspring.

Being confronted with the various approaches to understanding Quimbanda I accepted its richness. I dare say that the cult and tradition has been passed on in riddles and fragments amongst genuine mediums and the most sadistic of sorcerers, as much amongst liars and pretenders as those few holding the torch of Phanes in the world.

I have been fortunate. I met several Quimbandeiros and Quimbandeiras and was inducted into the cult of Quimbanda in several forms or modalities, ranging from the way it is practiced in a family tradition in Umbanda as well as in Candomblé. From my experience of the various ways of Quimbanda I find a great degree of discrepancy, and in this discrepancy an even greater union, because we are speaking of death, memory and spiritual richness when we speak of Quimbanda. We find legacy along both axes on the cross, and I have ceased to search for a genuine and original Quimbanda because the original Quimbanda is where a true and effective connection with spirit is established; flesh and spirit turns into a crossroad of fire, balancing the pylon against heaven. So in this book about Exu I will, as I did with the mysteries of Pomba Gira, give my rendering of these marvellous debts of death in honour of the kings and generals in the Seven Kingdoms of Exu.

There is a tendency to emphasise a particular origin for Quimbanda, in particular the African, by locating it in Angola. It is important to track down our ancestry, because it sheds light and understanding on who we are and sometimes answers the questions about why we are that way. In this way it is no different from any cultural legacy. The origins lie there as memory, as tracks on the map, as wisdom. However, a new culture is different from the culture it sprang from, just as a child grows apart from its parents. It has a past and a future. As such, Quimbanda was born out of the native, African and European paths that crossed in Brazil. As Exu and Pomba Gira venture out in the world they need to get used to new habitats, and we find a mutation and adaptation taking place. There is a lot of resistance towards this process of adaption, but all terreiros state that we are born with an Exu and Pomba Gira which walks with us in life, whether we are aware of this or not. The key lies in providing an unfaltering link between man and spirit so a truthful legacy can be passed on, because the legacy of Quimbanda rests in man's nocturnal history and the trials of passion, in the laughter as much as the tears. Quimbanda is a cult that plays itself out on a canvas of human skin still dripping with the blood of memories. It is because these spirits are the most helpful of allies, because of the memory they understand, and because of the same memory and understanding we can turn this mirror upon ourselves and become wise. That is, if we dare. The way towards wisdom suggested by Exu is one of hellfire and brimstone, one of ruthless honesty and bravery, where the most vicious of all enemies is your self.

I have in this book, as in the other titles, taken as my measure and source the material published about Quimbanda and black magic between 1940 and 1970 because I feel it is here we find the cult known as Quimbanda in its most vibrant elegant and beautiful expression. Here we find the cult of the streets, mediums of merit and an insistence that a hustler and a prostitute can have as much dignity and saintliness as any nobleman, bishop or sage. Adopting these avenues of Quimbanda also enables a rich depiction of Exu where he can be understood from within Christian mythologies, alchemy and astrology as much as historically and culturally. It is my intention to give this, my complete understanding of Exu and his grammar, in this book.

With this focus in mind I will return to the knowledge and counsel of masters like N. A. Molina, Aluizio Fontenelle and Antonio Alves side by side with the wisdom and experience of Tatás and Yayas I have met over the last decade. This is naturally mediated through my own experiences and understandings of this enigmatic spirit of masculinity and volcanic conquest.

So, with this I give this book, this testament and grammar as a gift to the seven legions. May it be received well in all courts by all Kings and Queens and all spirits, baptised and pagan, who guard the ever-burning Fig Tree in Hell.

Sarava!
Tatá Sigatana
Cabula Mavambo Ngobodi Nzila

*Now from the sixth hour there was darkness
over all the land unto the ninth hour.*

The Gospel of Matthew 27: 45
& The Harrowing of Hell: 11

I

Black Sun Rising

QUIMBANDA is a cult of earth and fire, a nigromantic cult where death walks the worlds as our friend, ally, or as our nemesis. Quimbanda is a mirror world of our shadows, where we constantly contemplate our own abyss. It is a cult where the legions of Mars play themselves out in the fields of Saturn, manic and intoxicated by the figs of fire and the sulphuric wines of Venus. As Pomba Gira is the Queen of the cult, the complete mirror of female substance and its variety, so Exu is the King of this cult and the ordeal of every man. In Exu man can witness his flaws and enlighten both his darkest corners and his highest aspirations. Exu has been demonised and misrepresented for many decades, ranging from him being seen as the evil forces of the netherworld, to being the slave of Orisa, to being seen as identical to the Orisa Èsú – whom he is the slave of! So, in order to define who Exu is with greater precision it is worth evoking Aluizio Fontenelle and his book *Exu*.

Fontenelle defines the class of spiritual beings making up the legions of Quimbanda quite elegantly in the passages where he speaks of spirits as being either evolved or un-evolved. In these passages he also remarks that there is a third class of spirits, whom he calls *spirits of darkness*. This spirit retinue is understood to be of a liminal type and they are described as spirits of tension that are seen as superior in the world of spirits, being beyond good and evil and with a peculiar interest in maintaining sub-lunar activity. Furthermore, Fontenelle emphasizes the need for building up your own good character, being focused on what is good and at all times being kind and honest. This is because hatred and violence build all too easily when we walk into the territory of these spirits. He states clearly that Quimbanda is black magic (*magia negra*) which he sees as different from the *mirongas* of Umbanda with its white magic.

2
The Black Roots of Quimbanda

BLACK MAGIC was seen by people like Fontenelle as a fusion of *curanderismo*, being proficient in herb lore and trafficking with spirits, and *feitiçaria* meaning sorcery. The technology is quite similar in the macumba of Quimbanda and the mironga of Umbanda, what varies are the spirits employed and the aim of one's working. These workings are often seen as different from the prayers and sorceries applied by Pretos Velhos (literally Old Blacks, predominantly forced immigrants of Congolese ancestry) and Caboclos (native Indians). This richness is made evident when he comments on the plural legacy of Umbanda and Kardec's Spiritism by evoking the importance of the Caboclo Penas Brancas (White Feathers) and the Preto Velho Pai Joaquim de Angola. So we find here a cluster of practices that can be *black* in many senses, and *low* or *high* in many senses.

This division most likely came through grammars of Solomonic magic brought by Italian and French immigrants and in particular the writings of Eliphas Lévi. It is here we find the distinction between high and low magic. In *The Keys to the Mysteries*, Lévi comments that high magic is the art that leads man back to the original moral laws. This is a core principle in the theology of Umbanda. So naturally the idea of low magic harks from the same sources and is where we find nigromantic arts like oracular communion with the dead (Necromancy), sorceries of all sorts and spirit trafficking. This magical and ecclesial influence upon Umbanda and Quimbanda is vital because it is in the nocturnal reading of the Holy Scriptures the legends of night unfold upon the canvas where the world is painted with Exu's magma.

Fontenelle was a medium and an Umbandista, so his perspective on Quimbanda was born from the Spiritist Christian dualism so typical for Umbanda where the battle between good and evil is seen as very real. It is important to refer to this time of change in terms of the openness of Quimbanda, since in the 1940s there were still severe restrictions from law enforcement on the practice of black magic and non-Christian religious activities in general. It is however vital that we do not discard the Christian elements related to Quimbanda in favour of some form of centrism. It was, after all, with Umbanda that the wide variety of works with spirits of darkness were recognised as pertaining to a specific realm, and were typified and accepted as a spiritual reality. What was quite wonderful with the Umbandistas was the focus on character and their non-judgmental way of interacting with beings, both spiritual and material. These attitudes display how these founding fathers were tied to the French gnostic tradition, in particular Martinism, with its exaltation of the anonymous philosopher that walks the world and heals in silence, work Lévi would classify as typical for one who works high magic. This attitude generated a loving kindness that enabled a succession of Quimbanda through Umbanda, unfortunately marginalised and demonised by society and seen as a hot and dangerous, yet necessary mystery for the Umbandistas.

In the 1920s a corner to the left outside the Umbanda temple was set aside for the restless spirits of Quimbanda. Here they were given cachaça, tobacco, blood and praise in the name of spiritual evolution. They were approached as impure and hostile spirits that should be somehow tamed into accepting the moral laws of creation. Possessions by the spirits of the 'left hand' were at this time violent, bestial and shocking. Rarely did the spirits speak, but instead answered questions with nods and grunts, though with a few exceptions, as some spirits came through and displayed a maturity and an uncanny knowledge. The relationship with the goetic spirits came into being, and through this the nocturnal history that can be read in the Holy Scripture was fortified. It was as if the French and Italian impulses from the latter part of the 19th century instigated the work that led to the birth of Quimbanda under the wings of Umbanda as a cult in its own right. It is also quite intriguing that the few houses and lineages of Quimbanda succession that claim to be of the root (*de raiz*) are all turning towards this French influenced nocturnal reading of the Holy Scriptures. As we proceed in this chapter it will become even more evident and understandable, because in this lies the spirit of heresy and otherness that affirms Quimbanda to be truly a sorcerous cult, a succession of Brazilian Witchcraft based on traditional premises. Again, we can find all this spoken of in Lévi's *Transcendental Magic* where we read the following:

In black magic, the devil is the great magical agent employed for evil purposes by a perverse will. The old serpent of the legend is nothing else than the Universal Agent, the eternal fire of terrestrial life, the soul of the earth, and the living centre of hell. We have said that the Astral Light is the receptacle of forms, and these when evoked by reason are produced harmoniously, but when evoked by madness they appear disordered and monstrous: so originated the nightmares of St. Anthony and the phantoms of the Sabbath. Do therefore the evocations of goetia and demonomania produce a practical result? Yes, certainly – one which cannot be contested, one more terrible than could ever be recounted in legends! When anyone invokes the devil with intentional ceremonies, the devil comes and is seen.

The Christian elements flow richly within Quimbanda to such an extent that Exu Rei, or King Exu, is directly associated with Lucifer and/or the Lucifer/Satanas polarity. It is popularly seen as a cult of Diablerie. Fontenelle uses the Enochian legend of the fall of the apostate angels and their exile as the motive for the beginning of Quimbanda. He even suggests that the name Exu is from the Hebrew term *exud*, which Fontenelle translates as meaning traitor (in reference to one of the Hebrew tribes). It takes on a similar meaning in Latin in terms of out or exit as in *exodus*, but can also mean outcast. Here Lucifer's fall from grace is presented as continuing through the history of mankind in the form of paganism and sorcery, igniting war, destruction and death. This leads to the Apocalypse where *the people of Exu* enable this last design of the cosmos to unfold and thus restore Eden upon the earth. The Devil as St Michael's warlord executes the divine verdict and becomes the vehicle for salvation. A theme of alchemical and cosmological importance centres on this story, and within the dominion of Exu, is revealed. At the same time Exu mirrors the world by anchoring his reflection in sin and human activity. These are painted in colours and shades that emphasize the tension between the spiritual and mundane, light and darkness, and thus give the illusion of duality so we can fight our own battle towards becoming whole again.

5
The Veiling of Corpses at Midnight

THE LEGENDS OF NIGHT, as we read in the Gospels, tell us that during the suffering and crucifixion of the son of God the heavenly host gathered around him; and so too did the infernal host. Up until this point the god made flesh denied temptation, denied the myrrh and opium offered to him, denied the wine and water as he gave up his breath on the spear of Longinus.

Joseph of Arimathea and Nicodemus, the Pharisee and Sanhedrin member attended his death and saved his blood, sweat and relics. Joseph continued his church, but through Nicodemus a different legacy was maintained. Nicodemus has an apocryphal text ascribed to him, the Gospel of Nicodemus where we find the important section, The Harrowing of Hell, which describes Christ's descent to Purgatory and Hell where the Lord of Hell is surprised by his powers. Here we meet the *scorn of the angels* Belzebub, who has been syncretised with Exu Mor. Exu Mor has in turn has been referred to as *the scorn of the angels, he who is spitting at the righteous* and *the destroyer of the pillars* to mention but a few of his names. But his tales go further, and deeper.

The apocryphal text tells us that to be hung on a tree, as Jesus did, was reserved for those accursed. So from his crucifixion at the gate of skulls, Golgotha, he opened the infernal and celestial gates at a precise astrological moment where his breath was given to both the above and the below. The Harrowing of Hell demonstrates that the death of Jesus shook Heaven as much as Hell, and that he had to enter into both domains to conquer. We are moving far from accepted Christian doctrine here as we venture into the lands of heresy and hidden truth.

Joseph and Nicodemus prepared the corpse of Jesus, wrapped it in linen and saved the relics, gathering wood, nails, body parts, and the dirt and flora that shot up through the blood drenched mud on the hill of skulls. Joseph continued the solar legacy of Jesus, but by marrying Mary of Magdalena he assumed the position of 'guardian of mysteries,' because woman is God's secret. Nicodemus held the secret of night and became the precursor of Bishop Cyprian of Antioch, the Saint of Necromancers. Both Nicodemus and Cyprian share the same spiritual afflatus, the same spirit guide, whom in Quimbanda is known as Exu Meia Noite, Midnight Exu. Joseph of Arimathea and Nicodemus are known in Quimbanda as Exu das Duas Cabeças, a Janus type of Exu that binds polarities like the serpents on the Caduceus.

With this knowledge revealed, the comments in the Gospel of Luke, corroborated by the Gospel of Mark, emphasising that Jesus was placed in a virgin grave, and the first corpse to be placed in the garden appointed to serve as a cemetery, gains necromantic dimensions. The first body to be buried in a garden transforms the garden into a bone meadow and forms the foundation of the boneyard. The first buried then becomes the king of the bone meadow, placing Jesus the Christ in a most interesting continuum: the mysterious succession of death, resurrection and salvation. From this revelation may those who already know its continuation walk on and those who don't know be satisfied with the veil of night being shattered in this way. And the shattering is yet another important aspect, because the shattering and rending of the veil of the Temple where the Ark and Covenant were found guarded by cherubim is the secret revealed by a nightly fire held by the spirit guardians of Quimbanda.

In the shattering of the temple, its veil torn, we find that particular quality of eruptive and destructive fire so present within Quimbanda. We see here a nocturnal and aggressive fire, a quality which is known as Exu Mor. This spirit has been associated both with the spirit that moved Hiram to build the temple of Solomon and with the fire that led to the destruction of the Temple, being the twin powers of Jachin and Boaz manifested in the blazing candle between the horns of the goat's head. This fire is in truth the guiding star of Solomon, the King, the goat of wisdom itself, the storehouse of celestial fire blazing between the horned pillars.

It follows that Exu Mor's identification with the icons of the Goat of Mendes and Lévi's Baphomet is not random, but rather suits this spirit well. In the same manner Exu Meia Noite (Exu Midnight) also gravitates towards physical forms that suit him, those learned in theology such as a rabbi, a priest or a bishop – or a devil. So, whilst Exu Mor is tied to King Solomon, Exu Meia Noite is tied to St Cyprian and St

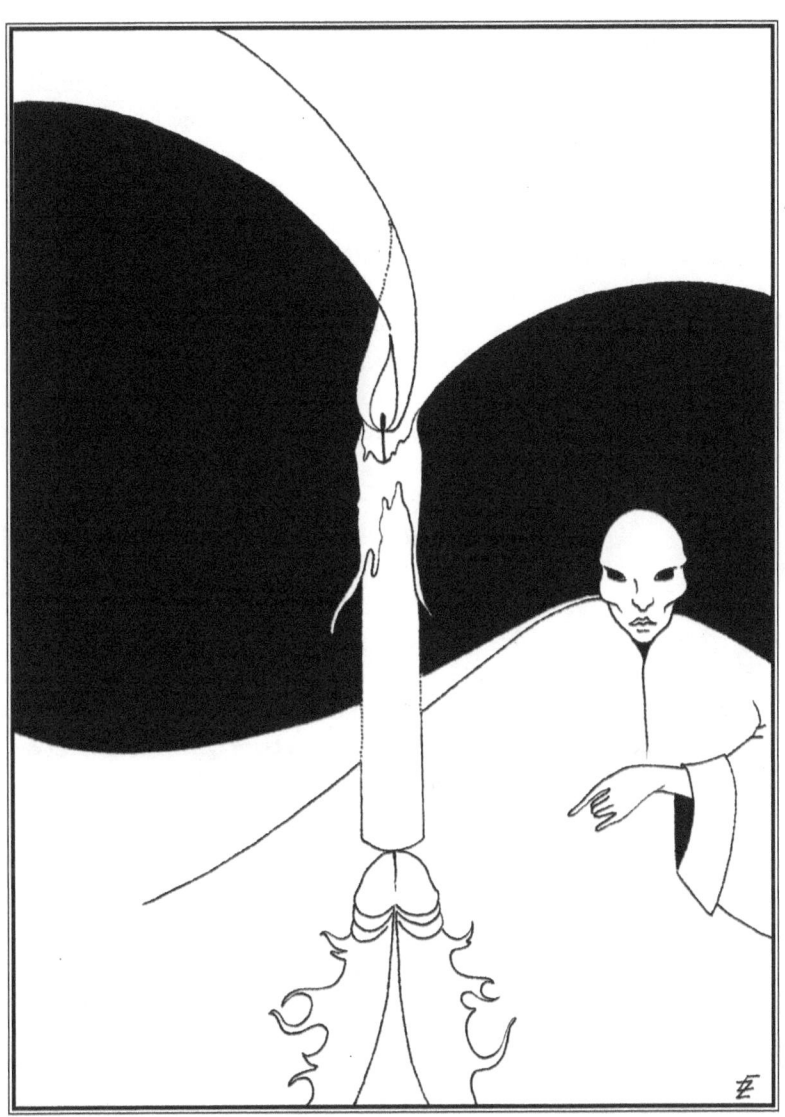

Nicodemus. It follows from this that the spirit of inspiration can be perceived as the diabolic caricature of Pope Alexander VI in a corona of devilish fire.

These examples and revelations leave Jesus, or rather his ensouled corpse prepared by the powers of left and right, as the Corpse King of Hell, a Saturnian influence in one sense, but a celestial in another. We find a Sethian ascent spoken of in this mystery, where his breath brought his spirit under the wings of St Michael, and some even say that he merged with his angelic patron.

In this secret matrimony between the draconic Corpse King and its Sun-drenched slayer we find the true identity of the Maioral or Chief of Quimbanda, the angel who threw the dragon out from heaven, because he knew the dragon all too well, and thus the two hands were folded upon the cosmic cross, the serpent fixed and the gates opened.

Sol Invictus – Father of the Dead

THE CONSEQUENCES of this nocturnal legend are quite profound as the crucifixion of Jesus the Christ takes on renewed dimensions explaining a necromantic mystery of supreme importance. It also reveals how Quimbanda affirms the traditional and classical dual bond between the Sun and the Netherworld, an association that harkens back to Egypt and Canaan. In this we find yet another traditional doctrine, namely the importance and interplay between the two luminaries of God, the Sun and the Moon, revealed here in a nigromantic context. I have chosen to use the term nigromantic rather than necromantic because the nigromancer has a wider field of spirit ingress and summoning as his field of activity than the necromancer. We are not speaking of solely summoning the dead, but a wider array of spirits and in particular the summoning and binding of familiar and teaching spirits.

The two luminaries, Sun and Moon, are the powers that mark the three dramatic hours of the Crucifixion. From the sixth hour (six being a mystical number of the Sun) and until the ninth (mystical number of Moon) an eclipse occurred as the Obsidian Butterfly made the world dark for three hours. The ninth hour is the time when the Sun enters the realm of Hell and the Moon rises from Hell to give its dim light to the night of sleeping matter. Here we find a great mystery hidden within the number of the Beast of the Apocalypse, 666, Sorath, the solar spirit that inflames the nous, being the spirit of the Sun in its perfection. Six is the Hebrew *Vau*, the letter of Tiphareth and Beauty. It was in this hour the eclipse happened and darkened the land until it reached the ninth hour, the number of *Teth*, the Moon and the Sephirah Yesod. By the sacrifice of beauty an axis was formed between the world of Formation and the Kingdom. It should also be remarked that six adds up to *Dob*, meaning bear, and might hint towards the polar position of the constellation of the Bear, the Greater and Lesser, being the Hyperborean mystical Sun and in this the regal nature of the bear as patron of kings. In the same way nine also gives us the word *Bo* which can mean an *entering* and *to come in* and *to go down*. Even more interesting is the fact that nine is the number of squares on the Kamea of Saturn, the darkened Sun. It is here we find the metaphysical mystery of the Maioral in Quimbanda being St Michael the Archangel who, for all purposes, is the Sun transformed into the fire of Saturn, the Dragon. I believe this reasoning explains the solar paternity of notorious witches like Medea and Circe and also why the *Book of Coming Forth by Day*, the manual for transition to death, is ascribed to the Sun as the ruler of Amenta.

Abel is solar, Cain is lunar and thus we have a play here in how the one affirms the other and the ruler of night presents very different rules from those which the Sun gives us. This means that the cemetery is really the Sun slain and it is the skin of the Sun that is draping the Earth and veiling the dead and manifests itself in what we know as the Calunga, the cemetery.

The relationship between Exu Rei and St Michael is one of balanced interaction where the one reflects itself in the other. St Michael the Archangel was considered a healer and divine physician in the early years of Christianity. Over time the role of judge and warrior took prominence. A similar idea can be found in Quimbanda, which is a cult of healing, composed of warriors. St. Michael is the Sun reflecting perfectly the darkness of the Maioral and is the angel that restricts and makes possible this dynamic interplay of these solar poles of white nights and dark days. He is the scales in the hand of the Maioral, and this is his ponto:

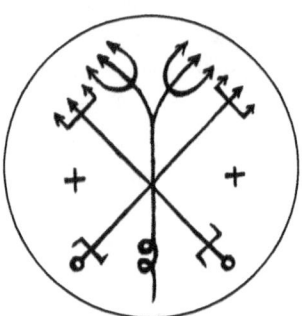

If we turn our attention to Canaan, we find Shamash, the Sun celebrated as *The Lord of the Spirits of the Dead*. We are speaking of the Maioral proper, Sol. This is further exemplified in how the Ugaritic Solar kings paid their obedience to Baal and Anath on the New and Full Moon. Here we meet the sun in the form of Shapash, a female deity who supports Baal in his might against Mot (Death). We find the concept of the Sun not only being female but going through a state of nigredo where she starts to shine again, but this time with the light of the knowledge of death. Her sister, the deity Kaseph or Keseph, meaning silver moon, became a name for Hebrew witchcraft and sorcery today known as *keshupherim* or *keshaphim*, an art taught by the Cherubim to Moses' father-in-law Jethro, the *sol niger* of the keshaphim (master of the lunar sorceries) and passed on to Moses. We should notice that the worship of Shamash was forbidden in the Tanakh and the penalty was death. So, we might conclude from this that the spirit of Moses moved Jospeh of Arimathea, but Nicodemus was moved by the spirit of Jethro, the Sun shining and the Sun darkened being present in the work of resurrection. In this we find a hidden history of Quimbanda and we gain an idea of who these Exus really are. As we see from this, they are not solely spirits who once walked the earth, some of them are spiritual entities divinely formed that have as their field of activity the earth. This is remarkably similar to the doctrine of the watchers in the Enochian transmissions, and this underlines the nigromantic aspect of Quimbanda as we are speaking of more here than just communion and divination with the dead as is entailed in simple necromancy.

De Nigromancia

In the light of this, let us look at the rather obscure text *De Nigromancia*, ascribed to the authorship of Sir Roger Bacon. This text (Sloane ms. 3885) dates from the 16th century and is highly interesting as it gives supreme importance to two of the most important saints in Quimbanda: St Michael and St Cyprian.

Cornelius Agrippa states that it is possible to ensoul a corpse if the carcass and blood is present and that it is also possible to draw the shades of the soul by vapours, liquors and odours, as well as song, sounds and movement. Whatever moves the soul will potentially move the shades of the soul as well, but without the need for the presence of a corpse or lifeforce offerings. Agrippa makes a distinction here between the necyomancer/necromancer and the sciomancer, the one who calls up the shades of the soul, as the Witch of Endor was reputed to do. Agrippa emphasizes the importance of the presence of body parts and bones, or the geographical location itself. Wherever some form of murderous cruelty, death or execution has taken place a point of necromantic power is established and shades can be called up there. Agrippa summarizes it thus:

> Therefore [Necromancers] easily allure the flowing down of wicked spirits, being by reason of the similitude and propriety very familiar: by whom the Necromancer strengthened by their help can do very much inhumane and terrestrial things, and kindle unlawful lusts, cause dreams, diseases, hatred and such like passions, to the which also they can confer the powers of these souls, which

as yet being involved in a moist and turbid spirit, and wandering about their cast bodies, can do the same things that the wicked spirits commit.

Another interesting acount from Agrippa is how a soul can be restored to the body, in other words, how to make a golem or how revenants and the undead were made to walk the earth again. He states in this regard that a high degree of perfection is needed in ones election of what harmonies, celestial and terrestrial, or what souls are used to animate a particular body or matter. What our Western sources communicate to us in riddles and enigmas finds a direct sympathy and resonance with the necromantic mysteries preserved in African faiths and in Palo Mayombe. As we see, wickedness walks hand in hand with necromancy, not only because it is sinful to commune with the dead but because the practice also enables the flowing down of wicked spirits, what in Quimbanda are known as *kiumbas*, and often dubbed *shades*. Certainly necromancy does invite challenges, so grave that Eliphas Lévi said the following of this nocturnal art:

> I regard the practice as destructive and dangerous; if it became habitual, neither moral nor physical health would be able to withstand it. The elderly lady whom I have mentioned, and of whom I had reason to complain subsequently, was a case in point. Despite her asseverations to the contrary, I have no doubt that she was addicted to Necromancy and Goetia. These are dead people whom we mistake for living beings; these are vampires whom we regard as friends.

So, we can see that necromancy is truly scary, not only because it works, but because it can lead to addiction to the art and obsession. For Lévi it is important to stress that these shades are not our friends, but vampires. There is much truth in Lévi's words, albeit presented in fearful terms, and it should be stated that yes, both unhealthy obsession and the energetic draining we know as the effect of vampires are real reasons for caution. I will also testify to the possibility of the flowing

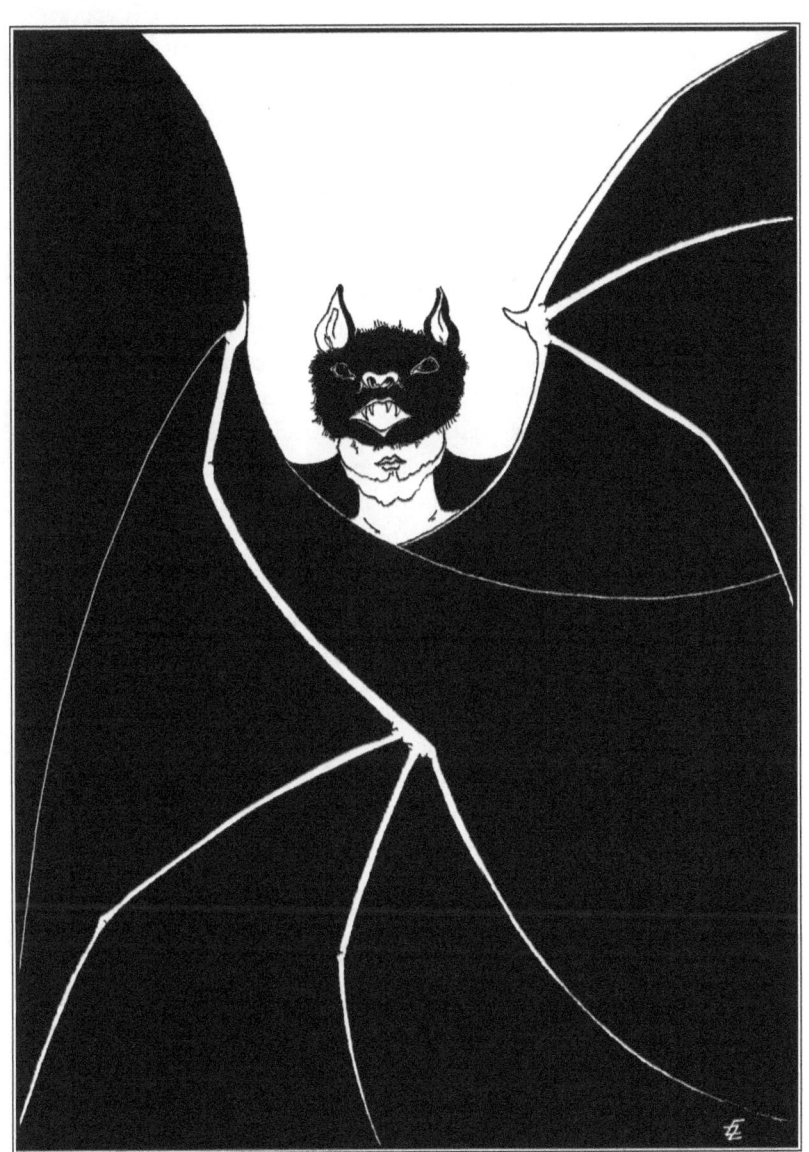

down of hostile spirits in our work with shades and bones. It appears to me that there are many spiritual moths out there that are waiting for opportunities to feed at the table of blood and bones within the bone garland. As we proceed in this work, we should learn to be well equipped to deal with these matters, so let us now return to *De Nigromancia* and what it has to tell us about this much maligned art.

We find recommendations and observations concerning the moon, which should be increasing in light, her first quarter is considered most auspicious for works of necromancy. Normally one can perform one's operations and experiments from sunset and until cock's crow. It is however most auspicious to enter one's circle or commence one's work in the hour of Venus. The book also states that the period from sunrise until its zenith holds a particular power, and indeed, this is the time for shaking off the fumes of death and purifying one's soul and body in order to return to the world of the living. It is also important to avoid impure days and hours. I have in this regard found the *Hygromanteia of Solomon* to be greatly rewarding for the practitioner. The counsel in *De Nigromancia* of avoiding unlucky hours and days is to be avoided because of the possibility of activating *volneris*, simply, a curse. This is especially so if malefica is done in hours that carry a malefic energy in themselves. It is perhaps natural to think that negative works in a negative hour will fortify the working, but it is imperative to be wise here so that a double negative does not lead to inadvertent self-cursing.

The book further counsels the fumigation of laurel, the same wood which forms the necromancer's wand. This is a solar tree, and reminds us that these operations are always better if the Sun is well aspected and favorable with the ruler of the hour we are working with. It reminds us that we bind spirits of air, fire and water differently. For example, if you want to bind spirits of water gather rainwater and place it at the centre of the circle, or do your workings close to running water. Likewise, if our experiment holds a particular planetary value we should make sure that we are working in the planetary hour where we find this particular planetary ray most potent.

Most important for *De Nigromancia* is the 14th of May, the feast day of St Cyprian. If we see this day side by side with the moveable Holy

Friday, the day of the Lord's expiation and the three hours where his spirit and breath were moving around over Golgotha, we can see a process of the volatile dragon becoming fixed. So, this time is naturally most auspicious for works of an initiatic nature as well. Another date given importance is the Sunday of the Myrrh bearers which in the Orthodox Church falls on the 3rd of August and is in honour of Nicodemus, who reddened the bones of the Lord of the graveyard.

Another recommendation given in the text is to take a small meal of bread, liver and red wine prior to workings with the dead. This is quite interesting because in several African traditions the liver is believed to be what holds the witches' power. Likewise the liver held a particular potency in Greek and Roman antiquity where it was favoured for divination. This connection between the liver and its particular power lives on in traditional medicines, such as Ayurveda, where the liver holds the mastery of the five digestive fires that purify the blood. The importance of fire and blood can be seen not only in its importance for health but also on a more symbolic level.

If workings are done outside the moon phases spoken of earlier, where one is working with the female planets, Moon and Venus (these timings being optimal for workings with Pomba Gira) the book advises other times, more male in vibration. In general Thursday and Sunday are favoured days, both being ruled by male planets and the circle is entered in the hour of Saturn. The summoner should then station himself in the North and their assistants in the south.

When the infernal hosts are called, and spirits such as Amazael, Aziel, Anathana, Azael, Tyer, Lucifer, Ashtaroth, Belial, Troglis, it is always done by the virtue of St Michael, St Cyprian or King Solomon. Curiously, we find a similar hierarchy in Quimbanda, but with more lenience given in approaching the spirits head on. This is possible when a relationship with one's Exu and/or Pomba Gira has been established and the secret name has been given. We have then managed to forge a vinculum with spirit that ensures familiarity, guidance and protection and the need for rite and drama is drastically reduced and takes place on a more intimate level. This connection often comes with the gift of second sight, be it in vision, dream, crystal or shade. In Quimbanda this is a gift given by spirit most often through the frenzy of possession, but there are other ways and means. Let us not forget that some people are simply naturally gifted with this ability.

De Nigromancia gives a formula for obtaining second sight that enables one to see the 'host of Heaven and Hell.' This formula requires that a viper is killed when the Sun is in Mars. The fangs should be taken and mixed with balsam and mandrake and then be consecrated and steeped in good quality oil in the first hour of the Sun, or during the first degree of the Sun entering Aries. This being done, the snake's blood (or the blood of bat or lapwing) can be used for calling up the legions of death and wickedness, and equally spirits of healing and wonder working.

The death of Jesus replicates the mystery of the two Suns guarded within the Sol Niger. It is here the spirit we know today as Exu Rei, or King Exu, enters and gains the power Jesus gives up at his moment of death. For three hours Exu Rei distributes the breath and blood of Jesus to his legions and replicates the mystery that enabled Lilith to spawn a multitude of demons on the shores of the Red Sea. This power is spread by Exu Meia Noite (Midnight Exu), the spirit teacher of St Cyprian who gives the power of kingship to a host of Exus.

Lastly, there is one stellar connection that should be mentioned: Orion. In Hebrew Orion is called Kesilim, which has the value of 120/730, but the numeric value is the same as that for *fools*. This temurah is not without reason. *De Nigromancia* takes as its focus the constellation of Orion, because it was here that the leader of the fallen host, Shemyaza was captured and affixed upside down, like the tarot trump The Hanged Man. Orion is the stellar patron of hunters and holder of the secrets that enable angels to be enfleshed. He replicates the mystery of vivifying corpses and bringing life to matter in cosmic form. The connection with the hunter stars also connects with certain Exus in the spirit catalogue responsible for opening doors and vinculums. I believe it is here in the image of Orion where the sage and the fool part, the wise one knows how and when to open these doors and possibilities, the fool opens whatever part of the starry hunter that suits his or her fancy with little care for the sorcerous rules and even less spiritual sensitivity. In this is found the divide between the slayer and the slain.

The Two Suns & the Fiery Grave of Asclepius

LET US RETURN briefly to the alchemical dimensions of Quimbanda, the black sun and the mystery of putrefaction, and afix this corpse in the heavens. Again we need to address the Sun as we see it shedding light upon the earth. Its power is dry and consuming; the fire that makes matter as dry as bones. The philosophical Sun that instigates the nigredo or blackening of matter, the putrefaction, works hand in hand with the calcification of matter where the flesh/matter is made wet and unites with the world soul in the form of the Earth herself. So we find here a mystery speaking of the importance of the consuming and mystical fire of the two suns at work here. It is this mystery that is encoded in the form of St Michael the Archangel as the Maioral of Quimbanda. This means that Michael himself becomes an alchemical and timeless personification of an eternal mystery, the great work itself, and the restoration of the philosophical sun within that enables and makes possible resurrection and immortality. The Sun rises and finds its peak at midday and then sets out for his journey into the night, this is a mirror of maturity and natural cycles.

You gain familiar spirits by workings with the angelic prince Alastiel. Little is said about this angel, so I assume that his name is from the Latin adjective *alatus*, which means that which possesses wings. This generic form fits well with Alastor, the vengeful and winged aspect of Zeus often considered to take the shape of a self-afflicted curse. So, this might be read esoterically as the angel prince Alastiel being the power that avenges malefica. This would explain why *De Nigromancia* states it is crucial to obtain a good rapport with this angel. I see here a similarity between the position Scirlin holds in *Grimorium Verum* and Exu Calunga and the three commanders hold in Quimbanda. This means that the importance of building a good relationship with a certain key spirit is what safeguards one's sanity and equilibrium in one's nigromantic work. It is the truth of the hermetic axiom *as above, so below*. An opposite, stellar alchemy takes place in the heavens and mirrors the work the nigromancer does upon and within the earth. It is here that both the stellar Sun and the draconian Helios are revealed.

Consider the stars which make up the celestial Hercules. Prior to this identification they were seen as the Chaldean Sun god Izhdubar, as the crown and star upon the head of Tiamat/Draco, which he was considered to have slain. The qualities of Hercules were later transmitted onto the constellation Leo by Ovid, which he referred to as the Hercules Lion, the Violent Lion and Bacchus' light. The transition of Hercules from the dragon slayer of the heavens into the solar heart of the constellation Leo where we find the star Regulus (also known as Cor Leonis or heart of the lion, one of the four royal stars) is replicated in Christian legends of St. George and St. Michael. The solar station is conquered by subduing the dragon and becoming its master. It is also interesting to bring attention to another of the stars in the constellation of Leo, Deneb/Denebola, also known as the tail of the Lion, seen as a fiery and destructive influence bringing misfortune to men, especially those in offices of the state. Denebola served as a regal reminder of the complexity of the royal station.

Hercules is to the west of Ophiuchus, the serpent holder, yet another potency standing on the head of Tiamat/Draco, and associated with Asclepius. Ovid mentions Bacchus in relation to the constellation of Leo and we should look at these themes, because in them further depths will be revealed. Asclepius in his power of holding serpents displays dominion, and Bacchus represents the oracular dimensions that take shape in possession and frenzy. So let us first examine the themes of Asclepius and Apollo which can shed light on another dimension of the nature of Exu.

In the Gospel of Nicodemus, the Harrowing of Hell, we read that Jesus was accused of throwing out demons in the name of Asclepius. This seems confusing, but as Apollodorus recounts:

> Asclepius became so skilled in his profession that he not only saved lives but even revived the dead; for he had received from Athena the blood that had coursed through the Gorgon's veins, the left-side of which he used to destroy people, but that on the right he used for their preservation, which is how he could revive those who had died.

Asclepius was the son of Apollo and the princess Coronis (the Crow) who died during labor and was put out to be cremated. Apollo cut his child from the womb of his dead mother, hence the name Asclepius, to cut open, and he was raised by the Titan-blooded centaur Chiron. Chiron was son of the titan Cronos and the nymph Philyra who was turned into the honeysweet Linden tree (*Tilia* genus) by the jealous Zeus. Chronos passed on virtue and knowledge from the golden age to his wise son Chiron, who in turn passed this knowledge to his foster son. The cunning of the healing arts were so great in Asclepius that he even revived the dead, and thus Zeus vanquished him with a thunderbolt for upsetting the natural order.

Concerning the death of Asclepius, who was turned into stars by the work of the thunderbolt, we should note that he was instantly deified. This is a phenomena we find in the cult of Quimbanda and in Brazilian folklore in general. Those who undergo immediate transfiguration are known as *encantados*, charmed ones who vanish in nature and remain in proximity to the earth as Masters and Teachers of certain people or small communities. The cult of Catimbó is particularly rich with these spiritual phenomena, but some Exus are also encantados and are therefore known as catiços. The Exu catiços are understood to be different from the Exus we will discuss in this book. The catiços are seen as spirits of nature that reveal themselves like Exus and call themselves by names of Exu, but they are not guardians of particular places of powers, rather they are forces of power born from nature itself. These Exu catiços are generally more violent than the classical Exus and must be directed with diligence to avoid harm to the medium.

Asclepius did not die, but vanished immediately into the nature he knew so well and was transformed into a cluster of stars known as the Serpent holder. His mother Coronis was also brought to the heavens in the form of the constellation Corvis who rides on Hydra's back. This is the star at Apollo's left shoulder. At his right we find the star Vega, brightest star in the Harp who holds the powers of Venus, often called Queen of Life, though prone to debauchery and sloth. This means that Apollo merged with Daphne, the nymph that was his first and true love and together they have the laurel as their symbolon, a union of Sun and Moon. The raven is one of the attributes of the solar and oracular Apollo, who also holds in his hand a Harp, the constellation next to Hercules.

The Harp is the constellation that holds the necromantic mysteries of Orpheus, his descent to Hades and his decapitated head coming ashore on the island of Lesbos. Its brightest star is Vega, which is the soul of Eurydice. Orpheus' head entered the land of women, Lesbos, after failing to rescue his beloved. Mystically the one beloved turned into the many beloved, and the lover of 'One' became the precious one of many. In this we find the intense relationship between the royal Exu guarding Pomba Gira, the Fig Tree in Hell, the woman of Seven Husbands.

It is my belief that Asclepius represents the archetypical first necromancer and it is this theme that is transmitted in the form of St. Cyprian. Apollo however holds the keys to a deep necromantic mystery where he holds the laurel staff and the Harp. The fact that Apollo is given Orpheus' gift and soul denotes his mastery of this journey to and fro in the halls of Death. There is however an interesting discrepancy here concerning Apollo's oracular pedigree. I tend to find Apollodorus in general more truthful and I am inclined to agree with him that this gift was given to him by Pan, and not by his father Zeus. Pan giving the grace of prophecy harmonises better with the serpentine mysteries that we find entwined in the oracular process itself. Python possessed this oracle, but Python was merely the mouth and tongue of Gaea (earth) and Poseidon (oceans). If we should dare to make a comparison within the legions of Quimbanda we find Exu Calunga, who draws heavily on the themes of Saci or Aroni to be the most likely of the portents of the powers of Pan, and through this Exu Calunga that carries their form. Saci is a midget trickster spirit that ensures movement in the woods. Aroni is the dogheaded messenger of Osanyin, the spirit of the forest. Both are ascribed the power of forcing the hand of chance. More will be said of them when we present the mysteries of Exu Calunga. Exu Calunga holds a prime position as a nucleus of power that he flung out above and below as a maelstrom empowering his 18 legions of Exus.

Exu and the Death of Bacchus

WHEN WE BRING Bacchus/Dionysus into this equation it is because of his death and descent to Hades which forges his connection with Haephestus/Vulcan, thus we come full circle with the relationship between the Sun, Asclepius, Hephaestus and the themes of death and dominion they represent in relation to the fires of Hades and the ecstasies of the night.

Vulcan was a limping god. The limping is said in Homer's *Iliad* to be due to his fall from Olympus when his mother Hera beheld his ugliness. The *Iliad* also states that his limping was caused by his father Zeus throwing him down on the island of Lemnos after he sided with his mother in a dispute. He was brought up in an underwater cave where for nine years he was an apprentice of the arts of the blacksmith and jeweller. He was raised by the aquatic Titaness Tethys and the mother of mermaids, Eurynome. He is perhaps best remembered for his turbulent relationship with Aphrodite/Venus, his wife, who was repelled by his ugliness.

There are several features here that reveal Exu themes. Firstly we have the limping, a quality ascribed to the devil but also as a sign of falling in itself. Hence we will know that an angel is fallen by its limping as much as we will realize that something has broken through from the other side by its limping gait. This theme is evident in the iconography of Exu where he is depicted with one human foot and one cloven hoof. It is also interesting to take note of the aquatic cave being the cradle for Vulcan in this regard. The deepest points of the ocean are in African faiths always associated with mystery and ancestry. Not only this, but as the oceans have the peculiar ability of eating light and not giving any back, the logical consequence will be darkness upon darkness, yet we find a curios metamorphosis taking place. The deeper we go and the less light we find, the more aquatic creatures generate their own light and their shapes become more and more outlandish and deformed. So, we find here a mystery speaking of how we can forge our own light in the field of ancestry and mystery, and I believe this is a trait of Vulcan we can apply to Exu.

Exu shares common themes with Dionysus as well as Hephaestus/Vulcan. Not only do they all bring the fire of immortality from Hades, stolen from heaven and thus manifest ecstasy and sorcery, there are several other factors that can help us understand this intriguing devil known as Exu. Dionysus was the one who brought Hephaestus back to Olympus, riding on a donkey, like Jesus did. This speaks of the intense relationship between the two outcast gods.

If we look closer at the substance that makes up Dionysus we find a relationship with Vulcan/Hephaestus. This is the fire at the centre of the world, or the flames in the netherworld. This theme is further stressed by Vulcan's wife Aphrodite behaving freely in sexual matters. We might see a 'wet' form of Vulcan in Dionysus. It is the earthy fire of the netherworld transformed into a moist fire of the heavens, where he is the mediator between his solar and lunar self properly identified with the star that dies and rises in the course of night, namely Venus. These considerations are important, because it sheds light on why the fiery and hot spirits of Quimbanda are called Exus. It is here we find the connection and subsequent forgetfulness about the reasoning behind it. The explanation is quite simple, since the spirits that make up Quimbanda are considered hot and unpredictable, a stabilizing element that could serve as the opener and closer of gates and crossroads would be ideal. The perfect candidate was the Orisa Èsú, the linguist of the worlds, dweller at crossroads, friend of wisdom and psychopomp. So, at some point it became customary to be initiated to the cult of Èsú in order to safeguard oneself and stabilise one's own practice with these volatile spirits of fire and night. The Orisa Èsú was gradually seen as the power that kept these forces in some form of order and thus these spirits multiplied, in conformity with the linguistic nature of Èsú, into legions and lines of spirits assembled from the netherworld, nature and the heavens. Today this legacy is in danger of becoming forgotten, yet in this we find the reason for Exu being the male potency of the cult. It is in the borrowings from the Yoruban cult of Èsú that are found both the foundation of Quimbanda and its understanding of Exu. This is visible in some form of *ebó* (sacrifice/offerings). The construction of the spirit vessels however is reminiscent of the cult of Osanyin and

Kongolose derived mysteries, such as Palo Mayombe. This is mediated and fused with native Brazilian, Kongolese and European practices and concepts leading me to conclude that we can hardly say that one form of Quimbanda is more valid or more connected to the root than any other, as diversity is its very nature. The importance lies in whether we are truly connected to spirit or not, because in this lies the key to who is riding who.

Every person alive is said to walk in the company of an Exu and a Pomba Gira. Consequently these spirits represent the essential quality of the soul and can manifest as what we know as lares, household gods, for good or for ill. Most Exus and Pomba Giras were once living beings that upon losing their shell contracted into a spiritual quality of some form. The form they were shaped into was still drawn to matter and hence resonates with the works of the human soul here on earth.

Since humans are more and more preoccupied with being more unique than what our unique being dictates, this generates an equal illusion on the other side of the mirror of the world of souls. From this merging of will crashing in the mirror between the worlds are born odd spirit characters, variations within the variations. We can find Exus with odd names, like 'baking oven' and 'Japanese sailor.' The presence of such spirit forms speak of a human desire to be different and unique, and how the fertile field of this cult is in giving birth to new spirits and discovering old ones. In this we find challenges that lead to growth. These matters are also caused by the many complex factors involved in the mechanism of possession. For now I will only state that it is important to keep in mind that Quimbanda carries a story of a cultural and historical forgetfulness within its constant renewal and recreation.

Necromancy certainly has its root in ancestor veneration and might be said to give us an opportunity to forge a spiritual ancestry through earth, blood and prayer, a work of sympathy where kindred souls on both sides of the veil make bonds. In this we need to show caution. As we do not have an intense harmony with every kind of person, so it is in the world of spirits. As above, so below. Some spirits are prone to harm and contempt the human race. But, more of this as the book proceeds. At this point we shall pause and bring all these threads together and let these threads find Africa in the Venusian lands of Vera Cruz, also known as Brazil. Naturally they shall find each other in the ecstasy of wine, the tearing of flesh and its renewal as death, plants and earth are given a voice. Quimbanda is a necromantic cult and all necromantic cults have an intense relationship not only with fire, but with the Sun as well as the Moon. In Quimbanda the two luminaries of heaven, Sun and the Moon, are given to Exu and Pomba Gira respectively, but its mystery spreads its wings to the eight corners of Hades.

On Obsidian Wings

THERE IS ONE OTHER ASPECT in the theme of the black sun and dual sun that should be mentioned as the chapter moves towards its close. In Aztec mythology we find the tale of Quetzalcoatl, the feathered Serpent, a most proper alchemical symbol in the form adopted. At sunset this deity took on the form of the black sun, going through a metamorphosis of night, and as the black sun venturing through the nights of the netherworld did so as a butterfly. This finds resonance in Brazilian, European and African beliefs of the firefly and the moth being spirit presences, one higher and loftier than the other. The butterfly is also frequently considered in contemporary occultism to represent the soul, and naturally the dramatic metamorphosis of the butterfly gives us much to contemplate. This butterfly was amongst the Azetcs seen as made of obsidian, a mineral extremely sacred to certain forms of Exu, and was called Itzpapalotl. The Aztec worldview counted nine layers to the netherworld, taking the earth's surface as the first where descent to the others was made possible by entering the mouth of a giant toad. These nine layers harmonise with the ninefold division of places of power within the seven kingdoms that will be used in this grammar to present the many Exus.

In this we find an opposition and a play upon contrasts as Quetzalcoatl is also opposed to the forces of the Tzitzimime and the Cihuateteo. The butterfly he becomes in his night travels is usually considered a solar orange. He is the monarch butterfly, which is a symbol of warriors who have died in battle, who carry the Sun on their backs from sunrise to sunset. Itzpapalotl carries the sun from noon to sunset.

Itzapapalotl was given rulership of a paradise world seen as the cradle of human creation, the place where the souls of children dying before their first year came, as well as women who died during labour. She is the mother of the moth and can show herself as a deer, as a bat or scorpion, hence her name sometimes being the *butterfly with claws* and the symbolic association between nocturnal butterflies and bats. Beside the butterfly form and the obsidian attribute, she is seen as a skeleton and a warrioress manifesting in solar eclipses. When she takes on her deer woman form it is to seduce men or mate with serpent spirits. Besides toads and scorpions she is also reputed to show herself as a masked white woman, with jaguar hands and eagle feet, cloaked and veiled. It is an evil and murderous energy. She is a defender of women and feeds upon men. This relates to mysteries pertaining to the Pomba Gira known as the Fig Tree in Hell and Exus like Asa Negra (Exu Black Wings) and Morçego (Bat). All these animals are crucial to working the cult of Quimbanda. It is a cult of nocturnal birds and amphibians, of creatures that cross water and earth and thrive upon fire and poison and hence I shall close with some observations in the form of a warning.

The Scorpions in the Track

THE KING OF THE CULT OF EXU is a most proper icon of change, exchange and transformation that can turn the suffering road of human existence into solace and triumph. I would say, as much as Pomba Gira is the solace of the world, Exu is the power of triumph. Triumph calls upon its own shadows of hubris, pride, solipsism and revenge. The shadow of triumph however is failure, and in failure we can start to nurture the most negative of all poisons; hatred and anger. In failure, anger and hatred take shape and when this ugly fire is too much to carry we project this outwards and the entire world is coloured by our sick vision.

Quite correctly and in conformity with its delicate gnosis few people are capable of dealing with this often unnatural infernal fire, hence they see only the poison, and they ingest this poison. They turn into scorpions, but not the kind of scorpions that stretch their axes up and down to the left and to the right, but instead generate a hard, dark shell around their soul and condense all their poison in the act of making a point, no matter how absurd, wasted, ridiculous or whatever. It seems to me that this is a mechanism contained within the poison itself and our reaction dictates whether we alchemise it or perish at its sting. When poisoning occurs we need to heal it. The best remedy is to work on our character and realize that poison can make a man immune, or a corpse. The path of poisonous fire is for the real man or woman, who in the fire of Hell turns gentle and understanding; who grows wise through suffering and ordeal, who sees themself as a warrior ready to accept life no matter what its cost. It is indeed the path of a dark knight, a poisonous path that either gives you the armour of a knight or the carapace of a scorpion.

*Truth is not a mere copy of reality:
it is always dynamic, involved in action.*

Roger Bastide

The King of the City of Dust

The history of Quimbanda is forged in forgetfulness, nostalgia and rebellious turmoil. It is a cult that has changed and adapted over the centuries under various names and ritual forms. The truth of Quimbanda rests in the dynamic interaction it always had with its land and people. Tracing the historical patterns that lead to modern day expressions of Quimbanda takes its toll. We need to consider several different forms of folklore across Brazil, social changes, and geographical variations. History is a fragile discipline as it aims towards explaining so much from assembling facts in the form of historical occurrences that hold meaning and significance. This demands a good analytical mind for the qualified assumption of meaning that lies at the heart of history. I draw upon the research of Roger Bastide, who in turn used the illuminating research of L.A. Costa Pinto, Nina Rodrigues and Gilberto Freyre. Perhaps the first dignified study of black cultures and *macumba* in Brazil was made as late as 1901 by Raimundo Nina Rodrigues who tried to counter the successive denigration of black culture in Brazil, yet Bastide, in spite of his 'racial' flaw is a vital avenue for approaching this subject matter. Bastide constantly stresses the problem of cultural memory and its forgetfulness, which I feel is crucial for a study of the historical provenance of Quimbanda.

Social turbulence lies at Quimbanda's roots. In 1611 there were discussions about making Native Brazilians free men and women, but not until 1789 was this promise made good. A far worse fate befell the Africans who were declared free men and women as late as 1888, and this after much international pressure. In all fairness it should be pointed out that the tutor of the Emperor and patriarch of independence the Freemason José Bonifácio remarked in 1823 that slavery was a *mortal cancer* in the country. Slave traffic was forbidden in 1850 and in 1871 the 'law of the free womb' saw its manifestation. This law stated that children born of slaves from that date on were to be considered free. In 1889 Brazil changed from crown property to fledgling republic. The first republic was riddled with scandals, oppression and tyranny.

The Belle Époque overlapped both crown and republic lasting from 1870 until 1930. This was a period of French and continental influence on art, music, philosophy and literature. With this beautiful epoch came the ugliness of Social Darwinism and the Africans, Cafuzos, Caboclos, essentially anyone with a non-European heritage, were discriminated against. In the same period we find black movements, Caboclo movements and the founding of Umbanda as Kardec's Spiritism spread rapidly through the urban centres of Brazil. The attempts at vanquishing African roots only made them stronger and it was a time where Quimbanda took the form which we know it in today, as a conglomerate of African and native wisdom oriented around a Kongo cosmology with greater or lesser influences from Spiritism. It is this conglomerate of impulses, rebellion and social turmoil that lie as tender nerves in what is known as Quimbanda de Raiz, that is, Quimbanda of the Root.

In 1930 the military staged a coup and stayed in control of Brazil until 1985. In 1985 the first democratic election was held and Tancredo Neves was elected and assassinated, as popular belief holds, making way for Sarney (who allegedly supported the military regime) to be the first president in what is known as the *new republic*. From here a democratic and social agenda took shape. It was only as late as 1988 that laws criminalizing racism and sexism were put in place in Brazil.

The Devil of the Cabulas

THE ACCOUNT OF THE papal representative Dom João Nery in *Espírito Santo* tells us that macumba was used interchangeably with the word *calundus*. Calundus were described as *sortilegious celebrations* predominantly of a *double black* concentration, due to both the presence of Africans and because of the black and diabolic nature of their rites and magic. In accounts and descriptions from the 17th century onwards we find recurring mention of the calundeiros celebrating a spirit known as Calunga Ngombe. Interestingly *ngombe* is a term referring to a Congolese dialect, and also a name given to the class of mediums and diviners in the same district. Calunga signifies both the abysmal waters of ancestry as well as the mysterious ocean itself. The practice of the calundeiros took place in calundos, nefarious and eerie compounds. Their practices were described as a fusion between black magic, spirit possession and Masonry of an African temperament. The term itself is derived from the North-Angolan city Calunda, but was used as reference to the slave compounds themselves. From the Calundas surfaced Cabulas, which we might consider the spiritual structure from within the Calundas. The Cabulas observed a traditional African hierarchy and structure whereas the cult was headed by a chief of the cult, called *embanda*. He was assisted by a *cambono*. The cambono was the master of ceremonies and appointed to be the General of the ritual, to ensure that everything proceeded in a safe and orderly fashion. The meetings were known as *enjiras* and those attending were usually dressed in white. They called upon Calunga (the ocean and potency of prophecy), Baculo (ancestors) and Tatá (disincarnated masters and teaching spirits). The goal of the rituals was to enter into trance and commune with spirit guides in order to secure protection and understanding. Bastide points out that Tatá came in many guises, such as Tatá Guerreiro (Father Warrior), Tatá Flor de Carunga (Father of the flower of Calunga), Tatá Rompe Serra (Father who breaks hills), Tatá Rompe-Ponte (Father who breaks bridges) and so forth. Macumba originally referred to the drum used in the enjiras. Gradually the term macumba fused with Cabula.

As macumba became more known and written about, the terms Tatá, Pai and Mestre became conflated to refer to the head of the cult, both physical and discarnate. The same structure as was common in cabulas and amongst the calundeiros continued under various guises, under the general label of macumba until the 19th century when it was gradually referred to as Quimbanda in reference to the practices of the cabulas. At the turn of the previous century the use of the term macumba held a distinctively African or Kongolese flavour, but with an air of black magic following it like a shadow.

The bad reputation of macumba is partly explained by the application of magical and sorcerous solutions to deal with very real problems of abuse, hardship and suppression. The macumbeiros appealed for the help of those spirits who could open roads and break down their oppressors. It is also important to pay attention to the ecclesiastical schisms in the 15th and 16th centuries when Northern Protestant Christianity distanced itself from what they saw as a Satanic Christianity in the Catholic Church. From this point on the Devil gained prominence and it naturally gave cause for concern, as it demonstrated that the Devil was able to divide the house of God. Prior to the reformation the power of the church was considered to be so strong that man had nothing to fear from the myriad of devils around him. With reformation, schism and ecclesiastical unrest, this perspective became rapidly altered and in the 17th century the devils lead by a supreme Devil became a real threat. Hence the Devil as enemy of the Church was gradually seen as a source of power, and a possible friend, of the calundeiros and macumbeiros.

These are the formative decades of Exu's diabolic iconography. As the Devil became more and more evil, that is, a threat to the white slave owners, the more the oppressed people, either exiled from Europe or imported from Africa, saw in the enemy of their oppressors a friend. Bastide commenting on this diabolic syncretism notes that the Yoruba Èsú was a natural and perfect form for merging these native and Kongolese spirits into a protective intermediary between God and men. After all, the spirits they summoned in their rituals were often spirits of healing, war, opportunity and attack, and none was better suited than Èsú to bring these requests to the feet of Nzambi (God). It looks as if the merging of the crossroad spirits of macumba and the Yoruba intercessor Èsú was a gradual process that began in the early 19th century with them emerging as identical with the birth of Umbanda. There are even examples of notorious Quimbandeiros in the 1970s going to Ketu, Nigeria to make initiation to Orisa Èsú to give maximum support to their work with Quimbanda. Èsú was seen as being not only the intermediary between God and men, but also between the Infernal and men. Èsú was considered to hold a neutral role, mediating the angelic choirs and the legions of Hell. From this the epitaph Exu was given to the myriad of spirits from crossroads, streets, lines and kingdoms that found their way into the structures of Quimbanda. This was all helped by the fact that the Orisa Èsú was being translated as *devil* and *Satan* in the first English/Yoruba dictionaries, and is a translation which is still given today.

Another consequence of the Orisa Èsú being given such a pivotal role was that this Yoruba Orisa was seen as a social force capable of resolving cultural conflicts. Exu became a fusion of the Kongo fire spirit Kadiempemba and the Yoruba Èsú veiled in the guise of continental demonology and Spiritism. Exu of Quimbanda rose as the equilibrium that united the negative or Bantu legacy and the positive, the Nagô/Yoruba legacy.

It should be pointed out early on that there is no such thing as African dualism or any Manichean idea behind any African faith or theological concept, unless it is for the sake of allegory. Where we see what might be considered dualism we will also see that such a state is a deviation from the natural order where everything is seen as rays and extension of a singular creative principle, a wise origin of all things. This contrast and possibility invested in the One, the source, is found in all spiritual manifestations be they, plant, beast, man or gods. Everything that is, is an extension of the source. Everything is paradoxical and ambivalent, and most ambivalent of all are mercurial principles like Èsú.

African spirits are always understood as natural principles, qualities are commonly ascribed to the principle giving how, where and why they appear and act. They are all dynamic, but for some this can be understood as arising from an ambivalence at the spiritual centre of the principle. In effect this means that a spirit can manifest and work across a great array of possibilities. In the case of Exu, it was his function as opener of roads, intermediary, linguist and sorcerer that was emphasized and thus it was within these qualities the spirit host took shape. The aggressive fire was likewise given constant attention in the rebellion against slave owners. So the protector of the Africans became the white man's poisoner, killer and a sorcerer. Through social need Èsú gained a following that broke the limits of his people and became more a general force, a god for the oppressed, for criminals and outlaws. Èsú became the conglomerate known as Exu. All these associations developed between the 17th and 19th centuries. We also see a cultural overspill where the Yoruba Èsú is venerated as Exu by people claiming Bantu heritage in the macumba houses in Rio de Janeiro as attested to by Bastide in the late 19th century. Here the most significant being to make *ebó* and give *padé* and *eko* to was Exu, a clearly Yoruban influence. We also see that Yoruba and Bantu ideas are conflated to such an extent that it is as if the malefic and protective aspect of Èsú have taken on a life of their own in their merging with the European Devil as the Exu of Quimbanda took shape. Exu rose out of the fertile Brazilian soil soaked in blood and sweat before setting forth on wings of sorcery and attack.

The Septenary Roots of Macumba

WITH THE ABOLITION OF SLAVERY macumba flourished. The mutually cruel fate in being both abandoned and left on the streets generated kin bonds of sodality between those who had been freed. In particular in Salvador, Bahia and in Rio de Janeiro, a rapid and powerful growth of houses of macumba took place. These were in effect successors of the cabulas, but now with an increasingly European influence which had been brought to the larger cities during the Belle Époque. Exu and his cult become endowed with a multifarious legacy of magical knowledge of indigenous, African and European pedigree. In this melting pot the European Devil turned into a sort of tutelary spirit for the macumbeiros as they continued the enjiras of the cabulas, but now with the book of St Cyprian and Spiritist techniques in their magical arsenal. Bastide recounts that some believed that the followers of St Cyprian were able to transform themselves into were-animals and St Cyprian was taken as a patron of black magic. Black magic (*magia negra*) was used interchangeably with macumba. From this melting pot Quimbanda grew, and because of this we find that Quimbanda is a variation upon a diabolic theme mediated in shades of white, red and black and the iconography tells the story of how the devil befriends the oppressed.

Èsú entered into this calculation and synthesis because he was messenger and intermediary, he was transformation, magic, and the qualities of the European devil were interpreted in these very terms. In the same timespan we see another Yoruba Orisa entering the realm of macumba, Omolu, testifying to an explosive exchange of wisdom and knowledge. Omolu is the owner of earth, sickness, healing and those who succumbed to smallpox. Omolu was thus adopted as the owner of the Cemetery.

The period from 1870 to 1920 was marked by a great interchange between magicians and sorcerers informing the multiplicity of macumba and therefore, Quimbanda. In the aftermath of the abolition of slavery a wave of French homeopaths and Spiritists descended on the urban centers in Brazil, in particular Salvador, São Paulo, Rio de Janeiro and Porto Alegre. With this French bourgeois culture came neo-paganism, neo-hedonism and decadence. With them were also the books of J.K. Huysmans and the romantic Satanism which had a greater social impact than is generally remembered. Huysman's *À Rebours* and *Là Bas* were published in Brazil in the 1890s and made a great impression on Masons and Rosicrucians who were intrigued by the descriptions of the black masses. The process garnered support from intellectuals like Teixeira Werneck and Eduardo do Campos, who propogated this romantic Satanism in their intellectual circles. Naturally, these impulses coloured Quimbanda as the movement gave added pathos to the diabolic imagery of Exu. Stefania Capone (2004) concludes in her study that macumba incorporated and reinterpreted European beliefs in conformity with an African worldview. I find this observation to be profoundly correct, and this observation also explains the current tendencies amongst Quimbandeiros to disagree about the origin of the cult. The roots are metaphorically Seven.

Quimbanda tell the story of oppression and rebellion, the split between the slaves and their owners, as well as the split within the African population itself which became even more complex when children of double heritage were born. I refer those interested to the monumental work of Gilberto Freyre, *Casa Grande e Senzala* (1933) which over the course of two volumes details with great insight the complex position of the freed slave in a restrictive society which needs to adjust to the changes. It is here we find social discourse concerning the possibility of the 'barbaric' black man evolving towards the 'dignity' of the white man. Imagine the reactions when such questions were posed for discussion and debate! Some freed slaves set out to demonstrate the affirmative in this proposition, others rebelled with an even greater hatred. Conflict and ambivalence followed in an attempt to set the scales right.

In 1863 Spiritism arrived in Brazil and not long after we find low spiritism taking shape. This low spiritism recognized two lines of emanating dead, which were respectively the Indian line (Caboclos) and the African line. The low spiritism was called this, both because of the type of spirits called upon and the more rustic (read: African/Black) forms of possession and trance that took place. The label *low spiritism* reflected the French idea of a high and low magic distinction, courtesy of Eliphas Lévi. The spirits that were worked within the African line were called Pretos Velhos, or Old Blacks, being the African ancestors looking after their living descendants. These could come through their mediums in benevolent forms like Pai João or the more vengeful ones like Pai Joaquim and Pai Kongo. This low spiritism is important to mention because it rapidly took shape on its own terms in the houses of macumba where native, African and 'pagan' spirits gained prime importance in the cult. The purpose of the work was always attack, protection and guidance.

The establishment of spirit lines crystallised Quimbanda from Umbanda. Spiritism was actually welcomed by many of a Kongo heritage as a way of reconnecting with their ancestors in a new way. It is known that the word Umbanda is derived from the kimbundu *ymbanda* which roughly means chief healer, used both as a verb and as a noun. Likewise the word *quimbanda* was originally a noun, referring to the chief healer, but can also mean medicine in a general and spiritual sense. The split between Umbanda and Quimbanda is noted for the first time in the macumba houses of Rio, where the macumbeiros of black and mixed ancestry, according to Bastide, simply accepted the constant accusations of being evil and embraced Exu as the king of the reign of terror and embraced his sorcerous legacy. Here the lines and legions of crossroad spirits from Hell, and Omolu and his armies of death from the cemeteries of cultural memory and forgetfulness seep in. Quimbanda represents a particular heritage that finds itself with one foot in Africa, the other in Europe and with a soul in ancestral memory. This should also suggest that the terms Umbanda and Quimbanda were in use long before Zélio was instructed in 1920 to establish Umbanda under the guidance of the Caboclo das Sete Encruzilhadas (Caboclo of the Seven Crossroads).

In the 15th century expedition to the Congo, King João of Portugal brought a version of the European feudal system with him, albeit in miniature. In this first foray he sent priests, philosophers, teachers, and farmers, representatives of all the social classes, with the aim of spreading Western style civilisation amongst the Africans. He also took some key Congolese back to Portugal to educate them and reinstall them into their original societies and thus establish them as part of a fledgling aristocracy. In this vein we see the first manikongo (the King of Congo) Nzinga Mbemba, who was sent to the Vatican and returned to the Congo with the Bishopric name Dom Henrique I in 1521. This might have seemed a clever plan of indoctrination, but the Congolese behaved in unexpected ways and Africanised the Christianity that the Portuguese were trying to impose. This was immensely frustrating for the colonisers. Controversy and superstition abided and no matter how much the Portuguese crown and the emissaries of the Vatican tried to educate them, the Bantu and Congo were considered incapable of the right form of veneration and religion. For the Congolese the Church, the cross, the prayers, the songs, the holy book were all nkisi, that is, medicine, a power for curing or healing, or for accomplishing their ends. This worldview that early anthropologists like Tyler saw as *primitive animism* was considered rustic and barbaric. The African continent was understood as a remnant of religion and culture from an earlier stage in human evolution. This coupled with the diabolic superstitions imposed upon Africans, both by the white man's observation of his behavior, language and skin colour created the cultural frustration that infuses Quimbanda.

Sorcerous Healing

It is commonly believed that the Portuguese mission in Congo was a cruel one and that the Africans were forced to convert. However, the cruelty came later, and this is documented extensively in my book *Palo Mayombe: The Garden of Blood and Bones*. In some cases they were forced to receive baptism before embarking on the ships that took them to the New World, but mainly the mission in Congo was one of seduction. The missionaries at first allowed the Africans to maintain their traditional perspectives upon the Christian mystery believing that they could alter their perception over time. This was not very successful and meant that Catholicism in Africa was already 'heretical' before the crossing. It was necessary to keep silent about one's African practices in the New World. It is clear that the saints' sacraments and relics of Christianity were already in a synthesis with the Congolese worldview when they arrived in Brazil. This is an important point to remember, because this twisting of Christianity contributed to making the diabolic aura around the Congolese grow even stronger. There was a tendency to view the form of worship the Congolese Christians practiced to be in error, both in the form of worship and in the theological understanding. This often led to the assumption that the African faiths were diabolic cults. Hence words like *kimbanda* which actually means *that from which the cure comes* was perhaps seen as a means for curing, but equally considered as the devil's remedy, and consequently evil.

In the work edited by Phaf-Rheinberger and Pinto (2008) it is stated that the Angolan/Kimbundu term *umbanda* had the connotation of *traditional medicine or cure*. The one who mastered this discipline was the Kimbanda. As we can see from the contemporary distinctions of Umbanda and Quimbanda, a massive amount of change occurred in order to re-establish these ideas as purely Brazilian concepts uprooted from Angola and readapted to the social and spiritual climate of Brazil.

Kimbanda means healer/medium/medicine/cure and it can be a person or a tool for curing, like *nkisi*, a spirit vessel, bundles of herbs, or a talismanic object. Kimbanda is something or someone who holds the power of transformation. The healing nature of kimbanda is different from that of a sorcerer, but the power applied is similar. We should also notice that there is actually little difference in meaning when it comes to the word *mbanda* and *kmbanda*. As the phonetics suggest, the difference appears to be more one of geographical origin, between upper and lower Angola. It can also be understood as being a prefix establishing the art itself and the one performing the art. This means the kmbanda is a master of mbanda. When Umbanda took shape in Brazil so did Quimbanda, but the context was now wholly different as the fusion between the kimbanda and the sorcerer, Muloji was assumed to be one and the same.

The arts of kimbanda were recognized to be about spirit trafficking and the facilitation of cures and healing, but also to effectuate attack and revenge. The kimbandeiro was a traveler in the other world and as such fulfilled a role similar to the shaman in native traditional societies where the shaman is the healer of the society and the time traveler along the ancestral line of the tribe. The earliest dictionaries of Kimbundu/Portuguese in explaining the term *kimbanda* states that this is similar in meaning to the Kikongo *nganga* and that the term *ndoki* is similar to *muloji*. Hence we see the sorcerous potency as a quality endowed in a person, and not as a practice. What is interesting in this is that the term *muloji* signifies someone who manipulates the power of fire and the spirits of 'offence.' It has a connotation clearly suitable for the more aggressive works of Quimbanda.

Kimbandeiros, at least in certain districts, were considered ritual experts and in particular with great knowledge of funeral rites. Frequent reports and known practices of the kimbandeiros were a skill in summoning graveyard spirits, both of good and bad intent. As mentioned earlier in this chapter, the spirit known as Calunga Ngombe held a central position in the cabulas. Being the spirit of prophecy and divination he was also used for diagnosis. Illness in Congo societies was not viewed only as corporal, but there were spiritual and ancestral components to illness as well, hence the Kimbanda would work with the dead and perform acts of sorcery in his or her healing work.

Bastide presents an interesting theory as to how the syncretism and synthesis in the New World was possible. He segments Bantu and Congo faith into two vital components; ancestral reverence and reverence of nature. Of these cornerstones the colonisers broke one, that of ancestry. Therefore ancestry became uncertainty, of crossing with other people, of abuse and rape. The whole ancestral pillar went through a radical transformation. In the same way the reverence of nature was redirected. The African nature spirits that served as access points to rays and realms within Nzambi were relocated. What was left was the most important element, the worldview of the Congolese that reoriented itself in this new landscape which was partly known and partly alien. As one of Bastide's informants told him when he was researching macumba in Rio de Janeiro: *we live in a new land now, we need to pay reverence to the spirits of this land.* It was this particular Congolese attitude that ensured the survival of their faith and influenced Catimbó, Candomblé and Quimbanda in Brazil.

The Congolese reverence for nature and its spirit also extended to the native Indians of Brazil and led to a magical and powerful addition to the cult of Caboclos, which in turn also marked Candomblé. With the arrival of more and more Yoruba and Fon people, Candomblé took a different shape and crafted itself on Yoruba principles though its roots were partly Bantu/Congo. Bastide claims that the Bantu/Congo perspective was one wherein spiritual opportunity was recognised and seized in the new religious movements of Brazil, for example Spiritism, where they saw the opportunity to take back their ancestors, but within a uniquely Brazilian expression. As Bastide wrote: *It is precisely the readiness of the Bantu to take on the colour of his environment that explains why.*

In order to demonstrate the importance of the Congo influence and worldview we can look at the example of the Cabinda nation. In the 19th century theirs was a unique form of macumba which worshipped stones. The Cabindas gave reverence to the sunflower and their rituals were called *macumba*, apparently in the sense of *going to a drumming*. In the rituals of macumba they would call upon saints known as Ganga-Zumba, Canjira-Mungongo, Cubango, Sinhu-renga, Lingongo and others. In these rituals, chants, music and dance were a constant companion to aid possession by tutelary spirits and ancestors. The description is similar to what the Bishop of Espírito Santo recorded at the end of the 19th century when he wrote about the Cabulas and their worship, which again is similar to what we find in Catimbó, another cult born from indigenous and Congo influences. Other deities they venerated were Nganga Nzambi (God), Zambiapungo (the spirit-ancestor of the Kongolese people), Lemba (a spirit of fertility), Calunga (spirit of the dead and the sea) and Zumbi (spirit of death). Interestingly for us, the priests were called Quimbanda. It is here we find the transposition of the Congolese Aluvaia and Bonbonjira as being identical with Èsú, although perceived from a distinctive Bantu perspective that is still alive and well in Quimbanda today.

Bastide suggests a common origin between Bizango in Haiti and Quimbanda. Yet in Haiti Bizango is not solely Congo, but equally Marabot, that is, of mixed ancestry. I believe he has noticed here something intensely vital and important about Congo spirituality, its ability to bridge similarities in an elegant and simple synthesis. He is also seeing the sympathy between the Congo spirituality and the native spirituality that perhaps cross-fertilized each other as Quimbanda took shape.

Yet from those flames no light,
but rather darkness visible.

John Milton

Wardens at the Gates of Night

From its history we can understand both why Quimbanda is subject to such great variations, and why it is so pragmatic. It is quite impossible to see one particular ritual or devotional format as more true or original than any other. From the accounts concerning the work of macumba we see basic themes repeating themselves. The focus of the rituals were to enter into possession with one's Tatá or guiding spirit, what today is seen as one's personal Exu. This relationship, this bond, is the heart of Quimbanda. It is this merging that gives birth to the Quimbandeiro and endows him or her with a unique set of powers. These powers are in resonance with the Exu itself and the lines and kingdoms close to the practitioner and the temple of Quimbanda he or she is born from.

Holy Herbs & Enchanted Saints

St Cyprian was an important saint in macumba given his ability to empower his adherents, especially in performing magical surgeries and animal transformations. Almost no one remembers this relationship in Brazil anymore, but the mystery lives on in certain brotherhoods called *sect rouge* in Hispania, as it does amongst some witchcraft families around the world. This capacity is in the secrets of spirits like Exu Mangueira, Exu Marabô, Exu dos Rios, Exu Meia Noite and Exu Capa Preta. Likewise, we find St Anthony, St George, St John the Baptist, St Catharina and others being given reverence in the cult. Yet contemporary Quimbanda does not necessarily pay attention to saints. We find a broad spectrum ranging from Quimbanda being maintained pure and without any (or minimal) outside influences, to small and isolated cults completely subdued by saints and orixas in some Umbanda terreiros. It is clear that the differences within the cult in existence today are the memory of the many lines which give a particular colour and form to any given *cabula/terreiro*.

The native Indians also shaped Brazilian spirituality. Today this heritage is generally referred to as Caboclos and includes full blooded

Indians and those of markedly Indian descent. Folklorist Câmara Cascudo suggests that the term is either from the Tupi *caaboc*, meaning forest dweller or *kariboca*, meaning child of the white man. Caboclo was originally the name given to children born from the union of Indians and Caucasians, but over time became a denominator of Indian blood mixed with any other. The Caboclos originated in the North of Brazil from Amazonas to Alagoas, but over time spread across the entirety of Brazil. Bastide records that since 1591 the ways of the Caboclos were documented by the Inquisition tribunal under the name of *santidade*, or holiness/holy works.

Santidade was said to have built its cult around a sacred stone they called Maria and initiation into the cult was a form of baptism. There were several Christian elements to the cult, such as the use of novenas, rosaries, and crosses. The Inquisition defined them as a 'polygamous cult' dominated by singing, dancing and the use of several sacred herbs in order to access the spirit of holiness. The cult worked with Caboclos, *encantados* (enchanted ones/fairy taken) and *eatiços* (literally windwalkers – in the sense of disincarnated Caboclos) and it was directed by *Pajés* (shaman-doctors). As Santidade faded away it took the shape of Catimbó. The typical altars of the Catimbozeiro would be two-fold, one to the right and one to the left, where statues, crosses, liquors, herbs and tobacco were present. It was also common to find amphibians and insects drenched in wax or resin present on the tables, being used as servitor spirits. They had, and still have, a separation of the week where some days were better for workings of 'the left' and other days suitable for workings of 'the right.' Monday, Wednesday and Friday were seen as auspicious for benevolent workings while Tuesday, Thursday and Saturday were good for malefic, hence the expression of *giving smoke to the right or the left*.

The ritual followed the same steps whether one worked on the right or the left. With songs and prayers, whistles, incense and sweet perfumes, dead Masters and Tatás, catiços and enchanted ones were called to take possession of the Pai/Tatá, guarded by the Master of ceremonies. Once in possession, the spirits frequently asked for tobacco and alcohol to sustain and support their temporary corporeal residence.

Besides tobacco, Câmara Cascudo noticed that since 1740 the use of the herbal substance *ajua* (perhaps ayahuasca) and *jurema* made part of the cult side by side with other psychotropic and powerful plants like *djamba* (cannabis). Djamba is said to be a Bantu addition to the cult, even though djamba is actually a Yoruba word.

Of the spirits called upon we have mentioned encantados, or enchanted ones, these are people who vanished mysteriously in nature without leaving any physical trace but continuing to influence this world from the other side. We might equate this to being fairy taken in Northern European legends. One interesting legend concerning the origin of the encantados tells us that after Jesus' birth Mary went to Egypt to hide him under the roots of the Jurema tree in order to save him from Herod. This gave the tree supernatural qualities and it became the mother-tree of all encantados. This means that Jurema wine can work as a portal for people and turn them into encantados. Vital to this discourse is to note that the encantados were frequently seen as divided into seven kingdoms, although some traditions give five and others as many as 63. In these kingdoms we find states, cities and villages, each with their particular Masters. Each master has his own line of mysteries which he controls. The Masters could be native Indians, like Master Tupan (God of thunderous creation), Master Mussurana (God of healing) or be Caboclos, like Master Germano and Mistress Angelica. They could also be African, like Father Kongo, or Indian/African like Master Pai Joaquim, this generated a multitude of lines of shared ancestry. There is most certainly a legacy here that we find in Quimbanda, as in one of the pontos cantados of Pai Joaquim where we sing: *Father Joaquim is black and jolly, as quimbamba.*

In Father Joaquim, Pai Kongo and so forth we find the class of spirits called Pretos Velhos. In them the wisdom of Africa resides and it is through this wisdom Quimbanda kept flowing and moving, guarded by the Bantu and Kongo heritage of the Cabula. Preto Velho represents the original image of a Quimbandeiro, a wise healer. The same influences are also found in Catimbó which works with tables to the left and right and *give smoke*. Unlike Candomblé there is little choreography or folkloric dress code in Catimbó. Its main focus is upon the mediums and the lines of departed Masters, generating a fluid and pragmatic cult that inspired Zelio's formation of Umbanda in the 1920s and, in turn, Quimbanda itself. Bastide concludes in *The African Religions in Brazil* that:

> Catimbó devotees do not constitute solidly united organic entities. They drift from one cult centre to another, as variations in the ceremonies or the neighborhood facilities may dictate. Here religious mobility is pushed to the extreme. The determining factors are individual preferences or need, daily life and its illnesses, love affairs, crops, unhappiness, and dreams of a better future.

The Muslim Waters of Quimbanda

THE MUSLIM NATIONS that arrived in Brazil, according to Nina Rodrigues and Arthur Ramos, guarded their mysteries whilst under great scrutiny. Their ability to guard secrets was so good that today their influence is hardly mentioned and only vaguely remembered. The Muslim persuasion was referred to as Mossourubi, Musulmi and Malê. Malê comes from Mali in the Niger valley which is dominated by the Malinka people (also called Mandinga) and rapidly became a synonym for macumba and black magic. Bastide points out that it was strictly speaking the Hausa people that brought Islam to Brazil, which is interesting given the Hausas' geographical proximity to the Yorubas and the tensions between these two people. As happened when Christianity met Black culture, so too a fusion of African animism and Islam surfaced in Brazil, already in a transformed state and then going through yet another transformation in the new land. We know that in 1840 in Rio de Janeiro there was a mosque to be found at Rua Barão de São Felix. The Muslims were additionally at times called *mina* in reference to the port in Bahia where they arrived. It might also connect them to the early stages of macumba which most likely was established in the harsh conditions in the northern parts of the state Minas Gerais, where they were forced to mine for precious metals which were then transported to Victoria, Salvador, Rio de Janeiro and at a later stage to São Paulo.

As late as 1912 the existence of a Malê sect is reported in the state of Alagoas that venerated 'Ali Baba,' not the protagonist from *The Thousand and One Nights*, but Ali, the cousin of the prophet, the originator of Sufism and mystical Islam. The Ali they venerated was seen as a child draped in red, wearing necklaces of *ofás* and an *alufa* referred to as *iman* or *almany* who presided over the ceremonies which included making arabesque paintings while singing hymns of praise to Allah and orixás.

Today these influences are rarely mentioned. It is as if the waters of Islam flowed completely into the spiritual climate of the time. This can be partly explained by the transformative quality Black Islam held, but also because the Hausa people were considered a great problem for the colonisers. From 1813 they started to ship many of these troublesome Hausa Muslims back to Africa, whilst eradicating many others. This led to the stronghold of Black Islam being fragmented, yet this allowed it to fully merge with the land and its spirits.

There are some accounts of celebrations of Ramadan in small closed communities in Bahia and Rio in the late 19th century that describe the prayers and also the charms and practical magic performed. The importance of *kissium* (prayer) and the Alcoran (Al Quran) is noted, as well as that they wear the abada and turban, and that they use prayer beads and observe fasts. Their public ceremonies were always performed in secluded places and they were reputed to be very private and secretive about their cult. The few accounts left speak of seeing supernatural light glowing upon the faces of the Malê and Alufás. Reports of mysterious giants of fire walking in their company naturally gave them the reputation of being masters of black magic. Some saw benefit in this and started to sell spells utilising the aid of spirits known as *aligenum*, better known to us as djinn. It is plausible that some of this heritage found its way into the constantly developing Quimbanda, but it is hard to deduce exactly what came through the Muslim sorcerers.

I find it reasonable to assume that this legacy is a memory encoded in the Malei line, and also in the Mossourubi (or Mossurubi). This assumption is fortified by some votaries of Malei Quimbanda being rather cautious with alcohol, tobacco and meat and even using prayer beads in works of contemplation and trance. It is also possible that at least some of the astrological lore that went through a theosophical reorientation by Lourenço Braga in the 1960s ultimately had a Malê or Alufa (Muslim) heritage. We can summarise this by returning to a quote from *Pomba Gira and the Quimbanda of Mbùmba Nzila*:

> There is yet another line, called Mossourubi, which is at root related to the Malê, Muslims from the area of Mali and Sudan that were particularly represented in the state of Alagoas. These people were also called Malinka and Madinga, and this referred to those Africans who were neither Bantu nor Yorubá. The Yorubás were known by the generic Nagô. Malê is quite similar to Malei, yet another line of Quimbanda, reputed to be the most violent and sinister of them all. The chief of this line is Exu Rei and his deputy Exu Marabo. Marabó is a term designating a sorcerer amongst Muslims in Sierra Leone and Ghana, equivalent to a juju man. Could it be that several of the lines found in Quimbanda today originate from this small group of Muslims from Yorubaland and Dahomey?

The Lines of the Morningstar

RISING FROM THIS MELTING POT of diverse influences, we find the Spiritist sect called the Followers of the Morning Star. This fellowship was heavily influenced by the French spiritist and occult movement and had at its core a doctrine that divided disembodied spirits into the following categories:

- *Guides*, who do not come down to earth, but ensure a certain celestial or planetary radiation which is accessible on earth.
- *Spirits of Light*, who are the messengers of the Guides.
- *Marumbos*, which are seen as disobedient and restless spirits that insist on staying earthbound.
- *Suffering spirits*, who cause illness and inspire evil.

From these four categories they saw five different irradiations or forces in nature that they parted into lines. These were:

- *The Line of Exu*, where all vice amongst mankind was found.
- *The Line of Souls*, where the suffering spirits were found.
- *The Line of Quimbanda*, which was seen as composed of spirits telluric in essence, but having the nature of the Moon and Neptune. They saw these as the planetary forces inspiring sin and addiction. This line was nothing less than black magic of the worst kind.
- *The Line of Uruanda (Arruanda)*, which was composed of spirits that have turned away from their evil ways and towards the light, ie undergoing a process of conversion.
- *The Line of Umbanda* that works only with spirits of nature which have become divinized and do the work of light.

In this organisation we find the *marumbos*, a corruption of maroon or marabou, with the meaning of black ancestry. It is also likely that the word *marumbu/marumbo* and *mironga* (spell work) are related. Likewise, the line of Quimbanda, which was at this time considered the African line ruled by St Cyprian, was as disobedient and restless as the marum-

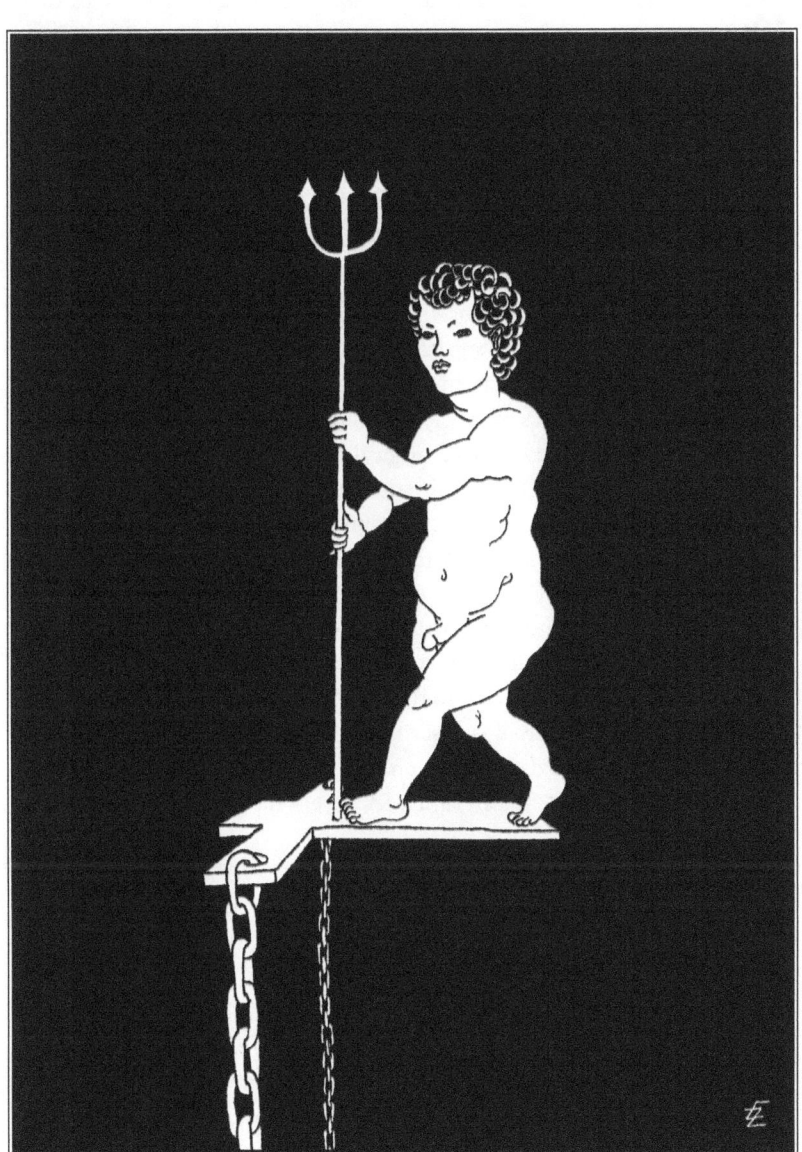

bos. The African heritage was acknowledged as a line in its own right, but was riddled with negative ideas and concepts. Clearly the idea of African cultures representing a primitive stage in human evolution motivated this hierarchy and the conversion of the Africans was now given a spiritual dimension. These tendencies were presented early on with a dilemma when the mediums working in the line of Umbanda also received the spirits of Pretos Velhos, Caboclos, Orixas, and even Exus.

Given these factors another hierarchy took shape, but was rapidly transformed. This hierarchy attempted to organize the African spirits into nations, such as Nagô, Cassange, Angola, Malê and so forth. These attempts at organizing the spirits were in turn redefined through the work of N. A. Molina, Antonio Alves and Aluizio Fontenelle which developed into the lines of classical Quimbanda still worked today. Beneath this lies a forked root of magical Christianity where Joseph of Arimathea was considered the mystical origin of Umbanda whilst the heritage of Nicodemus prefigured the mysteries of Quimbanda.

In this process Exu takes on the role of Satan and Lucifer, understood to be the murky subconscious of God himself. He is the cosmic quicksilver that threatens the natural order. Because of this the spirits in the line of Quimbanda were seen as cosmic fluids of a sinister disposition that could be converted to the light by being treated as the slaves of Orixás and Angels. Exu is described as a part of our animal soul, an instinct aiming towards survival, protection, defense and attack, what the Umbandistas came to call *pagan*. So, here is the divide, in the words of Fontenelle:

> Quimbanda perpetuates the determination to maintain the old African traditions, while Umbanda seeks to break away from the wild and uncivilized influence of Quimbanda.

Lacking a kinder word, it seems to me that a form of spiritual racism is moving the spiritual climate. But it is also worth noting that the African roots were so far spread into so many conclaves of spiritual life that it was impossible to remove them.

It should be clear by now that the idea of lines arrived from several different origins, such as the cult of encantados, Santidade and Catimbó as well as Spiritism. The Followers of the Morning Star are but one example. This too is found in Kardec's spiritist theology, where one of the pillars is that spirits generate phalanxes based upon common affinities. In the same way as we humans form groups and relationships based upon intellect, shared interests or vibrations, so it is on the other side.

Already in 1925 Leal de Souza had generated a proto-line where macumba and Spiritism merged with Candomblé influences as they were presenting the first lines of Umbanda.

- *The Line of Oxalá* (Nosso Senhor do Bomfim)
- *The Line of Ogum* (Saint George)
- *The Line of Euxoca* (Oxossi) (Saint Sebastian)
- *The Line of Xangô* (Saint Jerome)
- *The Line of Nhan-San* (Iyansan) (Saint Barbara)
- *The Line of Yemanjá* (Our Lady of Conception)
- *The Line of Almas* (Souls, the African Line of Saint Cyprian)

What is salient here is that the Yoruba spirits, the Orixás, are given an elevated position while the Bantu and Congo heritage are bundled together into one line, the line of souls which was in practice the line of Quimbanda.

In the following decade the lines changed, and so did their content. We find the Line of Oxalá turning completely Catholic and not only venerating the legions of Saints like Anthony, Rita, Catherine and Expeditus, but also departed Africans who during their life were good Catholics. The Line of Yemanjá turns into a line of multiple legions wherein we find sirens, undines, Caboclos of waters, and mythological creatures like the Boto and the spirit Jara. The lines also hold a particular affinity with Mary Magdalena, Venus, the Moon and Polaris. The Line of Iyansan is substituted with the Line of the Orient seen as being commanded by Joseph of Arimathea, and here we find nearly every kind of people from Eskimos to Europeans, Japanese to Arabians. The Line of Oxossi and Xangô were filled with Indian spirits and Caboclos while the Ogums were considered guardians of lines like Malei, Nagô and given places in nature. Lastly the Line of Souls, defined as the African line, lost its saint and was seen as ruled by Father Cabinda, in reference to the slaveport in the Congo delta. Here, in Cabinda, we find legions of Angola, Guine, Congo, Mozambique and so forth, all with their Masters and Fathers.

In this climate Quimbanda takes shape, as in a glass darkly it shows its resistance, with wings, claws and African blood it rises within seven lines, which were detailed in the mid 1930s as being as follows:

• *The Line of Souls* ruled by Omolu and his legions of cemetery ghosts and ghouls.
• *The Line of Skeletons of the Cemetery* ruled by João Caveira (John Skull) and his legion of hungry ghosts.
• *The Nagô Line* ruled by Gererê and spirits haunting crossroads.
• *The Mossorubi Line (Muslim)* ruled by Exu Kaminaloá and his legions of crossroad demons.
• *The Malei Line* ruled by Exu Rei and Marabô with their legions of vicious and dangerous spirits of aristocratic and decadent leanings.
• *The Line of Caboclos Quimbandeiros* ruled by Pantera Negra (Black Panther) and his legions of savage spirits, both African and Indian.
• *The Mixed Line* ruled by Exu das Campinas (Exu of the Plains) and his myriad of hostile spirits.

Seven is a recurring theme and a number with great significance. There is good reason to assume that the seven lines and seven kingdoms were partly influenced by the *Book of Revelation* where we find the seven churches that are given seven messages and each possess seven weaknesses and strengths. As the Seven Churches of the Apocalypse designated specific types of congregations or communities, so did the seven original lines. and from this the hierarchies.

The Seven Infernal Kingdoms are divided into seven night hours, each holding a particular vibration where given works are said to be more effective. In the middle ages the night hours were divided into the following decans or parts and similar observations can be noted in some houses of Quimbanda even today:

> Crepusculum
> Vesperum
> Conticinium
> Intempestiva
> Gallicinium
> Matutinum
> Diluculum

Only Intempestiva, the dead of night, the blackest hour is considered auspicious for the night flight, whereas the twilight hours are seen as mixed hours that can be used for a multitude of workings. The two hours marking the twilight of the Sun's rest would be benevolent hours and conticinium being the hour of contemplation and fortifying the focus of the work taking place at the Intempestiva, the *inopportune hour*. This gives us the hour of cock's crow, Gallicinium, where light returns to the world over the next two hours, which are excellent for purifications and sending to rest what is restless. Gallicinium is given the colour black, Matutinum, red and Diluculum, white.

The Seven Lines of Quimbanda

THE LEGIONS OF EXU are organised into specific lines. These are the hierarchies that will be presented shortly, but there are also hierarchies within the hierarchies. Each and every Exu is a chief in its own line of mystery with its attendant spirits. This is also true for each and every house of Exu and Tatá. For instance, in a house where Tatá Exu Morcego is sole chief, a unique hierarchy, albeit with common denominators, will establish itself. Likewise, if a particular set of mysteries is worked, let us say roots and healing, one would organize the Exus at least into a kingdom or even a line of healing spirits where Exu Curadôr, Exu das Matas and Exu Pimenta would be high up, given their expertise in these matters. This means that whatever Exu is the head of a given temple is the king of that place. Your personal Exu is the king in your life and as such is in charge, being at the top of the hierarchy for you. The hierarchies change according to which Exu is the most prominent in the various temples and terreiros. We might see the terreiros as distinct districts in the realm of Quimbanda, each with its own chief. These spirits are organized in many different ways: just as spiritual and social organisations can vary in form, so do they. Furthermore, one should be aware that the hierarchy is not carved in stone. It is a dynamic organisation, and just as military officers change rank over time, indeed so can Exu. This is accomplished by the constant addition of new Exus to the legions, which induces a healthy dynamic into the organisation of the various legions. Thus, the system turns into a dynamic relationship with Exu and Pomba Gira, which is based upon personal congress with these spirits. The simple secret is that every Exu and Pomba Gira is a king and queen in his or her own realm. The organisation into hierarchies is actually far less important than the personal relationship the votary forms with Exu. Knowledge of the original hierarchy may come in handy when work with a given Exu is failing. One can approach an Exu higher up in the hierarchy than the Exu worked in order to reinstate harmony. For instance, if a problem is experienced in a work with Exu Carangola, it is possible to rectify matters by appealing to Exu Caveira or Exu Tranca Ruas as they are senior in the hierarchy.

Another element is that each Exu and Pomba Gira is seen by Umbandistas as having roads themselves. This means that there is an Exu Caveira of the Souls, just as there is an Exu Caveira of the Crossroad and so on. This manifold segmentation exists in order to give added quality and direction to the power worked with. For example, the power of Exu Caveira in his natural habitat, the Cemetery, will be different to finding this force at the shores of the ocean.

Another organisation of the spirits of Quimbanda is in terms of kingdoms. The kingdoms are as follows: Encruzilhadas (Crossroads), Cruzeiro (a reference to the large votary Cross in the middle of the cemetery), Matas (Fields/Weeds), Calunga (Cemetery), Almas (Souls),

Liras (Harp) and Praia (Beach). This classification will be used in the spirit catalogue given in this book. The kingdoms also present the Exus and Pomba Giras in their original station, as guardian spirits of specific portals in nature and places of power. In the kingdoms we meet original powers, whilst in the lines we meet teaching spirits. It is useful to have a good grasp of the kingdoms, because no work is done unless licence is granted from the kingdom we work with. Exus from other lines and kingdoms can then enter as parts of the spirit host when a particular work is done, depending on what kind of work is done in the kingdom. Just like an army distributes its soldiers and commanders depending on the type of expedition being undertaken, so it is with the spirit host established in kingdoms, workings and in life. These positions will not necessarily be the same as their rank in the hierarchy but are mediated by the temperament of the Tatá and the terreiro.

It is finally worth observing that the lines replicate the mystical number nine as the seven Exus have a king and a queen that begins and ends the lines. This nine-fold division is found again in the organisation of Exus placed in kingdoms.

Here follows the traditional seven lines of Quimbanda:

First Line
The Line of Malei, headed by Exu Rei

This line is said to be related to the practices of Catimbó and has lately gained a reputation of being a school of black magic, a sort of dark side of Quimbanda. The colour of this line is black, red, dark green and gold. This reputation can however be disputed, as the line consists of some of the most wise and benign powers of all the legions, but it is also because of the aristocratic and wise quality of these Exus that makes work with kiumbas (i.e. husks, larvæ) perhaps more safe in this line than any other. These spirits are associated with reptilian spirits of the night, and also with the beast-like forms some men become after their death. Some people do not turn into pure souls upon death, but rather become creatures of nightmare. This line is said to consist of the spirits of sorcerers and witches. Personally I find reasons to see this line as one inspired by the proto African lines and the heritage of the Malê (Muslim) people. Because of this I am not in agreement with Exu Rei being the ruler, but rather Exu Marabô the Elder. Some say that these spirits make the high council amongst the Exu and they are organised as follows:

1 · Exu Rei das Sete Encruzilhadas
2 · Exu Marabô
3 · Exu Mangueira
4 · Exu Tranca Ruas das Almas
5 · Exu Tiriri
6 · Exu Veludo
7 · Exu dos Rios or Campinas
Pomba Gira · Pomba Gira Rainha das Sete Encruzilhadas

Second Line
The Line of Souls, headed by Omolu

This line works with the transition of souls between the planes; as such, all of these Exus are at times understood to be omolus, spirits of the Cemetery. The colours of this line are red, black and white. The work in this line is of a healing nature and we find much Yoruba influence here. For instance, the *padé* is frequently used, as is the food known as amalá and various forms of white *ebós*. These Exus are excellent teachers of the art of mediumship. It is a fine balance in the line between stable benevolent forces and more eruptive benevolent forces. This line can be worked when we seek to understand the mysteries of death in all its facets. They are organised in the following way:

1 · Exu Mirim
2 · Exu Pimenta
3 · Exu das Sete Montanhas
4 · Exu Ganga
5 · Exu Kaminaloá

6 · Exu Malê
7 · Exu Quirombô
Pomba Gira · Pomba Gira das Almas

Third Line
The Line of the Cemetery, headed by Exu Caveira

These spirits live in the cemetery and take the form of skulls and skeletons. Their colours are red and black with hints of yellow. This line is marked by the undead, revenants, vampires, and night creatures of all kinds. In the line of the cemetery we find death in a most active form. These spirits can be evil, sexual and dangerous, but they are also some of the most effective spirits to work with in solving impossible situations or unblocking roads. When this line is worked it is important to observe regular regimes of purification and magical baths as kiumbas frequently come on hard when this line is worked. These spirits are organised as follows:

1 · Exu Tatá Caveira
2 · Exu Brasa
3 · Exu Pemba
4 · Exu do Lodo
5 · Exu Carangola
6 · Exu Arranca Toco
7 · Exu Pagão
Pomba Gira · Pomba Gira Rainha dos Cemitérios

Fourth Line
The Line of Nagô, headed by Exu Gererê

This line is reputed to be one of the more advanced of the lines, being from the area of Nagô on the border of Benin and Nigeria. The colours of this line are black and red. These Exus control the magical arts, astral travel and are well versed in the art of Vodou. Exu Gererê is often confused with Exu Ganga, but is in fact a slight corruption of Gégé, designating the work with Vodouns in Candomblé. The spirits in this line are said to be Gangas, in the sense of being sorcerers or magical medicine. They preserve a form of Vodou of Nagô origin and at the same time are a more 'pure' expression of Yoruba faith. The Nagô line is reputed to be very hard, demanding and dangerous in its crude Kongo sorcery.

1 • Exu Quebra Galho
2 • Exu Sete Cruzes
3 • Exu Gira Mundo
4 • Exu do Cemitério
5 • Exu Capa Preta
6 • Exu Curadôr
7 • Exu Ganga
Pomba Gira • Pomba Gira Maria Padilha

Fifth Line
The Line of Mossorubi, headed by Exu Kaminaloá

This line consists of spirits who have the power to influence the minds of people, to cause diseases and inspire insanity. Its colours are red, black and dark blue. Those working with this line tend to develop excellent skills as dreamers and diviners. It is a line of Arabic influence where we find both the warrior and the sheikh. It is also said that this line tends to bring in Asian influences to the life of the one who works it, such as Buddhism and Bön-po. Pomba Gira Rosa Caveira has an affinity with this line. Whenever you need to attack another person's mind to cause insanity and delusion, cancer or diseases of the blood, these spirits know the ways. Here I believe the hierarchy is slightly off, or perhaps it has simply changed over time. I would personally move Exu Morcego to be first in command, followed by Sete Portas, then Sete Sombras and then Dos Ventos. The spirits of this line are as follows:

1 · Exu dos Ventos
2 · Exu Morcego
3 · Exu Sete Portas
4 · Exu Tranca Tudo
5 · Exu Marabá
6 · Exu Sete Sombras
7 · Exu Calunga
Pomba Gira · Pomba Gira Maria Mulambo

Sixth Line
The Line of Caboclos Quimbandeiros, headed by Exu Pantera Negra

This line consists of Indians and Quimbandeiros who are experts in the art of healing, cursing and shape shifting. The knowledge of the wild lies here as well as the legacy of the Caboclos and their sorcery. Their colours are black, red, green and white. These spirits often take the role of personal guides for the people they choose to walk with. Most stories relate that these spirits were more concerned with inflicting pain and harm on people when they walked the earth, but in their disembodied state they have turned into helpers and healers, yet they retain a poisonous sting. Most of these Exus are found in the woodland and they always take the shape of Indians. They are as follows:

1 · Exu Sete Cachoeiras
2 · Exu Tronqueira
3 · Exu Sete Poeiras
4 · Exu das Matas
5 · Exu das Sete Pedras
6 · Exu do Cheiro
7 · Exu Pedra Negra
Pomba Gira · Pomba Gira da Figueira and/or Cigana

Seventh Line
The Mixed Line, headed by Exu dos Rios or Exu das Campinas

This line does not consist only of Exus in the strict sense of the word, but also a great variety of malefic spirits and entities of crude composition that can be used in works of attack and malefica. These spirits can also become guides and teachers for the Quimbadeiro, but many of these Exus have a reputation of being unreliable, as they feed upon destruction, obsession and havoc. It is not possible to list the names of spirits of this line as they seek out the Quimbandeiro along personal paths. It is however interesting to note that this line is the redefined African line from the 1920s, here considered a collective of myriad spirits. It seems that the constant spirits in this line are Zé Pelintra and Pretos Velhos Quimbandeiros.

Lines of Umbanda related to Quimbanda

For the sake of completing this presentation it is worth seeing the relationship Quimbanda has with Umbanda in terms of lines. This organisation considers Quimbanda as a slave line of Umbanda and hence Orixás are considered to be the true chiefs of Quimbanda.

- *The Line of Oxalá* is related to the line of Malei.
- *The Line of Ogum* is related to the line of the Cemetery.
- *The Line of Oxóssi* is related to the line of Caboclos Quimbandeiros.
- *The Line of Xangô* is related to the line of Mossorubi.
- *The Line of Yorimá* is related to the line of Souls.
- *The Line of Yemanjá* is related to the line of Nagô.
- *The Line of Ibêji* is related to the mixed line.

In addition to this, Ogum serves a distinct and important function as the guardian of ritual procedures, and his manifestations in terms of lines are as follows:

Ogum Malê · The Line of Malei.
Ogum Megê · The Line of the Cemetery.
Ogum Rompe Mato · The Line of Caboclos Quimbandeiros.
Ogum Matinata (and/or Rompe Mato) · The Line of Mossorubi.
Ogum Megê · The Line of the Souls.
Ogum de Nagô · The Line of Nagô.
Ogum Xoroquê · The Mixed Line (Linha Mista).

There are also other Ogum spirits, more tied to the lines, such as Ogum Beira Mar who is seen as guardian of the line of Yemanjá and the ocean shore and Ogum Yara who is a protector of rivers, waterfalls and female Caboclos and women in male-oriented occupations, like hunting, the police and military.

When a given Exu is taken as a focal point the hierarchies tend to change accordingly and are then moved by the given Exu possessing a radiation that calls upon a unique hierarchy. For instance, if we take Exu Meia Noite as a focal point for a working we would also have access to Exus like Mirim, Pimenta, Malê, Ganga, Kaminaloá, Carangola and Quirombô. Some of these are not even listed as having a ruling position in the kingdoms, so with that in mind, here follows the presentation of a few Exus who fall outside of the arrangement in the spirit catalogue.

Exu Carangola (Sidragosum)

An Angolan Exu, as the name indicates, Carangola is reputed to make people disorientated and confused. He induces hysteria and madness of various kinds. Some say that he is the spirit that inspired the whirling dances amongst the dervishes; this is because he enters possession with a similar swirling movement. He is also knowledgeable about the domains of Exu Caveira and is said to have been a Rabbi, or at least well versed in the mysteries of Kabala. He is one of the more obscure Exus and is best approached under the auspices of Exu Caveira, as he has a reputation of being difficult to control. Often he does whatever he pleases, unless Exu Caveira is present to restrain him.

Sacred Items: Expensive cloth, trident, cigar, whiskey and marafo.

Iconography: A middle-aged Exu with full beard, ponytail, dressed in a multi-coloured cape but dominated by red. He is holding a trident and a book.

Ponto Cantado of Exu Carangola

O meu senhor das armas,	*My Lord of arms,*
Eu é fio de Angola!	*I am the son of Angola!*
Eu é Exu,	*I am Exu,*
Exu Carangola.	*Exu Carangola.*

Ponto Riscado of Exu Carangola

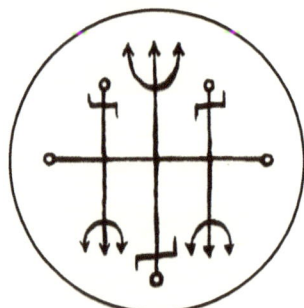

Exu Pimenta (Trimasæl)
Exu Hot Pepper

Pimenta is the chemist amongst the Exus, an expert in the arts of alchemy and herbs, a field in which love potions and magical powders are his specialty. Some say that his 'body' is too fluid to enter any horse and possessions usually take the form of inspiration. His colour is a hot red and his appearance is said to be that of a young handsome man who likes champagne and sweet marafo. He is one of the more powerful healers amongst the Exu and serves as a good guide for the person he takes under his wing. He is a gentle and wise spirit, but can be unpredictable. He often works with Exu Malê and Exu Curadôr.

Sacred Items: Cachaça (*marafo*), whiskey, herbs, roots, trident and medicine bags.

Iconography: A young red-hued Exu in a loincloth, holding a medicine bag and a trident.

Ponto Cantado of Exu Pimenta

Todo mundo quer,	*Everybody wants,*
Mas só Umbanda é que agüenta,	*But just Umbanda can take it,*
Chega, chega no Terreiro,	*Arrive, arrive in the Terreiro,*
Chega, chega Exu Pimenta.	*Arrive, arrive Exu Pimenta.*

Ponto Riscado of Exu Pimenta

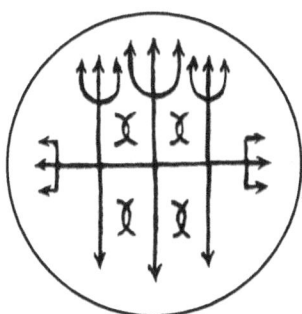

Exu Pinga Fogo
Exu of the Dripping Fire

Exu pinga fogo works in the African line of Souls, known as Yorimá. In this line we find the Preto Velhos from Congo, like Pai Arruda, Pai Congo and Pai Guiné. Exu Pinga Fogo works closely with Pai Guiné, and the herb Guiné (*Petiveria alliacea*) is sacred to them both. This, along with tamarind, eucalyptus, banana leaves and alfavaca (*Ocimum basilicum*), though a fusion of cloves and basil can be used as a substitute. He also likes garlic, so a fumigation or bath for him can be made with garlic, guiné, eucalyptus and alfavaca. He likes lead and tin for metals, and in the mineral kingdom he likes onyx and hematite. The latter is a stone he at times uses for healing purposes. It is said that he has had royal incarnations in the past, but since he was given to stealing, this became his end.

Pinga Fogo likes any form of pointed objects, be they needles, knives or spears. He works in the Campo Santo with Pretos Velhos and with Omolu. Here he works in the line of souls, but he is applied at times in workings that go counter to the purposes of elevation and transition so important in this kingdom.

Sacred Items: Cognac with honey, cigars and cachaça, candles and *guia* (necklaces) in black and white with traces of red.

Iconography: A middle aged red-hued Exu with torn clothes holding a torch and a trident both dripping with fire.

Pontos Cantados for Exu Pinga Fogo

Não bata na pedra,	*Don't knock on the rock,*
Da pedra sai fogo,	*From the Stone flows fire,*
Quem é que está na gira,	*Who is it that is here in this gira,*
É Seu Pinga Fogo.	*It is Exu Pinga Fogo.*
Eu sou Exú Pinga Fogo,	*I am Exu Dripping Fire,*
No alto do chapadão,	*At the summit of the big plateau,*
Comendo jaca madura,	*Eating ripe jaca,* (a fruit)
E jogando as verdes no chão,	*And throwing the green ones on the floor.*
Eu sou Exú Pinga Fogo,	*I am Exu Dripping Fire,*

No alto do chapadão,	At the summit of the big plateau,
Engolindo bolas de fogo,	Swallowing balls of fire,
E guspindo elas no chão.	And spitting them out on the floor.

Ponto Riscado of Exu Pinga Fogo

Exu Pantera Negra
Exu Black Panther

Some say that Exu Pantera Negra is not really an Exu, but a Caboclo Quimbandeiro. Others say he was a Cherokee chieftain that had to flee from his tribe after abusing his sorcerous powers and took up residence in the north of Brazil. He is reputed to be able to heal incurable illnesses and effectuate magical feats of cruel and dramatic dimensions. He clearly has a deep relationship with Pajelança, the indigenous faith amongst the Indians in and around the Amazon. This relationship is testified to by his ponto of firmeza, the song that summons his presence, which is in Tupi dialect, where he is called Yawara Pixuna. Pantera Negra has a double leaning, both towards the aristocratic Malei line and the Caboclos, and works well with spirits of both these inclinations. Being a natural authority he tends to inspire fear in his votaries and respect amongst the Exus. He has a close relationship with Exu Pedra Negra and Exu Marabô.

Sacred Items: Tobacco, gin, whiskey, ayahuasca, jurema, feathers, resins, thunderstones, jaguars, panthers, mountains, and waterfalls.

Iconography: A dark hued proud Indian dressed in flamboyant feathers and dark coloured leathers, flanked by a black panther and a large obsidian rock.

Pontos Cantados for Pantera Negra

Procure em todas as bandas,	Search in all places,
Em todas vai encontrar,	In all you will find,
Meu nome é Pantera Negra,	My name is Black Panther,
Que baixei pra trabalhar.	That came down to work.

YAWARA Ê !
YAWARA Ê !
HEY YAWARA
YAWARA PIXUNA
PIXUNA Ê, YAWARA
YAWARA, YAWARA!

Força, saúde e bem estar,	*Strength, health and well being,*
A legião vai te dar,	*A legion will always give you,*
Pantera na terra, pantera na agua,	*Panther on earth, panther on wáter,*
Pantera no fogo e pantera no ar,	*Panther on fire and Panther on air,*
Te venzo com o poder de Jaguar!	*I win over you with the power of the Jaguar.*

Ponto Riscado of Exu Pantera Negra

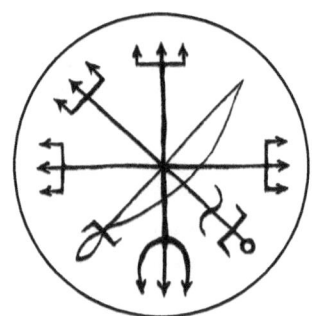

It would be difficult for me not to conclude that the most perfect type of masculine beauty is Satan, as portrayed by Milton.

Charles Baudelaire

IV

The Fig of Fire

In one of the pontos cantados for Pomba Gira Figueira do Inferno (the Fig Tree in Hell) we sing: *shake the fig, shake the fig, and let us see Exus falling from the tree*. This verse demonstrates how attached Exu is to Pomba Gira, Woman of Seven Husbands, and it also states the powers of the Queen of Quimbanda. If she shakes, Exu will fall. Pomba Gira represents the totality of female possibility. Her rays penetrate through solemn whispers in the boneyard and the burning lust of vampires. She is as much the stern Queen in control as riddled with debauchery.

Libertine Spirits of Truth

Over the years Quimbanda has gained a reputation for being one of the most welcoming of all African-rooted traditions in the diaspora. It is a cult free from judgment of people in all their diversity. This has also led to some unbalanced focus on the sexual element and we can today find examples of people stating that, for instance, Pomba Gira has a preference for homosexuals, prostitutes, transgenders and transsexuals. But this is not so. In truth, they don't care about colour, social status or sexual orientation, they care about heart and honesty – that painful truth many have difficulties admitting to themselves.

She is a spiritual force that encourages honesty of self, and Exu supports her ways and makes them stable. It is almost as if we see a reversal of the traditional symbolism here where the male is the pole and the woman is the possibility, what we see taking shape here is about the mystery of the pole itself. The pole is encouraged to be erect by the pounding heart, blood and soul of woman.

The openness in Quimbanda is not only due to the social conditions amongst Kimbundu speaking nations but also a consequence of the cultural diversity in Brazil that managed to uphold a form of adoration for women, albeit in the shadows of the machismo so typical in Latin countries. Macumba, later identified also with Quimbanda, gives us a myriad of stories of men protecting women, going to death for women and women having multiple lovers. No matter how you wish to look at it, the essential nature of many Exus is that they, as the fallen host, adore women. Hence they call upon the demonic as they recognise woman as heart and soul, purpose and meaning. I dare say that even the vilest of Exus will tell in the end the story of woman being the bed where his anchor caught.

Deep within Quimbanda we find a celebration of heart, soul and woman. So there should not be any mystery as to why anyone feeling the eyes of a judgmental society upon them will feel at home in the wild court of Quimbanda. In this untamed court she is Dominatrix and Solace, the soul pure and free of judgment. With her blood-dripping whip she tempers men and woman to be free and true in their pursuit of setting their ecstatic fate on fire.

The fact that Quimbanda does not discriminate between genders and sexual preferences goes back to its African roots, where amongst most Kimbundu-speaking people sexual preferences were not seen as problematic. In other West African districts, especially in the southern parts, the tendency was to see homosexuality as an attack upon nature, a form of grave disrespect towards the earth and the conceived natural order. In some districts death was the punishment for this. It should also be added that in Brazil the development of Quimbanda was taken care of by Kimbundus who were quite open in their approach to life, and fused with the equally carefree native inhabitants in Brazil and exiled people from Europe. So, the open-mindedness of the particular African strain and the liminial situation of exiled Europeans fused with the natural and joyous ways of the native Indians made prejudice difficult to establish.

Pomba Gira has embraced the voluptuous, the sexually dangerous and libertine. In doing this she becomes the sensual and erotic dagger that cuts both ways. This doesn't mean that she is a spirit that encourages us to cultivate vices, rather she forces us into situations where direct confrontation with vices and the sensual world of the soul gives us opportunities for gaining a deeper understanding about ourselves and our world. By assuming this form she brings a testimony to the world about the value and worth of being true to yourself and your choices in the labyrinth of fate. There is nothing right or wrong in her world, there is simply acceptance and denial. Her whip drives you away from social acceptance to self acceptance.

Since she is a liminial spiritual reality thwarting the extremes of experience and life, certainly a female prostitute – or any sex worker for that matter – would benefit from developing a relationship with Pomba Gira because she represents all facets of womanhood and guards woman in all situations. Likewise, Exu is prone to guard honourable males, in whatever situation, as long as heart and truth is present.

Over the last 30 years or so a tendency has surfaced where Quimbanda is used to effectuate our desires. It has become about binding objects of desire and pulling down the tower so it can fall upon the heads of our personal enemies. Prior to this, Exu was placated to lift sorrows, to make the crooked straight, to give money and not poverty. As the world changes, so do our demands. Naturally they can do all these works for you, but all invasions into natural currents come with a cost and a consequence. When we make a Quimbanda working for, let us say, the binding an object of desire, we need to observe what drives us. In this, we should understand that in the premise of the work we automatically summon a blessing or a lesson. The clearer we are about this, the less crooked our road to desire will be.

In a cosmological myth from Uganda, Charlotte and Wolf Leslau retell how Kabezya Mpungu, equivalent to the Bantu and Kongo idea of God, Nzambi Mpungu, had four children: Sun, Moon, Darkness and Rain. He then created the first man and woman and decided to withdraw from his work. Prior to this he called his four first creations together and asked what they would do in his absence. They all revealed that they would abuse their power and allow their quality to reign forever. Kabezya Mpungu made them agree to take their allotted part and placed Mutimba, 'heart' in his place. Mutimba felt lost in the world and declared: *Oh how great is my desire, said Heart, to commune with him. But since I cannot find him I will enter into Man, and through him I will seek God from generation to generation.*

It is curious, and quite beautiful, to see that the heart, the throne of the soul, is placed amidst powers that each had a tendency to overflow and thus generate disequilibrium whereas the Mutimba has a direction upwards, to the source.

The Gardens of Hell

A QUIMBANDEIRO IS A HEALER, hence the realm of medicine and plants should make part of the corpus of their knowledge. The herbarium of Exu is one of cures and poisons, of calmatives and psychotropics that ease or agitate mind and passion. The herbs and sticks, trees and scents favored by Exu are fiery and Saturnine, Solar, Jovial and Mercurial. We find plants announcing death, as in poisons and trees like yew and manioca brava (*Manhihot esculenta*). We find hellebore, mandrake and the melons of São Caetano (*Momordica charantia*), side by side with Crown of Christ (*Euphorbia milii*), mint, macadamia and laurel. I have decided to give a herbarium of Exu based on the particular property of the plant as it resonates in quality with Exu, hence herbs and plants, leaves and trees from all corners of the world will be given here along with their uses and qualities as applied within Quimbanda. In Quimbanda Exus take on the form of bats, crows, and undefined hybrids: part animal, vegetable or mineral like Exu do Lodo, who animates the muddy beaches and Exu Brasa who comes to life within embers. There seems to be a wholly different metamorphosis present amongst the Exus and hence their garden is also different from the flora we find in Pomba Gira's adytum. So with this be welcome to the garden, where Exu walks the night.

ACONITE, WOLFSBANE or MONKSHOOD (*Aconitum napellus*) is not native to Brazil but its lycanthropic gifts make it an interesting plant that prefers to grow amidst the rocky soil in the gardens of Hell, likewise DIGITALIS which carries similar properties as the bane of the wolf. It is said to have been born from the saliva of Kerberos in his confrontation with Herakles.

Ash (*Fraxinus ornus*) is the tree said to have wounded Achilles. It is also said that it sprang from the blood of the castrated Ouranos. This tree can be used in works of stability and protection and to ward off hostile energies.

Alecrim/Rosemary (*Rosmarinus officinalis*) is a plant that brings strength of soul and mind and is particularly sacred to the kingdom of Calunga and the ocean shore. Its use in works of love is well attested to in its reputation as a plant ally of streghes in Italy. The plant also holds the capacity of what we might call grace and is as such a wonderful herb to use to sanctify spaces. The plant is frequently used as a component in sacred baths to clean temple and home and it can also be used in works of attraction as it ignites the fires of love and passion. For cleaning the tronco of Quimbanda or to get rid of negativity in one's home 2/3 rosemary can be used together with 1/3 raw tobacco macerated in 3 dl of vodka and added to water.

Alfazema/Lavender (*Lavandula sp.*) is used to attract the line of Souls and is a powerful expeller of negativity. It has natural disinfectant qualities, brings the mind to rest and provokes dreams. It can be used as a fumigation or an infusion.

Aroeira/Mastic (*Pistacia lentiscus*) is indispensable when seating Exu. Its resin is said to be the concentrated fire of Exu, but its powdered bark can also be used, as it has similar qualities to the resin. It has the ability of seating what is restless, and naturally it can also be agitated. It holds great protective qualities and jars of charged bark and resin can be placed at the gate of the house to ward off negativity.

Abacate/Avocado Tree (*Persea americana*) is not often used directly in the cult, but its medicinal qualities are vast. An infusion of the leaves will fortify the immune defence system and invigorate the whole body. The fruits can be used in cases of impotence and lust under the aegis of Exus like Sete Sombras, Pedra Preta and Sete Cobras. The working should be done at the foot of the tree.

BANANA counts a vast kingdom in its own right and carries calmative properties and blessings of long life. Snakes and vipers love this plant, as do many varieties of insects. It is possible to work with Exu Serra Negra at the foot of the banana tree in aggressive spells. These aim to cut a life short and involve knives, oils, sulfur, gunpowder and works done with the plant's leaf and the name of the target.

BASIL/ALFAVACA (*Ocimum kilimandscharicum* and similar) is a basil of African origin, also known as Black Opal. The types of basil most favoured in works of Quimbanda are those which possess a distinct aroma of camphor, citrus or clove combined with the basil flavour. These varieties of basil hold magical qualities superior to the common basil and have a great transformative potency. They can be used as a general herb for all types of work, be they for defence, attraction or attack. It is particularly sacred to the line of Malei, Nagô and Mossorubi. There is a great variety of uses for this herb and one classical method is to make a bundle of seven fresh sticks which is then wrapped in red and black cord and presented to Exu. The bundle rests with Exu overnight flanked by three candles, and the following night the name of the person one wants to influence is placed within the bundle. The names must be written crossed seven times preferably on the bark of an appropriate tree and placed inside the bundle as pontos are sung. The bundle is then left in a bowl of vinegar, salt, pepper and guiné (*Petiveria alliaceae*) to generate turbulence, or in honey, rosemary, cloves and roses to bring about attraction. Exu must be given a seven-day candle and cachaça and red wine and the working is left for three days and then disposed of in the proper kingdom.

BARLEY (*Hordeum vulgare*) is a little-used ally, but is slowly making its way to the Cult through barley wine and beer offered on rare occasions to Exu Mor and Exus in the lines of Malei and das Matas.

BEANS (*Vicia faba*) are the necromantic gateway par excellence, especially black beans. They can be used as a means for warding off one's land by throwing them at the front and back door of one's house, and/

or at the gate. It is known from several Books of Cyprian and grammars of the Black Arts that beans planted in the sockets of skulls produce plants with unique powers. Black beans are especially used in Quimbanda as part of food offerings to all Exus; they are however most prized by Omolu and his spirit hosts.

BOLDO (*Plectranthus barbatus*) also known as TAPETE DE OXALÁ (Carpet of Oxalá) is a great purifier of spirit, mind and the intestines. This plant can be used as a calmative infusion and it heals the liver and brings respite from nausea.

CALAMUS (*Acorus calamus*) once used to make the pipes of Pan, it holds qualities sympathetic to the line of Mussorubi and is adored by Exu Veludo in particular. It can be used in workings where one seeks to influence the mind and thoughts of others and is also worked well in the Malei line and in the kingdom of the Calunga.

CARDO SANTO (*Argamone mexicana*) is an herb sacred to the line of Malei, said to hold the power of tangling people up in confusion and fear. It is also used in the treatment of malaria and is mildly toxic. It is a cousin of TRIBULUS TERRESTRIS. Exus like Morcego and Asa Negra have a great affinity with this plant and can be used to generate mental turbulence.

CARQUEJA (*Baccharis trimeira*) is a great plant, bitter to the taste, but holds cures for hepatitis and diabetes. It greatly fortifies manly vigor. It is adored by all Exus, perhaps because of its phallic shape and equally masculine qualities. It is an excellent herb to use as an infusion in its own right, or soaked in cognac or cachaça to fortify the spirit of the quimbandeiro.

CIPÓ CABOCLO is both a reference to the vines of the *Davilla* family as well as the JAGUBE/CIPO MARIRI (*Banisteriopsis caapi*), which is an integral plant for the creation of ayahuasca together with CHACRONA/ RAINHA (*Psychotria viridis*). These plants are sacred to Exu Pantera Negra in particular, but make part of the sacred communion with spirits in general and are in this capacity acknowledged by all Exus.

CHERRY (*Cornus sp.*) gives a red fruit, slightly acid but sweet, loved by Exus in the lines of the Soul and Malei and is revered in the kingdom of das Matas and Lira.

CORIANDER/COENTRO (*Coriandrum sativum*) is revered by all inhabitants in the Kingdom of the Lira and das Praias. It is a powerful plant, a fusion of Saturn and Venus and can be used in works of domination and seduction. Exus like Sete Liras, dos Infernos and Zé Pelintra hold a particular affinity with this plant.

CRAVO DE DEFUNTO (*Tagetes minuta*) belongs to the kingdom of the Calunga and das Almas with its cacapacity for guiding departed souls, but it also quickens land bound spirits. It can be planted in order to make a border between the living and the dead and as such serves as a field of communion.

CYPRESS (*Cupressus semprevirens*) is a tree revered as the staff of Asclepius and is sacred to Apollo. It shares necromantic qualities of dominion like the Laurel, but also carries the additional property of serving as a compass for the departed. Its sappy texture is excellent for works involving the restoration of, and communion with, the dead.

CRISTA DE GALO/COCKSCOMB (*Heliotropum indicum*) taken as an infusion is good for antiseptic purposes. Exu Quebra Galho and Exu Sete Portas are drawn to this plant and it is said that the plant is good for elevating a sunken soul, i.e. as a remedy for melancholia.

DORMIDEIRA/SENSITIVA (*Mimosa pudica*) is a vicious plant of mildly toxic qualities. It is in itself a cure for insomnia, but magically it is used by thieves to pass unnoticed and also in workings where there is a need for rendering someone blind to some shady business or clandestine activity. You can work this plant under the auspices of Exu Gira

Mundo where the flowers of the plant are used as a focus for targeting those one seeks to 'sedate.' It is also possible to use this plant to quicken dormant emotions, here the flowers are worked with honey, apple and sweet red wine with the help of Exu Porteira, Exu Veludo and Exu do Cabaré.

ELDERBERRY/SABUGUEIRO (*Sambucus sp.*) is a tree considered to be wise – but also punitive. It is held by the kings and queens, and also Exu Quebra Galho who marks the boundaries. The branches of this tree can be cut at twilight and made into a bundle in the image of a whip and used to torment people. Its fruits can be used as a part of a padé to sweeten people, even for making them amorous.

ELM (*Ulmus glabra*) is a dreaming tree and is a ladder the inhabitants of Hades climb in order to commune with us. It is also said to be the tree that guards the garden of Hesperides and can be used as a general ally in the kingdom of das Matas.

ERVA DE SANTA MARIA (*Chenopodium ambrosioides*) is a herb favored by Exu das Almas and in general in the kingdom of Encruzilhadas. It is rich in iron and holds curing abilities for soft and mucal membranes like the eyes. It is said to be a plant that can aid in the elevation of bones and hence, necromantic and mediumistic workings.

EUCALYPTUS/EUCALIPTO (*Eucalyptus*) is a potent disinfectant, but also holds the powers of earth and is as such a beneficient plant ally for any works done in the realm of Quimbanda. It is a wood that catches fire easily and its oil eases tense and fiery muscles. It is particularly adored by Exu do Cheiro, Exu Kaminaloá and Exu Sete Encruzilhadas.

FEDEGOSA/SICKLEPOD (*Senna obtusifolia*) is an herb cherished in the kingdom of the Cruzeiro. It is a plant that calms the passions and gives second sight. Exu Caveira and Pomba Gira Rainha da Calunga are in particular drawn to this herb. Fedegosa and coffee share many sympathies and can be used as substitutes for one another. Actual coffee is however more favored in the kingdoms of das Almas and Calunga.

FENNEL (*Ferula communis*) is the plant Prometheus used to hide the fire stolen from the gods within. It is considered to be of a fiery core and can be used as a staff. Its seeds can be turned into a calmative infusion well suited to wash relics and sacred items. It can be used in the kingdom of the Encruzilhadas.

FIG (*Ficus caprice*) is the gift from Hell to the Quimbandeiro. In the same way as it represented Persephone in Antiquity it represents the queenship of Pomba Gira. It is a plant sacred to the Maioral, to Exu Calunga and Exu dos Infernos.

FOLHA DE FOGO/FIRE LEAVES (*Climedia hirta*) is another indispensable plant for the manufacturing of the assentamentos of Exu and Pomba Gira. This is the vegetable fire that gives life to Exu.

GINGER/GENGIBRE (*Zingiber officinale*) is a root loved by all Exus and Pomba Giras. It is the root of fire and can be used as an infusion with alcohol to make a much adored fluid for their fire to walk on. The root is also used for making images of those one seeks to influence and the doll, with its volts, are sunk in containers of bitter or sweet fluids, prayed and sung upon with candles and tobacco for seven days in a row.

GARRA DE POMBA GIRA/CLAWS OF POMBA GIRA (*Martynia annua*) is used to bring stability to the fire of Exu and Pomba Gira, and it is indispensable to seating her. It can also be used to stabilize erratic energies in the form of offerings of cachaça or earth containing these seeds.

GRAPE (*Vitis vinifera*) is revered for its properties of being a conduit of the spirits that ensure manifestation for Exu and Pomba Gira. Grapeleaves can be used as plates for offerings, and can also make part of any working being done in all kingdoms.

Guiné/Henweed (*Petiveria alliaceae*) is a radical protective plant. The powder of the root is a toxic hallucinogen that can provoke disturbance of the mind and lead to insanity and catatonic states. It has great disinfectant qualities and can be used to effectively break any spell and return the energies to the sender. It is a plant much adored by Exu Morcego and is mostly used in works of direct harm and active protection.

Henbane (*Hyoscyamus niger*) is clearly the herb of St Cyprian. Though a herb that does not grow naturally in Brazil, its bitter lycanthropic qualities lead me to introduce henbane to my own tronco and I saw a myriad of winged Exus delving into my gift, which means Exu Morcego and Exu Asa Negra as well as Exu das Cobras do find an affinity with this plant which can be used for good and ill, but most of all for shape shifting.

Heliotrope (*Heliotropium sp.*) carries the dominant powers of the Sun and can be used as a general agent for sweetening situations and dominating negativity. It is particularly revered in the kingdoms of Calunga and das Praias.

Hellebore (*Heleborus sp.*) plants are prized by Exus like Morcego, Kaminaloa and many others given their capacity for inducing madness and frenzy. It is a key to night and the incomprehensible fire at the heart of the Fig.

Hemlock (*Conium maculatum*) was the herb Socrates drank and on its wings he went to the other side. Hemlock is the skeleton key to the kingdoms as testified by the reverence paid to it by necromancers for more than three millennia. It belongs to Omolu and Exu Sete Cruzes and is a powerful agent in provoking fatal illness and death.

Ivy (*Similax aspera*) is a vine whose red berries were turned into garlands worn in the *orgia* of Dionysus. It is a plant adored by Exu Tranca

Ruas, Tranca Tudo and Exu Gira Mundo. It can be used to open roads and make roads confused.

Juniper/Zimbro (*Juniperus oxycedrus*) bears leaves like knives and needles and aromatic and strong berries which are sweet to Figueira do Inferno, and when scattered on red hot embers give off smoky vapors that call the serene attention of Exu.

Jurema/Jurema Preta (*Jurema hostilis*) is the gateway to the other world – hence her chalice merges you with the other side. It is a common sacrament in Quimbanda and in particular for those working with Caboclos, spirits of the land and Exu Pantera Negra. As with ayahuasca we have here a sacramental gift adored by all lines and in all kingdoms, because the spirit known as Jurema is the third arm of Pomba Gira da Figueira do Inferno.

Laurel (*Laurus nobilis*) is endowed with the gifts of the Sun and makes the necromancer victorious in his or her arts. The plant belongs to the Maioral and Exu Rei and is revered in the kingdom of Encruzilhadas.

Lemongrass/Cidreira (*Cymbopogon sp.*) is also known as fever grass because of its ability to ease fever and the condition that caused it. It can also be used to make an ointment for full body application when one is preparing workings, especially of attack and defense.

Life Everlasting (*Helichrysum siculum*) serves several purposes with its power of imbuing bones with the lifegiving powers of the Sun. It can be used in the delicate process of reanimating skulls and bones for the purpose of communion.

Malva (*Malva sylvestris*) is a plant adored by Exu Veludo and the inhabitants in the kingdom of das Matas. It is also the plant of Tranca Ruas for its ability to sweeten the ways towards a goal. It is a powerful plant that opens opportunities, and brings prosperity and love. The ways it can accompany works are too numerous to state. This plant is a grace in the realm of Quimbanda.

Melão de São Cætano (*Momordica charantia*) is a protective plant of poisonous potency and belongs to Omolu and the kingdoms of the Calunga and das Matas. The plant is used in workings of death and elevation of death, but also to repel hostile spiritual influences.

Manioca Brava (yellow manioc) and Manioca (common manioc) are the twain roots of a plant of immense importance. Mani was the name of a Tupi warrior who sacrificed himself for the welfare of his tribe which was suffering hunger and drought. The young warrior was buried and from his corpse grew the plant called Manioc and as the plant sprouted the great Tupan brought rain and lightning to the earth. Manioc means the *house of Mani*, hence the manioc root became a first fruit of the land. This fruit was divided into white and yellow, the white being blessing of life, and the yellow being the blessing of death. The manioc is the food of the Gods, it is considered the food of the Golden Age and its twin quality being a symbol of the Tree of Wisdom that brought death and time to the world. We see its importance today in the making of padé, the prime food offering in Quimbanda, which is either made with manioc flour or corn flour. Both plants hold similar majesty replicated in their amazing endurance in hard conditions.

Mamona/Castor (*Ricinus communis*) hás a shared affinity with Omolu and Exu Rei. It is a plant that manifests the serenity of death and fire. Accordingly its leaves can be used for serving offerings and as the field of workings itself as much as a component for the assentamentos of Exu. The plant is slightly toxic but contains wonderful properties and can, like orange peel, be used as fuel, denoting its powerful fiery qualities.

Mandrake (*Mandragora sp.*) is not native to Brazil, but yet its potency must be noted. I personally brought this root to the feet of Exu and have found it to be revered as an equal by Exu Mor. It has entered into a curious symbiosis with the yellow manioc, which would indicate a mutual recognized ancestry.

Mangueira/Mango Tree (*Mangifera sp.*) is the sacred tree of Quimbanda par excellence as its fruits are seen as gifts from the Sun itself; hence the tree represents dominion over death and the dead. It has a status similar to the laurel. Initiations in Quimbanda must involve the Mango tree, it is considered to hold a potency almost ancestral in importance and must be a part of any well-made assentamento. Exu Mangueira is a great stabilizing force that calls upon the entire field of wood dwelling Exus for good and for bad.

Mint (*Mentha sp.*) has always carried connotations of Hades and the Netherworld, being the tongues of Hell spreading its rhizomes underground. Interestingly many mints are rich in estrogen and it is a plant unhealthy for the male fire if used in excess, with its relative pennyroyal being an abortifacient.

Mulberry/Amoreira (*Morus nigra*) tells the story of the Babylonian lovers Pyramos and Thisbe who met secretly at a Mulberry tree. An unfortunate incident with a lion caused Pyramos to be killed by his own sword and Thisbe, seeing her dead lover, followed suit. Their blood was drunk by the tree whose berries turned dark red. It is considered a devilish tree of wisdom and can be used in works of defence as well as attraction. It causes fatalities to occur. The tree is sacred to Exu Mor, Exu Morcego and Exu Meia Noite.

Myrrh (*Commiphora myrrha*) is a spiny resinous shrub that gave birth to Adonis and is used in works of reddening bones and tools to quicken the dead. The herb is sacred to the lines of Cemetery and Souls.

Oak (*Quercus ilex*) is the most important tree for Dryads, amongst many people and cults it is considered to be the King of Greenwood. It is the tree which the golden fleece was hung upon and guarded by the Dragon. It speaks of ancestry and death, being the ancestor of priests.

OBI/COLA NUT (*Cola acuminata*) is used for divination – and so is onion – which in Quimbanda is considered equal in fire. Whether a four lobed obi is broken and used for divination or two onions are cut in two making four, it is still an oracle of fire. The obis symbolise stability and prophecy – it is a seed all spirits respect – and so it is with onion.

OLHOS DE EXU/EYES OF EXU (*Abrus precatorius*) give characteristic seeds looking like red eyes with a black pupil. The whole plant carries intense properties and is said to carry the totality of Exu's transformative quality and is therefore used to manifest this force.

OLIVE (*Olea europea*) is most sought after in the cult for its oil, which can be used as a conductor for making sacred oils. It can be used as a substitute for palm oil and is to be preferred when working with the Malei line.

PARSLEY (*Apium sp.*) was the sacred herb the Goes used to wash bodies with. It is also turned into amaci (sacred water) to repel ghosts and larvaes (*kiumbas*). A bed made from pine and parsley can effectively be turned into a deathbed which calls upon the aid of Exu Sete Cruzes.

PINE (*Pinus sp.*) is a majestic and wise death tree, sacred to all the kingdoms, but in particular Calunga, because this tree is the life sap of death and murder. It is a tree that holds the souls of those who suffer violent deaths.

POMEGRANATE (*Punica granatum*) is the fruit with which Hades seduced Persephone. Ovid also tells that when the unworthy use the seeds they will be turned into screech owls. It is a plant revered in the kingdoms of the Calunga and das Almas.

POPPY (*Papaver somniferum*) is highly sacred to Pomba Gira, but is also used by several Exus for good and for ill, for communion and to give good and bad dreams. It is particularly sacred to Exu Morcego, and the kingdoms of das Praias and Encruzilhadas.

Rose (*Rosa sp.*) being the death flower of Adonis and said to be amongst the flowers Persephone gathered when she was seduced by Hades. It can be used to kindle and bring an end to passion and is revered in the kingdoms of the Lira (Harp) and Calunga in particular.

Sage (*Salvia sp.*) is sacred to the Malei, Cruzeiro and Cemitério lines where this plant can be used to exorcise hostile spirits or to direct them. Sage can be used in offerings or as a fumigation. Magical baths made with sage, salt and lavender will expel any hostile negativity around you.

Succulent/Cactus is a wonderful plant used in works of protection or to affix a victim on poisonous thorns. The more poisonous the cactus is the better suited it seems to be and the working of the cactus is simple. You anoint the plant at the foot of Exu as your wishes are placed upon the thorns of the plant.

Walnut (*Juglans regia*) shares properties with Chestnut (*Castanea vesca*) and is a tree adored in the line of the Cemetery. It holds the power to command spirits of all sorts and serves well as a conduit for communion, and also to stabilize erratic workings and situations. It is a tree sacred to Exu Mor and Exu Capa Preta.

Wormwood/Losna (*Absinthum sp.*) is the superior plant in the line of Malei, and in particular of Exu Marabô. Not only because it is a component of his favorite drink, absinthe, but also because wormwood has the ability to infest the mind with delirium and wickedness. As such it can be used as a gateway for kiumbas.

The Seven Protectors is a popular collection of herbs usually counting:

Arruda/Rue (*Ruta graveolens*)
Pimenta/Chili Peppers (*Capsicum sp.*)
Alecrim/Rosemary (*Rosmarinus officinalis*)
Basil/Manjericão (*Ocium sp.*)
Espadade São Jorge/Sword of St George (*Sansevieria trifasciata/ Sansevieria zeylanica*)
Abre caminho/Open roads (*Lygodium volubile*) also known as Periquitinho de Ogun literally 'Ogun's little parrot'
Guiné/Henweed (*Petiveria alliaceae*)

At times alterations are made and we find Levante (*Mentha viridis*) and Comigo Ninguém Pode/With me no one can do anything (*Dieffenbachia piétada*) making part of the herbal gathering. These seven or nine herbs should be part of the household of any quimbandeiro. These herbs can be worked together with most of the Exus and Pomba Giras, especially in works of protection.

Which way I fly is Hell; myself am Hell;
And in the lowest deep a lower deep
Still threat'ning to devour me opens wide,
To which the Hell I suffer seems a Heav'n

John Milton

The Shadows at the Graveyard
Towards the Embers of Beginning

It is important to understand that initiation into Quimbanda – to set fire to one's step at the threshold of Hell – invites Fate to move in wicked and enigmatic ways. Initiation in Quimbanda is to accept that suffering, turmoil and transformation are equally important parts in our progress as human beings as any form of spiritual or material blessing. I believe this lies at the root of Kongo spirituality, and is a fundamental understanding necessary for any healer. A healer must comprehend the suffering he or she aids people to rise above, and in this he or she must know Hell intimately and have discovered solutions and solace to aid in their ascent. It is in this deep metaphysical truth we find the idea in Umbanda that the Exus and Pomba Giras need to be evolved, to be turned to seek the light.

Simply put, the world of matter is Hell. The view from the stars is that we are living in Hell, but we look beneath our feet and find soil and bones, the memory and knowledge of ancestry and sages kept alive on earth, living on in trees, flowers and poisons. Quimbanda is about realizing this truth and it gives you the allies you need for coping with this in a way that brings fulfilment. The path is a hero's journey through the field of stars. It is because of this element, so rarely spoken of, that I see quimbadeiros falling prey to the impulses of the lower self, which calls upon us to be at one with the forgetfulness of earth and rivers. We call these forces *kiumbas*, they are obsessive spirits that can do our bidding... or we can be their prey. We have nine of them, aligned to the kingdoms – which is good, because then you can realise the constitution of the negative influence. Realising the nature of the problem leads to its origin and from this we find solutions taking shape.

I have witnessed a handful of different forms of initiation in Quimbanda, some elaborate and others head on and direct. I find both to be equally valid as long as they enable connection with spirit, because this is the entire goal in initiation in Quimbanda, that you meet your Exu and/or Pomba Gira and are consumed by them in a lifelong merging. There is really no going back from this. A going back brings you haunting and weird forms of suffering. When your foot is in the dirt and embers you are there to stay.

A proper initiation in Quimbanda must always challenge your fire, to temper it. This is effectively done with *amaci*, magical baths, and the nocturnal rites. It is a play upon the purity of spirit and flesh while the soul is caught in purgatory. It is a purging that has to be accomplished, and it must be done with a play upon Moon and Sun. Whether short and intense or long and brooding, a true initiation will accomplish this goal; with the Sun and Moon on your shoulders you will at some point be burning within, because your Exu is there with his coals and embers, to make two One. So what is the gain? What is the purpose? Why would anyone deliberately place their foot in the fire and walk on? The answer is simple: dominion. Dominion is to take control, it's not about the hunger for power at large, it is about dominating what is yours, be it soul, flesh, star and even Fate herself. Fulfilling this promise is no small accomplishment and this is why so many walk away from the path direct.

The quimbandeiro is a healer to the greatest extent of what this word can mean. In this are shared sympathies with what we generally call shamanism. The quimbandeiro searches out remedies for healing a society of one or a thousand. Still, we have the taint of black magic all over this, because indeed at root Quimbanda is black as Africa, the womb of the world where wisdom rests and has been continued. It was through Africans and the indigenous nations in Brazil it was continued, and underwent a social reform in the early 20th century where the diabolical imagery became a point of focus.

The proposition is this: why not have dominion of your world – not *the* world – because this is not what is offered to you. Again people perceive wrongly. The dominion is really about your world, to take what is yours, truly yours, and in this work for your desires to become manifest. But this does not entail delusions of global supremacy; it is a question of being in control of your world first and foremost, not the world of others. Here we encounter the idea of black magic for it is the magic of domination. It calls upon the powers of Saturn and Earth. The wisdom of time and the bones of ancestry speak loudly as you gain dominion; it is a call to know thyself as much as to know thy world and thy perimeters. Beneath it all is the voice from the first tree, the Fig of Hell, telling you, seductively: it is all about Love. A conflict is born that you must bring into One, in truthful observation of your declared dominion as stated while your feet are burning in compassion and hatred, twin snakes from alien lands. This is Quimbanda.

The Earth in Flames

IN QUIMBANDA places of power are often referred to as kingdoms. In every kingdom we find a great herd of protectors, guardians and supporters of a specific power, often attributed to a specific line. The line is always a composite of legions dancing around a focal point, a potency of particular importance within the line that calls upon obeisance from other powers. The lines reflect the multicultural ancestry of Quimbanda and in the past it was common to initiate people in conformity with the line they were working within. For instance, the line of Mossorubi, which is the line of Muslim influence, would diverge to some degree from how one was inducted into the line of Caboclos quimbandeiros, native spirits and Nagó, Yoruba spirits. One would then work with the spirits in the particular line one was admitted to, but crossovers often happened as in the kingdoms all lines ultimately meet. In essence initiation followed the same main points, but the context varied in conformity with the line. Unfortunately much of this lore is lost. It is but a memory that asks the pragmatic workers of contemporary Quimbanda to yet again establish ways of lineages. One example might be the Malei line that over the last 30 years or so has gone through a significant 'Africanisation' in its modus operandi and forms of initiation.

It is more common today that each house has its own format, a variation upon the basic secrets that make up unique initiations. I have witnessed initiations spanning a week and initiations spanning a night, they can each be effective as long as the centre of the secret is revealed, as blood and fire mingle, as a truthful connection is made with Exu.

When this connection is made with your Exu, initiation is conferred and a unique hierarchy takes shape. The lines and legions of Quimbanda re-establish themselves in conformity with the temperament of the newborn Tatá and also in resonance with the personal Exu of the quimbandeiros and how this Exu is connected to lines and kingdoms.

This means that we operate with two different hierarchies, one of a more general order, as given in this book, but in the private affairs of the cult the hierarchy is different. What is typical is that the role of the maioral will be filled by Exu Lucifer, Exu Mor or Exu Rei das Sete Encruzilhadas and the Exu of the Tatá will be the Exu Rei under the direction of the maioral in question. The personal Exu of the Tatá will be the King of the particular house, and the personal Pomba Gira its Queen. From this lines and kingdom tend to mingle until a given line stands out and can then be seen as the line of the house. As this happens the secrets of the house reveal themselves to the Tatá and fortify the tronco.

The kingdoms are nine and the spirit catalogue in the last chapter presents the Exus in conformity with kingdoms. A kingdom is a realm of power with a multitude of singular powers. A kingdom is not confined to graves and natural locations. In Quimbanda we also value manmade urbane constructs as holding particular powers, especially places that are passionate and hot. Every hot and turbulent place, where transformation is the keyword, is inhabited by an Exu or Pomba Gira. But we should be careful in assigning transformation just to seductive love play and bar fights. The rush of inspiration coming from reading a philosophical text that ignites new perspectives can also be a product of the transformative quality of Exu, as can sudden creative sparks that came from seemingly nowhere.

We should be mindful that occupations can call upon the presence of potencies in given kingdoms. For instance a gardener will be attached to the kingdom of the Wilderness (das Matas), but his Exu might be Marabó, hence his line is, strictly speaking, Malei, and from this a unique constellation surfaces. A prostitute will work in the kingdom of the Harp (Lira) even if his or her Pomba Gira might be Calunga, hence a crossover between the Cemetery and the Harp is established. I have found the observations of these nuances to be immensely valuable and useful in realizing both our presence in the world and who we are.

Exu is a flame guarding places of power all over the earth and the inbetween. This is also true for the practitioners themselves, set aflame in the transformative fires of Exu in a perpetual state of becoming.

The Frenzy of Possession

POSSESSION DEFINES A CONDITION where we are taken over by spirit resulting in an altered state of consciousness, and where we are allowing the higher and the Other to take us over. A genuine possession is commonly said to be signified by being completely taken over by spirit and the medium having no recollection of what was said or done during the event.

There are however other forms of possession; one is termed *two headed possession* in which the spirit goes in and out of the medium. It is considered an unstable and unreliable form of possession due to its lack of consistency, and in this it may be as difficult for the medium to be truthful as it is for the spirit. It is often a confusing matter and it is better to train the medium to be able to hold the spirit either in a complete possession, or what in Quimbanda is referred to as being *in vibration*. Being in vibration means that something is hanging onto you. This form of possession is very tangible. The medium will feel a weight attached to the nape of the neck and the area of the kidneys and liver. Something is literally hanging on your back. This form of possession can be understood to be a form of agreement between the medium and the spirit where the medium is aware of what is going on, but has decided to allow tongue and body to be at the disposal of the spirit. The medium remains as an inner observer, yet even in this state the medium's recollection tends to be foggy and blackouts tend to occur. In my experience this form of possession is a real state, but difficult to maintain as the tendency to succumb totally is present at every second. Possession has a negative connotation in the West as it implies a pushing out of our venerated, and often overrated, rational consciousness.

We are constantly reminded that possession is something evil and harmful. The ideas around exorcism do not help either. But in truth, possession is a merging with nature, celestial or infernal, where spirits and ancestors can use the living flesh as a conduit for prophecy, to do workings, to give counsel or to celebrate life and love.

If we look at the Greek understanding of the terms exorcism, *exorkizein,* and demon, *daimon*, we see that an exorcism was once understood to be a binding of a spirit by oath and a daimon was seen as a spirit/soul somewhere between man and the celestial, in the sub-lunar sphere. I speculate that the sub-lunar dwelling of the daimons is perhaps what has caused psychology, since Iohannes Weyer, to see it as a form of mental illness. Likewise, modern psychology is gradually getting more interested in this phenomenon given the increasing popularity of African-rooted traditions and their adoption by Westerners.

From a professional and practical point of view I note the similarities, but also the differences between possession and mental illness. For instance, the pathological symptom of hearing voices is usually a trait of some schizoid disorder. This can also occur in a spiritual practice, but for the one suffering from a schizoid disorder there is difficulty in separating the dimensions as imagination, fantasy and reality are constantly fused with little or no discrimination. For the practitioner working with possession and trance state this is not the case. Of course, possession by hostile spirits can happen. In Quimbanda we call them *kiumbas* and the Romans called them *larvae* and this bears further discussion.

First we must consider benevolent spirit possession and turn to Weyer's teacher, Henry Cornelius Agrippa, because possession was clearly commonplace in Western magic, as it is still amongst the few genuine traditions of witchcraft alive today. I am aware this might come as a surprise to many, hence my citing of Agrippa, because the many nuances he discusses are present in possession work in Quimbanda.

Agrippa discusses the nature of possession under what he terms *frenzy*. He defines the cause of frenzy as superior souls falling on our souls and making use of the body and tongue of the person whom the soul has fallen upon. The fact that he sees this as a *soul merging* is, I believe, of great importance.

In the past prophecy and soothsaying were part of this complex of states, with the Pythoness at the Temple of Apollo in Delphi being perhaps the most well known example. Agrippa makes a distinction between being taken over by a demon and by being moved by the Holy Spirit, he seems to make a distinction here in terms of the quality of the predictions of the oracle, where predictions of the future are supposedly from the Holy Spirit and other forms of inspirations are from demons/daimons. His attitude is born from the theological dilemma of his time concerning celestial and demonic magic where seeing the future was reserved only for God. This questioned the worth and lawfulness of prophecies made by daimons. Soothsayers and those who cast lots were especially targeted because their practices were seen as an invasion into God's sole domain. But this is only one of the effects of frenzy. Agrippa continues, saying that there are three ways for demons souls or spirits, holy and unholy, to make use of this 'vacancy' when the alien soul enters our body and soul. They are frenzy, ecstasy and dreams.

It would be good to pause here and look more closely at the idea of the soul. It is common to envision the soul as singular, but this model does not fit with the West African idea of the soul. Kongo faith holds that our soul is a complex of souls, a gathering of quickened powers that have a nature similar to lightning. The idea of the soul is perceived as a cluster made up of a harmony composed of various extensions of Nzambi giving us thoughts, memory, emotional states and otherworldly capabilities. In this, there are natural powers, connections with plants, minerals and animals that generate a unique soul that goes through a transformation from its pure flame at birth until its destination in death. Upon death, parts of the soul return to nature and Nzambi and yet other parts can merge with the ancestors, or even become walking deities. Death does change the constitution of the soul. A parallel to this can be found in the Scandinavian concept *hugr*, which is commonly translated as soul. The hugr is a composite of thoughts and spirit that can be contemplative and passionate. It is constantly followed by the double, *fylgja*, which comes in a variety of shapes and guises from all realms in nature and also from the invisible realm. Again we speak of a composite; the soul is an aerial fire, a bundle of active nature that lies at the heart of who we really are. Because of *fylgja*, it is possible for the *hugr* to go out *hamferd*, literally *skin leaping*, and the soul can then change shape as it rides the night.

The perception of frenzy being caused by spirits, gods and demons coming down is also found in the writings of Ovid. Plato also spoke of frenzy and possession. In *Phaedrus* he defines this state as a *freedom of the mind* where the body is loosened, as if it is escaping a prison, and in this state of freedom transcendence is experienced. We are provoked by a divine spirit that makes us transcend the physical boundaries. This can be done by dreaming, by ecstasy, by the use of herbs and the variety of spirit possessions and inspirations.

The frenzy is born from four different celestials, or potencies; these are the Muses, Dionysus, Apollo and Venus and each of them inspires in the medium a particular form of possession. Agrippa says of the frenzy of the Muses that it tempers the mind and brings the superior to the inferior, and that it is associated with lily, moonstone, soothsaying and divination. Verbena is a plant that facilitates this form of possession. We can say that this form of possession is similar to the idea of 'inspirations' we find in Palo Kimbisa and Palo Cruzado. The Muses are the nine children of Mnenosyne (Memory) and are themselves considered aloof ancient spiritual potencies. This form of possession is best utilized for generating art, scrying and divination. It can be a deceptive form of possession and demands that the medium is well trained and capable of discernment to avoid mixing the planes. Dreams pertain to this form of possession.

The second frenzy Agrippa discusses is mercurial and issues from Dionysus. It is largely attributed to shapeshifting and astral travel. It is similar to the shifting of hamr we find in Nordic practices and the idea of using the power of Oso in Yoruba cultures to travel the night. In Angola, this is the most noted attribute of the Muloji, the sorcerer; to be able to go forth at night in ghastly forms and cause havoc. This form of possession is also used in Quimbanda, but only after midnight, and the soul must be brought back to the body before the cock's crow. The body of the Tatá is anointed and washed in sacred herbs, veiled in a white shroud and either the Exu of the Tatá is called upon the shrouded body – or Exu Morcego and Exu Asa Negra, as well as the entire retinue of the line of Malei can be called upon – to undertake the night flight.

Agrippa writes that the technology for Dionysian possession rests in the use of solemnities, conjurations and expiations. He also adds that this form of possession enables us to hear our daimon, like Socrates did, or even see our daimons and spirit guards. This state can also cause involuntary possessions, where the spirit enters for moments into vacant vessels to deliver a message or a prophecy. This has several degrees ranging from a blackout on the part of the vessel, to hearing the voice of the daimon and being the mouth that brings forth a message. This is quite typical to see in young mediums who experience spirits slipping in and out in the process of attaining balance in exercising the mediumistic gift. It is also here we find the two headed possession we spoke of previously.

Agrippa deems the frenzy of Venus to be more subtle and makes the possessed one like God, because of the power of Love. In *Asclepius* we see this form of possession described as follows:

> Man is a great miracle, an animal to be honoured and adored; for he passeth into the nature of God, whereby he becomes God; he knows the rise of demons, and he knows himself to have his original with them, despising the part of his human nature in himself, having a sure confidence of the divinity of the other; the soul therefore being converted, and made like to God.

This sublimation is brought on by being possessed by the Holy Spirit itself, the possession of Love. This form of possession ignites prophecy and miracles. When this possession takes place the atmosphere will change, either the temperature, or at least goosebumps and electric shivers in the bones will be experienced by all those gathered. This is what we understand as a full possession, but it is of a subtle and aerial kind. At times the spirit dawns upon the medium so smoothly that nothing more than a gust of wind is felt, as the spirit lodges itself within the medium in seconds.

The frenzy of Apollo inspires voices, words, singing, music and harmony. Agrippa says that the method is to give sacrifices, food offerings, adorations and invocations. This will cause the mind to rise until the placated virtue is encountered and this will then inhabit the vacant body. He also speaks of how one can be possessed by image, that gazing on a certain spirit-endowed image can ignite the spirit within to connect with the spirit of the image. It is the frenzy of prophecy proper. It is a frenzy that divinises or evolves the vessel even after leaving, and the golden residues of the visitor are left with the host, so to speak, and the medium grows in accurate perception. This state is what we call a full possession, but is denoted by the spirit being far more active in words and actions than when imbued with the rays of Venus. We find the use of wine and herbs as conduits of this form of possession and communion with the spirits of nature, in particular water, as well as vigils in caves and the consumption of sacred food.

To these four basic forms of possession Agrippa applies degrees that give an added nuance to the frenzy. He says that the degree of Mars has positive effects on the imagination and is as such a trigger for creativity. The degree of Jupiter induces the gift for consultations and counsel. The degrees of Saturn were related to contemplation and the ability to absorb wisdom, images and riddles. Agrippa also commented that there is a speculative trickiness here that can be self-deceptive. Finally he comments that the degrees of the stars and of the primum mobile would indicate a more direct connection, close to manifesting a god, spirit or demon in the flesh. There are two ways of looking at his comments about the degrees. One is that we can recognise the starry influences from the behaviour of the medium. The other is that he suggests the possibility of utilising astrological elections for one's possession work. In my opinion this can only positively enhance the connection with spirit.

Sick Shells, Hungry Husks & Seething Souls

QUIMBANDA'S VIEW OF THE SOUL and afterlife has similarities with Roman cults and Kardec spiritism, but it all rests firmly on a Kongolese worldview. This means, that as there are good and bad people, so there are good and bad spirits. Not all souls are interested in our welfare and some are downright deadly. We might say that the idea of Tatá as disincarnated priests and masters is similar to the idea of the Roman *lares*, household spirits and guardian spirits. I find this reference very illuminating for how the idea of Tatá is understood in Quimbanda. The lares were spirits of land, blood, spiritual affinity etc. In many ways we can say that the gathering of lares to a specific person, household or temple is identical to how the constitution of the soul was understood. The unique gathering of lares would protect, guard and inspire the person they assembled around and the household and temple they were set to guard. Amongst the lares we also find penates, ancestors and familiar spirits, although these are a distinct class within the spirits that guard the hearth.

Finally there is the concept of larvæ or *cascarão* (empty shell, husk), which are also called *kiumbas*. This class of spirit is dread and darkness, formless and restless in their vengeful and liminal state. As I related earlier in this discourse, Quimbanda was originally seen as the dark mirror of Umbanda populated with resentful spiritual forces that needed to evolve by doing good work in the service of the spirits of light. The larvæ-like spirits of Quimbanda are known as *kiumbas*, derived from a ki-kongo word meaning *skull* or *works of the skull* – designating a vacant space for welcoming any type of spirit. But in Quimbanda, kiumbas designate a particular class of spiritual malefica and fire. Hence we find the idea of some force, both good and ill, becoming tangible and workable. The *kiumbas* are understood as being similar in function to the ghosts of people murdered, in agony, suicides and any other form that can lead to the spirit becoming restless and negative. They are also those spirits released from people unenlightened whilst on earth and hence they pass on in a darkened state and have little or no direction, only a quality of anger and despair about them. These spiritual realities can be used for workings and sent on errands, but they are never particularly loyal and are more like a beast on a leash, so care must be taken and support from one's guides must be in place when such brute powers are manipulated. In Brazil a common belief is that from Ash Wednesday, after Carnival and until the night when the Passion ends, these forces are particularly active and many refrain from doing workings during this period as negative intrusions may occur. The *kiumbas* are presences which naturally gravitate towards places of power guarded by Exu. We might see them as representing legions of negative and mindless vibrations resonating with Exu. The *kiumbas* are said to be particularly active in the night hours between roughly 2 a.m. and 5 a.m.

Each class of *kiumbas* has a particular force assigned to a kingdom. The work with *kiumbas* should not be done by inexperienced practitioners and I deem it crucial to first have one's Exus seated (i.e. you must be initiated). The *kiumbas* have a particular clinging quality to them and rapidly infest the practitioner as he or she is turned into food for these hostile spirits. The qualities of the *kiumbas* as they are found in the kingdoms are roughly as follows:

- *Kiumbas of the Calunga* are said to be powers consumed by hatred and violence. Here we find powers that provoke enslavement and domination.
- *Kiumbas of das Praias* are revealed in debauchery and provoke perversity and hot-headed sexual sadism.
- *Kiumbas of the Encruzilhada* are said to be consumed with agony and wrath, are in a constant state of being purged, and are prone to share this pain and cause confusion, despair and violent accidents.
- *Kiumbas of das Almas* are recognised by inspiring the feeling of being a victim in people and cause people to engage in self-destructive behaviours, if not outright degradation and violence.
- *Kiumbas of the Cruzeiro* are said to be consumed by disease and pestilence and can even cause damage to the immune defence of the practitioner as well as inspiring risk taking behaviour.
- *Kiumbas of the Lira* boil with violence and vengeance and can inspire violent tendencies and addictions of all forms in the practitioner.

- *Kiumbas of das Matas* are greedy and gluttonous spirits that can provoke the practitioner to fall away from their centre and be turned into a slave for these hungry husks.

Whenever work is done in these realms it is wise to observe the time when they are particularly active. It is also important to take note that when these kingdoms are worked the quality of the working will draw the attention of a myriad of spirits, even kiumbas. It follows that it is crucial to monitor oneself after works are concluded and be honest with yourself. Be aware of any negative or odd changes in your state of mind or heart, as these powers can attach themselves with great ease to the practitioner and contaminate their life and home. Observe ritual diligence in dispelling them, either by the use of amaci (magical baths) or offerings. Strategies for expelling these influences are similar to what we find in European lore in the remedies given for expelling vampires and ill-intentioned ghosts. Offerings of thorny roses, coins and beans, or throwing flax and sea salt over one's left shoulder three times as one leaves the kingdom is a good ritual strategy to apply, especially when more harmful or fiery workings have been performed.

The Loathsome Kiumbas

THE SEVEN OR NINE KIUMBAS can be viewed as a response or variation of the seven deadly sins. In order to understand the substance and work of the *kiumbas* we need to understand the metaphysics beneath the seven deadly sins. The name *kiumba* was understood by the Kimbundu-speaking people to be something filled with *ndoki*, in this case skulls or bones radiating a given energy, seen as powerful and at times negative. *Ndoki* is yet again a quite neutral word signifying power, presence and such like, but the kind of presence a *kiumba* was said to hold in itself was of a darker kind, and hence the usage of the term in modern Quimbanda as something malevolent.

The *kiumbas* can also be seen as powers related to the primordial nine or seven sins, each one finding a subtle or direct relationship to the circles in Dante's *Inferno*. Let us look at these *kiumbas* through the looking glass of Quimbanda, because these cosmic powers carry the potentiality of destroying grace, and this is as equally true for the work done with kiumbas as for the one using them.

Limbo is the realm where the unbaptised are found. *Anima sola*, the lone spirit in flames tied to the embers with chains is the proper image of this. Limbo has seven gates that lead to virtue or vice. It has been equated with purgatory, with the fairy realm, the abysmal waters and Hades; all these interpretations hold truth. In the works of Dante we find most Greek philosophers here, but also Ovid, Orpheus, Julius Caesar and Dante's guide Virgil himself. Limbo is a place where man is given a chance to temper his weaknesses. Wantonness, to be indecisive and weak, was in Antiquity considered to be the stepping-stone to misfortune and ambiguity. Limbo represented a chance to take control of one's passions and desires.

Beyond the first circle, all of those condemned for active, deliberately-willed sin were judged by the serpentine Minos. The structure of the circles, especially the lower ones, is in accord with the classical (Aristotelian) ideas of virtue and vice. When going through some of the well-known sins it is easy to see how they replicate the nature of the kiumbas in the kingdoms.

Luxuria (Lust) was in Dante's *Inferno* a place where restless tornados and strong winds impaired the desire for quenching the appetites, especially those of sex and lust. To be overcome by sensualism is the sin here, and Dante sees Cleopatra and Helen of Troy, Lancelot and Guinevere and also Tristan and Paris. It induces a state of frustration and despair. We find this current being born in works of bindings and where passions and lust are magically provoked.

Gula (Gluttony) is the realm where we find the three-headed dog Kerberos who represents self-indulgence and megalomania. This influence is noticed when a person seeks to dominate for the sake of domination, to block other people's roads because he feels in the right and thus justified in destroying other people's good fortune. There is a form of envy taking place here that heaps misfortune upon misfortune.

Avaritia (Greed) was seen by Dante as the result of ignoring the celestial in favor of the pursuit of temporal power. Robbery, treason and disloyalty are natural consequences of this quality and naturally we find priests, popes and nuns in this circle of Inferno; those who have used what is holy to become thieves and secure material wealth. This is unfortunately a common occurrence amongst many who work with spirituality as their main source of income; hence they call upon kiumbas to interfere in their happiness.

Socordia (Sloth) is a failure to utilize one's gifts, talents and fate; put simply, laziness. It is a sad condition where the kiumbas of disbelief have entered a person's life and generate carelessness and fits of despair.

Acedia (Melancholia) is denoted by an uneasiness of mind, self-hatred, lack of care over one's appearance and suicidal tendencies. These are *kiumbas* we find in the Calunga and at the Cruzeiro.

Ira (Wrath) is marked by vengeance as *love of justice perverted to revenge and spite*, in the words of Dante. Here we find hatred, anger and self-destructive behavior as the most prominent qualities with kiumbas. In *Inferno* we find these people in the joyless river Styx where they are in constant battle with one another, futile battles that never end. The influences of these *kiumbas* are noted by the same effect: warmongers, dispute and battles of ego – unfortunately another common feature amongst practitioners that work fiery cults and faiths.

Invidia (Envy) is a desire to deprive other men of their good fortune. In Dante's *Inferno* their eyes are sewn-up with wires. We find here the *kiumbas* inspiring the potency of the evil eye, a dislike for people more fortunate than ourselves and a failure to acknowledge the good works of others.

SUPERBIA (Pride) – or Hubris in Greek – is a boastful love of self, perverted into hatred for others. It is similar to *vanagloria* (vainglory/vanity), which denotes a boastful attitude and narcissism. This is well known as the sin of Lucifer which caused the fall. Actually Superbia is a quality that causes one to misunderstand one's station and purpose, and the fall in question is one where the *kiumbas* provoke the person to 'fall away from him or herself' and become a stranger in their own domain hiding behind masks (larvæ) of grandeur and ill-will directed towards others, especially if they are recognized as worthy or superior.

All of these sins are measured against virtues, and central for the play upon vice and virtue is the idea of *arête*. *Arête* designates the road of virtue to reach excellence, to be the best that one is capable of being. A part of this work rests in dominating one's passions and negative inclinations and not being mastered by them. The hallmark of a true Tatá, someone who has mastered the cult of Quimbanda, is found in this form of excellence of character. This will be the token that the serpents of fire have been tamed, the *kiumbas* chained, and that they adhere to the Tatá as the viceroy of the Maioral.

*The mind is its own place, and in itself can make a heaven of hell,
a hell of heaven... He who reigns within himself and rules
his passions, desires and fears is more than a king.*

John Milton

VI

Nocturnal Mercury

Quimbanda is an initiatic tradition, but there are still many things that can be done by the votary who seeks to establish a connection with his or her spirit. When your personal Exu or Pomba Gira has become clear it is perfectly fine to work with them, but if guidance is absent, the votary should limit the work to the spirits that are naturally close to him or her. We all have these spirits around us, and our personal spirits tend to enter into agreement, working with us in harmonious ways; but we cannot say the same of other representatives of this large family of spirits. Some of them are tricky and others very unruly. It is important to keep in mind that the work a votary does is restricted and that the focus for one's work will be a particular Exu or Pomba Gira. Yet still here danger abides, because we are working with parts of our soul that are easily led astray in delusion, passions and vice, without being necessarily provoked by kiumbas.

No matter how we seek to understand Quimbanda, at the centre we find the eternal demand of character and knowing yourself. This is true for the one who works Quimbanda as an infernal communion, as much as for the sorcerous warrior. A successful working depends on character and discipline. When we know ourselves we are able to generate stillness and all that we need to apprehend becomes comprehensible to us. We will know what needs to be done in a given situation and will use cunning in how to approach the spirits and the working itself.

From any kind of working we make, whether good or ill, residues remain. We make a mark on the world, no matter how small, by working a given bond. It can be like ripples on the water or a cat scratch on a diamond. Good workings tend to generate residues that bring more abundance, whilst negative workings generate residues of darkened light which attracts the blind and obsessive powers that naturally get involved in malefica. It is important to have enough discipline to invest time in cleaning up these residues so they don't infect your body or soul. Quimbanda, being a cult of nocturnal fire, will when worked naturally stimulate the same fires in the practitioner.

The Magical Arsenal of Quimbanda

THE MAGICAL ARSENAL of Quimbanda consists of cleaning spells, bindings, attack of all sorts, sympathetic magic, prayers, petitions and workings called *despacho/ebo*, or offerings of various forms. This arsenal is typical of any sorcerer who offers up a lament and demands in a dance with gifts and sacrifice. We feed the spirits with alcohol, tobacco, herbs and flowers to force a given road to manifest for our workings. This can be given on their point, the written signatures called *pontos riscados*, and fed with prayers and songs, called *pontos cantados*, or they are done in their realms in the world or at their tronco and temple. The wise quimbandeiro who possesses a true and genuine connection with his spirits can perform marvellous acts with a cigar, a few candles and a bottle of cachaça, and the misguided one will slaughter a farm just to twist creation a scant degree to his will and then have dark clouds falling on his shoulders as a negative pattern of repeating misfortune becomes established.

I adhere to the idea of the quimbandeiro being a warrior, a spiritual and sorcerous warrior, but with this understanding demands present themselves. In order to use one's arsenal wisely, one also needs to understand the purpose of the work being done and in this the circuits and bonds of energy applied, as well as the function of the tools used. In Sun Tzu's *Art of War* the first chapter deals with this calculation, which I deem crucial for the sorcerous warrior. Sun Tzu writes:

> It is a principle of the art of war that one should simply lay down his life and strike. If one's opponent also does the same, it is an even match. Defeating one's opponent is then a matter of faith and destiny.

The quote goes deeper than what is written, because the true enemy is always the enemy within. No war in the world of magic can be done successfully if the enemy within is not defeated. When we defeat the enemy within, serenity of mind arises. This serenity enables us to use the passions as tools of the mind. The question is then: how to reach this state of mind? A cold and calculated use of the fire that accepts with no desire? *Hagakure* gives the following answer:

> This is the substance of the Way of the Samurai: if by setting one's heart right every morning and evening, one is able to live as though his body were already dead, he gains freedom in the Way. His whole life will be without blame, and he will succeed in his calling.

This advice holds true for how to deal with the sorcerous weaponry of Quimbanda. After all, the quimbandeiro is the living embodiment of a legacy of wisdom, the memory of death living on in his or her body and soul and moving in his or her life. So, the quimbandeiro is absolute warrior, but he or she must first defeat themselves, and this opens us to the true essence of Quimbanda: it is an art of healing. So, a good understanding of purification, healing baths, fumigations and works for bringing opportunities of goodness into an ill-starred life must be present in the arsenal of a true quimbandeiro. The quimbandeiro works in a world of contrasts, and knows how to kindle a fire as much as how to drench a fire whether with water or alcohol.

The Sorcerous Technology of Quimbanda

A QUIMBANDEIRO will have at his or her disposal a range of sorcerous solutions for accomplishing a given goal. It is at all times wise to calculate matters of justice and strength and to be honest. An important difference between Quimbanda and more freestyle sorcery which uses sorcerous techniques relying on the practitioner's own soul power is that in Quimbanda we involve a spiritual potency. Hence what we bind and loose is bound to a greater extent than what occurs in a simple bonding between the practitioner and an object in a sympathy or antipathy, as we are adding a named spiritual intelligence that works with us as in a pact.

The Exus are spiritual guardians created by Nzambi, so whatever we bind or loose under their gaze will have a cosmic effect and also be bound and loosened elsewhere. This ripple effect is quite marked in Quimbanda and a working towards its intended goal has a tendency to move in mysterious ways. This is dependant on the insight applied in the preparation and execution of a working. I feel that often when mystery is involved in the working it is because spirit also wants us to grow wiser in the work, so it is particularly in works of binding an object of desire and works rooted in revenge we see this take shape.

It is rare to see fairytale results from binding workings, and this is largely due to the resistance in the object of desire. The less natural the sympathetic relations of the bonds worked the more mysterious and less predictable the result tends to be. So, a binding is often ruled by principles that shift the bonds and re-forge them in a greater harmony, and this can be a process where it is important to take advantage of the opportunities that open and work actively with them. For instance, a binding is done on behalf of a man that wants his wife back. This might seem like a noble cause, but what if the man was abusive? How does this change the way we plan the working, and in this case, is this the working that needs to be done, or is a change in behaviour perhaps a better working in such a case? Likewise, when one is obsessed with the object of desire, what can we expect from a working that is from the beginning fed upon by *kiumbas* as a result of the quality of the energy that infuses the working? It is important to think before doing, not all works should be done and not all works will give the desired results. On the contrary, a messy and rotten bond is likely to generate undesired results, and if the result is manifest, it will come with a bundle of unpleasant energies. I think everyone wanting to create magical love bindings should first read Mrabet's *Love With a Few Hairs* as a part of their learning process.

Revenge is likewise a bad fuel for magic, and it is bound to bounce back. I know of one fairly recent case where the man in question was hell-bent on murdering a certain juridical official because of false accusations. He went out in the Campo Santo and made the working called Dead Man's Box, which you will find later in this chapter. Within a week a scandal broke concerning the target; he suffered from a stroke that crippled him and took away his ability to talk. The Tatá who did this was most satisfied and revelled in his success only to find his own health decaying rapidly. Works of vengeance must be cold and calculated; the hot fire tends to call upon *kiumbas*. When consumed by the fire of passion, pride is fettered and we forget to take simple precautions such as salting our steps to mislead the *kiumbas*, or entering into the necessary regime of purifying baths and the doing of good deeds to help restore the natural balance.

This is just an example of many which testifies that these are real forces, and we should work with them with care, knowing why we are doing what, and calculate everything involved and in particular the nature of the bond we are working with.

On a more metaphysical level, the basic structure of a Quimbanda working is that the subject invites an earthly fire to execute a goal. In this process we need to know the nature of the subject, their motivations, character, emotional balance and so forth. Then in selecting the force to be applied we have numerous variations of this earthly fire; but it is all about fire, passion, heart and blood. This is the fuel we are using to accomplish our result. It is therefore crucial to know as intimately as possible the works and possibilities of the fire you are applying, hence my recommendation of approaching Quimbanda as a cult of spirit communion and approaching the spirits as tutors, the true Tatás and Yayas, experienced in life on both sides of the mirror. If we do this we will find that the fires of revenge and desire will be tempered and be replaced by understanding, and in the end better solutions will be provided to accomplish our goals. In this way we will eradicate the biggest pitfall in Quimbanda: to be turned into a mindless toy of the spirits, for the fun of it. The Exus are a law unto themselves, they can be applied to work dynamically in the natural course of the world, but they can also twist it into the macabre and grotesque. We might say that with these spirits there is no such thing as a free lunch; it is an exchange, and the better we bond in communion with them and take them on as teachers the better will this dynamic exchange flow, as they bring balance and cunning to our life instead of anger and drunken foolishness.

The Spirit Table

THE SPIRIT TABLE, also known as a *boveda* in Caribbean spiritism and *mesa branca* (white table) in Kardec spiritism and its Umbanda crossovers, is not a universal trait of Quimbanda but a practice adopted by a number of houses in the previous century as a means for reconnecting with ancestors and also for training mediumistic abilities. The spirit table is not a table that is worked directly, but a field for communion with one's legacy of blood and spirit. It is a simple technique and something that will benefit any practitioner. To set up your spirit table you need to find a corner in your house. The hallway and kitchen are the most favourable, whilst the bedroom is the least favourable. In this corner set up a small table and cover it with a new white cloth, or a cloth owned by someone departed in your family, and dress the table with it. Present on the table should be a white candle and religious tokens representing your blood lineage. Photos of deceased family members should also be placed here. Under the table you will place a small dish of tobacco soaked in alcohol and coffee that will be changed before the table is used and thrown out afterwards (the plate is brought back and sea salt is added to it). This dish serves to attract hostile influences that will feed upon this offering instead of you, or what is given to the ancestors. On this table you will also have eight or nine glasses, all but one being of the same size and type. The last one should be bigger than the others. For common use the smaller vessels are placed in a circle around the bigger one and are filled with fresh water before the table is used. You will normally offer bread, coffee and alcohol, but this must be mediated by the preference of departed family members. In time the table will gather symbols and tokens of what is a spiritual legacy as well, meaning, if boxing is a vital part of your life you might add pictures of famous boxers, as you will do with saints and thinkers that have influenced your life in meaningful ways.

The practices are fairly simple and the basic procedure involves prayers, readings from sacred texts, and contemplation. It will be largely beneficial to compose a hymn, poem or prayer honouring your blood ancestors, and use this as an opening whenever the table is used. The spirit table is a practical and pragmatic tool for communing with the spirits and the more the practitioner researches their blood ancestors and applies this knowledge in the use of the spirit table the better the results will be.

One technique is particularly auspicious for developing mediumistic skills. You will elect a time, whether every day or every week, but it must be the exact same day and hour. You will then light the white candle, offer bread and coffee and fill the jars with water. Tap on the table and state that you are there for the sake of communion. You will then stay quiet for a designated time, at least 30 minutes, and simply remain attentive. Over time you will develop skills of discernment where you will easily separate your own thoughts and inner states from the spiritual influx. It is this state developed by this simple practice that opens the power zones of the body to allow the spirit to enter. It is advisable to keep a spirit book to hand where you can note down your experiences with the spirit table.

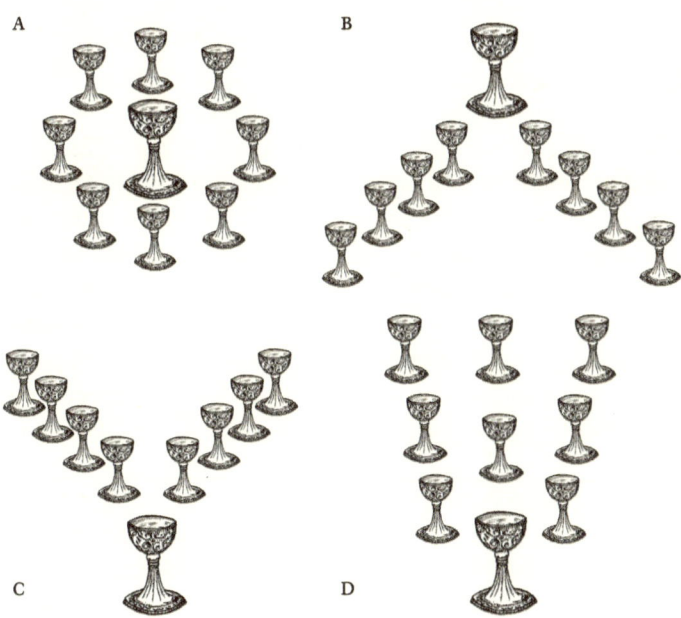

The spirit table is never worked, but it is possible to arrange the table in ways that give the attending spirits a particular direction (see illustration p.109). For instance you can fill the vessels with ice cubes and add bay laurel, basil and a domination wood asking in the form of prayers to gain support in adversity, for example in a court case. Ice added to the vessels in a circle can also be used to calm down and exorcise hostile and overly hot spiritual influences (fig.A). You can also arrange the glasses in a V shape by placing the larger vessel at the back of the table (fig.B). This is said to neutralise hostile spiritual influences and negative ancestral spirits. If this shape is reversed, by placing the larger vessel in front allowing the V-shape to take shape towards the back it is said to call upon benign spirits and positive ancestors (fig.C). It is also possible to arrange the glasses in the form of a pyramid for works of elevation, both of spirit and the soul of the practitioner (fig.D). Here prayers are presented and novenas directed towards patron saints.

The Vessel of Devotion

BRASS VESSELS for imprisoning spirits in the goetic tradition find their counterpart in Quimbanda where vessels of copper, iron or terracotta are prepared to seat the spirit. The idea behind this is to anchor the spirit by constructing the vessel in a way harmonious to the spirit's substance and then call it to dwell within. This is not a spirit trap or an Aladdin's lamp used to imprison djinn. The spirit vessel – or *assentamento* – is like preparing a body for the spirit to reside within.

The vessel of devotion is not an assentamento, but a seat of comfort for the spirit that can assist in making the relationship with it harmonious. It takes three weeks to construct and you will need to reserve the time from sundown to midnight for three successive Fridays to make this vessel.

First you need to locate a suitable vessel, which is a deep dish made from terracotta, clay or porcelain. On the first Friday wash this vessel in alcohol and raw tobacco and place two candles inside it, one red and one black. Light the candles and present a glass of cachaça or similar to the vessel and state your purpose in the following way:

Masters and Fathers of the powers of Quimbanda
It is me (state your full name three times) *that is gathered here*
before you
Guide my hand and eye as I walk out in your kingdoms
Lead me well so your seat can also be made well
Salvé Exu Rei!

Then take cachaça, tobacco and three coins and walk out in the world to find a crossroad that calls your attention. Here you take earth from the four corners of the crossroad, pouring the cachaça and leaving the tobacco and coins at the centre of the crossroad. Upon returning home add the earth to the vessel and place the vessel with the candles lit by your bed. Allow the candles to burn down. This is done three times, using three different crossroads a different one each successive week. Upon returning from the third journey, draw the ponto of Exu Rei, which is a crossroad of male tridents, burn it and add the ashes to the vessel together with dried chilli peppers and tobacco.

On this third night offer three candles, one red, one black and one white and place them around the vessel. The vessel is now ready and can be used as a seat of devotion for the Exu of your choosing. The vessel is placed upon the ponto of the Exu or in front of a charged effigy representing him and worked as a means for communion.

Healing Waters

MAGICAL BATHS or *amací* should form part of any spiritual and magical tradition. After all we are speaking about the world of matter, so our matter should be at all times in a good state to be worked with and worked by! It is amazing how many problems and difficulties can be solved by the physical and spiritual cleanliness created by *amaci*. Water and herbs can fortify the soul, ease the mind and agitate the spirit. It is most wise to make water and herbs an integral and indispensable part of the spiritual practice. The way of making the amaci follows the same pattern; prayers are simply said or sung as the herbs are macerated. Certainly some waters are more complex, but what is needed on a day-to-day basis is quite simple and most benign. Here follow a few healing waters I have found to be most effective:

Amaci for dispelling ghosts and kiumbas
You will make a bath of the following ingredients: sea salt, tobacco (*Nicotiana sp.*), basil (*Ocimum gratissimum*), odundun (*Kallanchoe crenata*), levante (*Mentha viridis*) and petals of white roses.

Amaci for bringing abundance and money
You will use the following herbs: folha de fortuna (*Kallanchoe pinnata*), honey, cowry shells, basil (*Ocimum gratissimum*), bay laurel (*Laurus nobilis*), leaves of grape (*Vitis sp.*) and leaves or flesh of the honeydew melon.

Amaci for preparing a working of Quimbanda
You will blend the following ingredients in hot water: cachaça, tobacco (*Nicotiana sp.*), chilli pepper (*Capiscum sp.*), ginger (*Zingiber officinale*), and leaves of datura (*Stramonium* or *inoxia*).

Amaci for restoring strength of soul and will
For this purpose you will make a bath of rosemary (*Rosmarinus sp.*), thyme (*Thymus sp.*), laurel (*Laurus nobilis*), spinach (*Spinacia oleracea*), boldo (*Plectranthus barbatus*) and coconut water.

Amaci for elevation and strength of the mind
You will make the bath with these herbs: levante (*Mentha viridis*), odundun (*Kallanchoe crenata*), anis (*Pimpinella anisum*), cherry (*Prunus serotina*), mulberry (*Morus sp.*), saffron (*Crocus sativus*) and coconut water, making sure that you wash your head with it very attentively.

Amaci for breaking the evil eye
You will take a bath in the following herbs and also use this as a floorwash. The herbs are: espada de São Jorge (*Sansevieria trifasciata*), rue (*Ruta graviolens*), lavender (*Lavandula sp.*) and rosemary (*Rosmarinus sp.*).

Healing Fumes

FUMIGATIONS are important and are ascribed to the influence of the *pretos velhos*. Here are a few traditional blends that are all used in the same manner. You will blend the ingredients together in equal parts and place on burning coals and fumigate the house, especially the corners and bathrooms. The ashes will then be given to the four corners of the house.

Fumigation for expelling negativity
You will need rue (*Ruta graviolens*), raw tobacco (*Nicotinia sp.*), barba de velho (*Tillandsia usneoides*), scrapings of bull horn, lavender (*Lavandula*), myrrh and sugar cane (dried and torn).

Fumigation for exorcising hostile spirits:
You will need garlic skin, asafoetida (*Ferula asafoetida*), guiné (*Petiveria alliacea*), folha de fogo (*Clidemia sp.*), filings of deer horn, barba de velho (*Tillandsia usneoides*) and horsehair.

Fumigation for bringing good luck to the house
You will need: guiné (*Petiveria alliacea*), rue (*Ruta graviolens*), raw tobacco (*Nicotinia sp.*), coffee beans and leaves, brown sugar, cow dung and rosemary (*Rosmarinus sp.*).

Fumigation to expel the Evil Eye
You will need: lavender (*Lavandula*), rue (*Ruta graviolens*), guiné (*Petiveria alliacea*), rosemary (*Rosmarinus sp.*), palo santo or frankincense, laurel (*Laurus nobilis*) and benzoin.

Workings of Magia Negra

Many today object to this term, but the magic of Quimbanda is black. It is of the fires of the night and pertains to the night. But it is our conception of black magic itself that needs to be altered. Black magic, also called low magic, is about using the material world in pragmatic ways to accomplish miracles and goals which encompass both the most amoral and worthy of aspirations. I will therefore present some examples of the variety of workings within Quimbanda, all of which have in common the practical use of our material condition. Some of these workings involve cruelty, and I do not endorse this, but yet, this is part of the history of Quimbanda and should be presented at least for its value, not only historically, but because it gives an insight into how the natural powers and kingdoms are believed to effectuate change by virtue of its properties.

Low magic and high magic are common denominators for black and white magic. High and white magic are the godly and lawful magic, with the black and low magic being forbidden and demonic. Essentially there is little difference in practice, it is only a question of the source of the power. The themes of black magic are sortilege, necromancy and spirit traffic with beings other than angels. The condemnation of the Black Arts as forbidden in past times was largely rooted in the idea that man was limited, and that trespassing into divine domains was ungodly and forbidden. This idea is in contrast to the Kongo worldview that sees everything that is as extensions of Nzambi, God. Hence the growth of wisdom can effectuate an unleashing of creative powers in mankind, and like Nzambi we can become creators and masters of life and destiny. In Quimbanda we work both domains, high and low, hence the existence of saints and the syncretism with Solomonic ideas and spirits. The understanding however is different. For the quimbandeiro it is about balance and not a battle between good and evil, high and low. It is simply a consequence of the realization that working night and fire constantly can lead to the practitioner being consumed by it, so sunlight and fresh air is necessary to keep the practitioner stable and wise.

From this perspective, whenever a human intercessor is affecting a cure it is as much black magic as if a person is causing magically-ignited havoc. The term *black magic* also denotes the racist judgments of earlier writers who deemed the wonderworks of Africans that had a material effect ungodly, nefarious and dangerous. Hence we have the double bind of *black* associated with low, or black magic as well as the people of a continent viewed as alien and dangerous by the Europeans. In the case of Quimbanda the repertoire of black magic is a synthesis of African traditional workings mediated upon the legacy of St Cyprian of Antioch.

For many of these workings lifeforce offerings are given to support it and to give the working spirit vital energy to execute its work with. We might say that a lifeforce offering serves as fuel for the work done and is an integral part of the cult of Quimbanda. As the saying goes, if there is no blood, there is no Quimbanda. The preferred lifeforce offerings of Exu are goats and roosters, but feathered animals in general as well as rodents can all be used. It should however be said that lifeforce offerings should only be performed by a Tatá or Yaya, this is because of the sanctity of the act itself and also because of the energetic circuit established that might be too hot to handle for the unsteady ones.

Dead Man's Box

For this working you will need to make wax figures of the target or targets and have present holy water, needles with heads, a piece of black cloth, a wooden coffin and a white candle. The work is better done on Mondays and in particular the Easter tide is auspicious for such workings. Perform this ritual in the Cemetery and make sure that payment is given to the Gate and the Cruzeiro. Then you need to locate a departed one who agrees to work with you. This being done you will light the white candle at the foot of the grave and baptise the dolls in the name of the targets and sing to the Exu chosen to aid you in this work. Prayers, songs and vivid visualizations need to be presented and it is crucial that you sense a controlled but raging fire building up within you. This being done the dolls will be baptised again. Wash the coffin in cachaça and place a layer of graveyard dirt in the bottom leaving it at the foot of the grave. With solemn prayers you offer breath and intent on the needles and insert them slowly in the desired parts of the doll. This done, the doll is veiled in black cloth and placed inside the coffin. A hand of tobacco and fresh red peppers must be placed around the corpse doll and the white candle placed inside. Again prayers, songs and vivid visualizations are offered as the candle is broken in two, placed inside of the coffin and the lid is closed. The coffin should then be buried at the foot of the grave as you make your statement out loud seven times in the name of the departed one and the Exu being worked. You will promise the departed one to return on three successive Mondays the following three weeks and offer up prayers and give water and coffee to the departed one. Upon the work being done you will arrange for a mass of the dead in the name of the departed one that agreed to help you.

The Killing Toad

Give Exu Porteira a yellow candle, three red roses, three cigars, one bottle of champagne, a box of matches and three coins. The working itself can be done with the help of St Cyprian, Exu João Caveira or Exu Tatá Caveira. It is also possible to apply all three of them. Give a black candle to Omolu at the Cruzeiro and ask him to guard you as you work. The offerings for João Caveira and Tatá Caveira are a bottle of marafo (i.e. cachaça), seven boxes of matches and seven black candles. The work should not be done at a tomb, but within the cemetery. When the place is located you will bring the offerings, mark the ponto with red pemba on black cloth and place the box with the toad on the ponto, and the offerings around the cloth. You will also place bread and water on the cloth. Now, in the form of prayers and spontaneous curses against the person you seek to harm, write the target's name on a piece of white cloth, crossing it three or seven times. The cloth is then placed in the mouth of the toad which you will sew up slowly with black thread as curses are spoken. The idea behind this malefica is to make the target wither away, so this purpose must be stated as a part of the prayers/curses. Then place the toad inside the box together with the bread and water and bury it. As the toad suffers and withers away, so will the target suffer and undergo misfortune.

The Invisible Snake

On a Sunday when the Moon is waning you will kill a snake or viper. In the first hour of the Moon, light a fire and place the snake in an iron cauldron and burn it to charcoal and ashes. This being done, mark the pontos of Exu Lucifer, Exu Capa Preta and Exu das Cobras on black cloth around the fire and call them. Sing and pray repeatedly over the cauldron the following:

> *Great Lords of the Abyss of Hell*
> *Lucifer, Capa Preta, das Cobras*
> *Heed my call and my yells*
> *May the soul of this snake*
> *Make my adversaries submissive to me*
> *With this their sight I do break*
> *And they shall not be able to see*
> *Salve Seu Lucifer!*
> *Salve Seu Capa Preta!*
> *Salve Seu Cobra!*

When the snake is turned into ash, consume some of it and cut some pieces from the black cloth where the pontos were marked and wrap the ashes in it. This will serve as a charm that can be worn on the body, or the ashes can be consumed when one needs to become invisible.

Break It! – A Work to Annihilate a Working

This working is done with Exu Tranca Ruas or Rei das Sete Encruzilhadas. It is done on a Friday, close to midnight. Bring with you a bottle of beer, a bottle of cachaça, seven red candles and seven black candles, six cigars, one meter of black cloth, one meter of red cloth, and six boxes of matches. You should start the working in front of your tronco, feeding your spirits and stating the intent of the working: to break a specific working. Then walk out and pay adoration to the first six crossroads you meet, leaving some drops of cachaça at each, and at the seventh stop. Here make the sign of the cross and on the left side present the red cloth, and draw the ponto for Exu Tranca Ruas, or another Exu you have a personal and good relationship with, to fortify and protect the work. Give three boxes of matches and the beer together with three black and four red candles and three cigars. Ask license to enter the crossroad to perform the work. Enter the crossroad and present the black cloth and draw the ponto of Tranca Ruas or Sete Encruzilhadas. Make a circle of the candles and light them, and present the cachaça on the ponto together with the matches and cigars. Here you should sing and pray to Exu, lament if you will and present your case. When done, empty the cachaça over the cloth and leave the crossroad by taking seven steps backwards, greeting the guardian of the working as you do so. Upon the seventh step, turn around and walk away without looking back.

The Magic of the Padê – Works to Gain Protection

The *padê* is a flour-based food dish that can be used in a great variety of situations. It automatically gives protection and gains the good will of Exu when presented. As such it is famous for its capacity for opening opportunities and removing blockages. It is a prized offering in all kingdoms and lines and in order to make a simple padê, you will do as follows:

Take flour of corn, cassava or manioc and heat it on the stove with generous amounts of palm oil. Hot pepper oil is added to this blend as are three finely chopped onions. The contents are then placed in a vessel covered with a black or white cloth and decorated with seven red chilli peppers, seven coins and onion rings. Cachaça is poured over it together with a slice of raw beef and it is presented in front of the tronco, at the crossroad or in the kingdom worked. There are several varieties of padê, but this one is a general one that can be used by votaries in a great variety of situations.

The Knight's Conquest – For Conquest of an Object of Desire

This working is a padê made in the same way as the previous, but with some alterations. This padê is not made with cachaça but with champagne and absinthe or chartreuse. You will also need generous amounts of honey. It is excellent with the Exus in the line of Malei and in the kingdom of the Encruzilhadas. Make the padê in the usual way, but when presented it must be accompanied by seven red roses free from thorns, and seven red and seven black candles. The roses should be tied with red cord and placed on the padê. To the padê you will also add an apple that you cut in two. Take out the core and place in the centre of the dish and with a virgin needle inscribe the name of the two people you wish to see merge – a virgin needle for each name on separate halves of the apple. Then cross the two names seven times on a piece of red cloth and place it inside the cavity where the core used to be, and drench it with honey and red peppers. Join the halves and tie it up like a ball with red cord and place it in the centre of the padê. Offer up pontos and prayers to the chosen Exu and take the padê to a place close to the dwelling of the target and hide it well close by. Some rose petals can be taken from the padê and left at the gate of the target. This will sweeten your way towards conquest.

The Hole of Enemies – A Work to Destroy Enemies

This working is done with any Exu of the Street or the kingdom of the Encruzilhadas, and works well with Exu das Sete Cruzes. On a Saturday night, under a waning moon, locate a desolate place; the more barren the location the better. You need to bring with you dark glass bottles, needles and small knives, one cigar, ten black candles and Affliction mironga, a powder made in the following way:

Take fæces of cat and dog, ataare (alligator pepper), chilli pepper, corredeira (*Euphorbia hirta*), bonedust (human), mamona (castor plant/ *Ricinus communis*) and a drop of mercury. This is burnt to ashes to make this powder. The Affliction mironga belongs to St Cyprian, Exu Meia Noite and Exu das Sete Cruzes and must be made on a Friday under their watchful eyes.

At the designated place pour a circle of cachaça around the spot where you will dig the hole. Into this hole break the bottles and pour cachaça over them. Arrange the candles in a circle around the hole and light the cigar allowing the smoke to enter the hole. Do this while calling upon the Exu that will assist you in the working. Write the name of the target on pieces of cloth or paper as you do this, cross the name several times and repeat several times, constantly merging your inner violent fire with powerful images aiming to destroy your adversary. Sprinkle the mironga over the glass and add needles, then the names. Add the rest of the mironga and more needles and knives. Make sure the knives are penetrating the name. Pour cachaça over it and place it all inside the hole. Over all this three black candles are placed and lit. Leave the working in silence with three steps backwards and purge yourself upon arriving home. Additionally, some of the mironga can be thrown at the door of the target after this work is done. This is bound to turn the life of the target into a living hell and caution must be demonstrated with such workings as this, as they are almost impossible to reverse.

The Table of Cure – A Work to Heal a Sick Child

This work is done with Exu Malé or any Exu or Pomba Gira in the kingdom of das Praias. You will need a new white cloth, a plain white cup, a bottle of white or transparent glass, three white roses, water from a stream, and three small white plates. Take the cloth and cover the table that is used for the working. This must be done with care and genuine intent to effect a cure. Place the bottle with the river water at one end of the table and the cup at its side. Place a white candle and three white dishes, one rose in each dish on the table.

The afflicted child should be presented to the table near the items offered. The following prayer should be said over the child:

> *Powerful emissaries of the kingdom of waters*
> *With all my powers and all strength in my heart*
> *I shall transform this water into your medicine*
> *With your blessing this water is now medicine for NN*
> *With this I greet you and thank you*
> *And I stay firm in my unwavering conviction*
> *So may it be.*

At this point offer up prayers and pontos to the Exu chosen to assist the working. The head of the child should be washed in the water and the roses taken to an ocean or river either by the child, or in the name of the child, whilst petitioning for a cure and healing. The water should be consumed in equal parts over the course of seven days to effectuate a cure.

Blinding the Evil Eye

It is believed that the evil eye, Ajô Cocorô, has its source in the heart, because the evil eye is a projection of what lies in the heart. Consequently, in workings of Quimbanda it is the heart that is attacked. One popular method is to take a fresh bull's heart and baptise it in the name of the person who has given the evil eye. It is even better, if possible, to drape the heart in a piece of clothing of the person in question. The heart is worked on Mondays or Saturdays and is bound with black cord and filled with the crossed name of the target together with sea salt, rue and rosemary. The heart is taken to a crossroad close to a garbage dump or close to a large swamp. Here Exu is called upon and given peppers, cachaça, candles and cigars. The ponto of the Exu is drawn on black cloth and the heart placed on top. As pontos cantados are sung and prayers are offered, the heart is stabbed repeatedly as you declare how this will break the evil eye. The heart is then wrapped in the black cloth and disposed of in a place of high activity in the kingdom of the Lira, for instance in some party strip or a place where the bars are crowded. This working is better done with Exus of the Lira, but can be used with the help of most Exus.

The Drunken Prophet

This is a technique, not strictly of a Quimbanda origin, that works well in the kingdom of the Lira. At times we are in need of answers and to use the powers in the kingdom of Lira for this purpose is a great way to obtain oracles. Go to your spirit table and tronco and light a candle for the spirit you seek counsel from. Then go alone to the Lira and seek out a proper bar or tavern. The tavern should be one where drunkards over the age of forty hang out; by this I mean those cheap and worn-down taverns. The intent made with prayers, candles, cachaça and cigar prior to setting out ensures that you will be guided to the right place. Take your time, reflect upon your confusion and enter when you find the place that holds your answers. Here buy yourself a drink and soak up the atmosphere, sense where the prophet, or prophets, are and go to their table with drinks for all – as the drunker the prophet is the better. Make a toast to life, love, death and all its mystery and see what happens during the conversation. If matters proceed slowly, buy a second and third round, direct the conversation towards your field of confusion and listen. Setting out with this intent will ensure a temporary possession of a vessel who will become your oracle and dissolve your confusion. Pay the prophet with yet another round of drinks and upon returning home give thanks to Exu.

Obsession Farewell

Obsession is perhaps the most harmful danger in Quimbanda and many fall prey to it. Obsessions are caused by kiumbas, and they need to be exorcised if they have contaminated someone with their particular obsession. It should be clear that spiritually inflicted obsessions can lead to insanity and death, so it is important to take this seriously and start the cleaning and healing process. The cure does not rest in some dramatic working, but in a change in spiritual routine and conduct.

Firstly, a deliberate wish for getting rid of the obsessive spirits must be in place and a daily regime of exorcising baths (*amaci*) must be undertaken. The afflicted must refrain from intrigue and gossip of any form and avoid intoxication by drink, drugs or negativity. Works of charity can also be a good option in such cases.

Lastly, the spirit table can be worked several times a day to cultivate serenity and the warding off of hostile influences. It might also be helpful to make a novena to one of the three prime saints of Quimbanda, St Michael, St Anthony or St Cyprian; this is because they serve as calm influences high up in the spiritual hierarchy. Nine days of diligent attention to ritual protocol will in most cases be sufficient to get rid of these harmful influences. Sea salt and rue can also be placed in the corners of the house for the period of purging. The nine days should be ended by making a floorwash where, in particular, the corners of the house and bathroom are washed clean. The floor wash consists of one bottle of cachaça or similar, generous amounts of lavender and sea salt mixed with pure, preferably holy water.

Sweet World

This working is best done on Fridays with the kingdom of the Lira or das Praias in particular. Take a blue candle and inscribe on it with a needle the name of the person you seek to sweeten. The needle is then inserted in the bottom of the candle and the candle is anointed with honey and placed on the dish. After, prepare a white dish and in the bottom of the dish draw the ponto of the Exu you will work with. Fill the dish with flax seeds, rice and nuts. Pour honey and palm oil over it. Next light the blue candle and give Exu three red candles and one cigar together with a glass of sweet red wine. This should all be placed in the kitchen, at the fireplace or stove.

This being done, write the name of the person crossed seven times on a piece of paper and place it in a pan filled with equal parts pure water and brown sugar or honey (be careful here, do not use pure honey as it is flammable, sugar-diluted varieties are better). Stir the name into this solution, praying and singing from your heart that the person will be sweet. The sweetening can be of someone infested with anger or someone who seeks to advance in matters of love. The ingredients are left to boil for some minutes, then placed in another vessel and given to Exu together with cachaça and palm oil. Allow it to cool down naturally and the sweetening is done and can be worked upon actively.

A Ritual for making St Cyprian your Patron

This procedure involves a nine day dedication for installing the saint. Obtain an image of him, be it a figurine or picture. You should also have at your disposal red and black cord, two white candles and one black together with St Cyprian oil that must have been prepared beforehand. The working must be done at midnight every day, starting on a Friday at the waxing moon, ensuring that the full moon is overseeing the completion of the work.

You will use as a nightly prayer the following:

Salvé!
Most Holy St Cyprian
I beseech you as my Patron
May you work upon me and keep me steady
May you lend me your powers
As I take you on as teacher, tutor and Tatá
Bless my house and my life
As you close up the minds and mouth of my enemies
Make my eyes double in vision
As my adversaries will be doubly blind
Great One, Blessed One
Most Holy St Cyprian
I beseech you as my Patron
I beg and pray
Heed my call
Amen!

While the prayer is said, anoint a one foot length of the cords (both red and black) with the oil and tie it to the effigy or picture with three knots. On the ninth night you will make sure that the image is reflected in the full moon and with prayers bathe the image or picture in oil and red wine adding the last strand of cord. Then place leaves of Acacia and Laurel between the cords.

Watch carefully during this period. If parts of cat, toad, snake or bat come to you in some way, these need to be placed in pouches of black cloth and tied to the effigy or picture with black cord. These can also be added over time as the relationship matures.

This being done St Cyprian is given water, bread, black beans and red wine as you burn incense of frankincense and myrrh before him.

St Cyprian Oil

Olive oil
Wormwood (*Artemisia absinthium*)
Dog's Mercury (*Mercurialis perennis*)
Pennyroyal (*Mentha pulegium*)
A pinch of bone dust
A pinch of sulphur
A pinch of goat horn filings
A pinch of copper filings
Pine or Cedar resin

In addition you need to remove the Book of Revelation from the Bible, draw his ponto on each page, leave a black candle on it and wait until it has burned down. You will then burn the pages and add to the oil.

Once made, this oil should rest with the image for seven days with a seven-day candle prior to use, or with Exu Meia Noite.

Ponto Riscado of St Cyprian Quimbandeiro

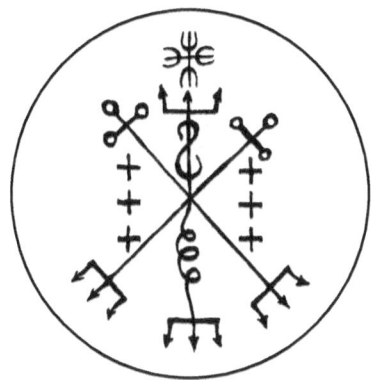

*Innocence, once lost, can never be regained.
Darkness, once gazed upon, can never be lost.*

John Milton

VII

The Legions of Hell

As we approach the spirit catalogue, there are a great variety of lines, kingdoms and hierarchies that cross, almost like a spider's web where the various agents in the web take control and prominence according to which intersection we approach them from. The traditional hierarchy sometimes gives the mysterious figure referred to as The Maioral as the head who is often, but not always equated with Capeta or the Devil, as well as being said to be Satanael. From the enigmatic Maioral flows a hierarchy of captains set over the massive legions of Exus which is as follows:

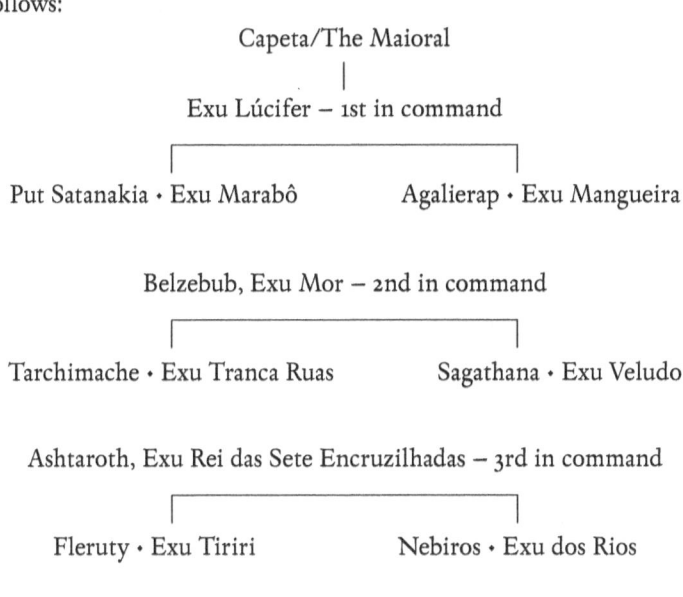

Capeta/The Maioral
|
Exu Lúcifer – 1st in command

Put Satanakia • Exu Marabô   Agalierap • Exu Mangueira

Belzebub, Exu Mor – 2nd in command

Tarchimache • Exu Tranca Ruas   Sagathana • Exu Veludo

Ashtaroth, Exu Rei das Sete Encruzilhadas – 3rd in command

Fleruty • Exu Tiriri   Nebiros • Exu dos Rios

Syrach • Exu Calunga • Gnomo • Kalunginha

This gives us three distinct lines connected to Lucifer, Beelzebub and Ashtaroth. Lucifer is attended by Exu Mangueira and Exu Marabô, or Agalierap and Put Satanakia. In the line of Beelzebub we find Exu Tranca Ruas and Exu Veludo as his generals, or Tarchimache and Sagathana as they are known in the *Grimorium Verum* and related grammars of the art. These again flow, like an inverted pyramid, into the kingdoms of Calunga and Omolu respectively in the third line, ruled over by Ashtaroth who is also known as Exu Rei das Sete Encruzilhadas, whose generals are Exu Tiriri and Exu dos Rios or Fleruty and Nebiros. This line also contains Klepoth or Exu Pomba Gira. We have yet another line in this hierarchy that is in the line of Ashtaroth but is ruled by Omolu and Exu Calunga, also known as Syrach. He has 18 legions of Exus under his command. They are together with their *Verum* syncretism as follows:

Bechard · Exu dos Ventos
Frimost · Exu Quebra Galho
Klepoth · Exu Pomba Gira
Khil · Exu Sete Cachoeiras
Mersilde · Exu das Sete Cruzes
Clisthert · Exu Tronqueira
Silchard · Exu Sete Poeiras
Segal · Exu Gira Mundo
Hicpacth · Exu das Matas
Humots · Exu das Sete Pedras
Frucissiere · Exu do Cemitério
Guland · Exu Morcego
Surgat · Exu Sete Portas
Morail · Exu Sete Sombras
Frutimiere · Exu Tranca Tudo
Claunech · Exu Pedra Negra
Musisin · Exu Capa Preta
Huictigaras · Exu Marabá

The legions under the command of the Boneherd, Omolu, include the following spirits, separated into two lines, each having a general appointed by Omolu to oversee them. In this case we have Exu Caveira and Exu Meia Noite being the two hands of Omolu that assist in curse and cure in the *campo santo*.

Omolu

Exu Caveira · Sergulath	Exu Meia Noite · Hael
Exu Tatá Caveira · Proculo	Exu Mirim · Sergutthy
Exu Brasa · Haristum	Exu Pimenta · Trimasael
Exu Pemba · Brulefer	Exu Malé · Sustugriel
Exu Maré · Pentagony	Exu das Sete Montanhas · Elelogap
Exu Carangola · Sidragosam	Exu Ganga · Damoston
Exu Arranca Toco · Minosum	Exu Kaminaloá · Tharithimas
Exu Pagão · Bucon	Exu Quirombô · Nel Biroth
Exu do Cheiro · Aglasis	Exu Curadôr · Heramael

Syrach/Exu Calunga and Exu Omolu share command over the seven lines of Quimbanda as a double root of the lineages. The lineages with their commanders are as follows:

Linha Malei · Exu Rei/Marabô
Linha Nagô · Exu Gererê
Linha Caboclos Quimbandeiros · Exu Pantera Negra
Linha Mista · Exu das Campinas
Linha das Almas · Exu Omolu
Linha dos Cemitérios · Exu Caveira
Linha Mossorubi · Exu Kaminaloá

These hierarchies do not however contain all the Exus and because of this I have found it more appropriate to separate the various legions in relation to their kingdoms. Some important Exus fall through the gaps in this way of organising them and some of those have already been discussed, whilst others will be discussed shortly. The spirit catalogue will describe all the Exus in the various kingdoms after a discussion of the higher triad with their nucleus of intermediaries.

It is important to pay attention to how the authority amongst the spirits constantly changes depending on which kingdom you are working in and the kind of work you are engaged in. As already commented upon, the natural dynamic within the legions of Exu is that roles and authority shift and new hierarchies are established within the existing ones. This dynamic is also at play when our personal spirits are brought to a given kingdom or place of power in a kingdom where we tend to have a meeting of kings and generals that assemble themselves in a unique way for the working. The seven kingdoms with their rulers and attendant Exus are listed below and as the spirit catalogue unfolds a more thorough explanation of the kingdoms will be given.

The Kingdom of the Crossroads (Encruzilhadas)
This kingdom is ruled by Exu Rei das Sete Encruzilhadas and Pomba Gira Rainha das Sete Encruzilhadas. In this kingdom, as in the other kingdoms, we have nine dwellings, with their inhabitants often called simply *people*.

The People of the Crossroads of the Streets · Exu Tranca Ruas
The People of the Crossroad of the Harp · Exu Sete Encruzilhadas
The People of the Crossroad of the Mound · Exu das Almas
The People of the Crossroads of the Track · Exu Marabô
The People of the Crossroads of the Woods · Exu Tiriri
The People of the Crossroad of the Calunga · Exu Veludo
The People of the Crossroad of the Market Square · Exu Morcego
The People of the Crossroad of Open Spaces · Exu das Sete Gargalhadas
The People of the Crossroad of the Beach · Exu Mirim

The Kingdom of the Cross (Cruzeiro)
This kingdom is ruled by Exu Rei dos Sete Cruzeiros and Pomba Gira Rainha dos Sete Cruzeiros, and refers to the central cross in the Cemetery.

The People of the Cross of the Street · Exu Tranca Tudo
The People of the Cross in the Market Square · Exu Quirombó
The People of the Cross in the Harp · Exu Sete Cruzeiros
The People of the Cross of the Woods · Exu Mangueira
The People of the Cross in the Calunga · Exu Kaminaloá
The People of the Cross of the Souls · Exu Sete Cruzes
The People of the Cross in the Open Spaces · Exu Sete Portas
The People of the Cross of the Beach · Exu Meia Noite
The People of the Cross of the Ocean · Exu Calunga

The Kingdom of the Woods (Matas)
This kingdom is ruled by Exu Rei das Matas and Pomba Gira Rainha das Matas. They govern all Greenwood except for what grows in the Cemetery as that carries a different quality and vibration.

The People of the Trees · Exu Quebra Galho
The People of the Parks · Exu Sete Sombras
The People of the Woods at the Beach · Exu das Matas
The People of the Meadows · Exu das Campinas
The People of the Highlands · Exu Serra Negra
The People of the Mines · Exu das Sete Pedras
The People of the Snakes · Exu Sete Cobras
The People of the Flowers · Exu do Cheiro
The People of the Plough · Exu Arranca Tôco

The Kingdom of the Cemetery (Calunga)
This kingdom is ruled by Exu Rei das Sete Calungas and Pomba Gira Rainha das Sete Calungas, or the King and Queen of the Cemetery.

The People of the Cemetery Gate · Exu Porteira
The People of the Graves · Exu Sete Tumbas
The People of the Catacombs · Exu Sete Catacumbas
The People of the Cremation Oven · Exu Brasa

The People of the Death's Head · Exu Caveira
The People of the Cemetery Greenwood · Exu Calunga (dos Cemeterios)
The People of the Grave Mound · Exu Corcunda
The People of the Pits · Exu Sete Covas
The People of Mirongas and Shadows · Exu Capa Preta (Exu Mironga)

The Kingdom of the Souls (Almas)
This kingdom is ruled by Exu Rei das Almas and Pomba Gira Rainha das Almas, also known as the King and Queen of the Mound (Lomba), because they tend to gravitate to places in the cemetery which are more elevated. We also find these Exus in hospitals, morgues and the like. This kingdom is about the grief and sorrow of the transition to death.

The People of the Soul of the Mound · Exu Sete Lombas
The People of the Souls in Captivity · Exu Pemba
The People of the Souls of the Wake · Exu Marabá
The People of the Souls in Hospitals · Exu Curadôr
The People of the Souls at the Beach · Exu Gira Mundo
The People of the Souls at Churches and Temples · Exu Nove Luzes
The People of the Souls in the Thicket · Exu das Sete Montanhas
The People of the Souls in the Calunga · Exu Tatá Caveira
The People of the Souls of the Orient · Exu Sete Poeiras

The Kingdom of the Harp (Lira)
This kingdom is ruled by Exu Rei das Sete Liras and Pomba Gira Rainha de Candomblé (Rainha das Marias) also said to be Exu Lucifer and Pomba Gira Maria Padilha. This kingdom speaks of art, music, poetry, inspiration, a bohemian lifestyle, but also the transmission of customs and folklore as in Candomblé.

The People of Hell · Exu dos Infernos
The People of the Cabaret · Exu do Cabaré

The People of the Harp • Exu Sete Liras
The Roma (Gypsy) People • Exu Cigano
The People of the Orient • Exu Pagão
The People who Hustle • Exu Zé Pelintra
The People of the Dumpster • Exu Ganga
The People of the Moonlight • Exu Malé
The People of Trade and Commerce • Exu Chama Dinheiro

The Kingdom of the Beach (Praia)
This kingdom is ruled by Exu Rei das Praias and Pomba Gira Rainha das Praias and its powers are related to the surface of the water, the ocean shore and the souls of people lost in the depths of the oceans.

The People of the Rivers • Exu dos Rios
The People of the Waterfalls • Exu Sete Cachoeiras
The People of the Stones • Exu Sete Pedras/Pedrinhas
The People of the Sailors • Exu Marinheiro
The People of the Ocean • Exu Maré
The People of the Mud • Exu do Lodo
The People of Bahia • Exu Bahiano
The People of the Wind • Exu dos Ventos
The People of the Islands • Exu do Côco

Capeta – The Maioral & Exu Rei

CONTROVERSY ABIDES concerning the nature of the Maioral, the true head of the cult. You can hear opinions which vary from it being Oxala and Nzambi to Satanas, the Devil and Lucifer. These are all masks of dispersion because the Maioral is in truth the Archangel Michael. This suggests a special dynamic between forces conceived of as opposing each other which is curiously enough a Bogomil idea. I am not suggesting an actual Bogomil component is found within Quimbanda, but there are clearly similar spiritual potencies and philosophies which moved the Bogomils as those which moved the masters of Quimbanda.

The Archangel Michael represents the spiritual fire of Heaven and the solar ability of overcoming, the necromantic gift par excellence, which generates this dual bond with the King of the World, this being Uriel, Lumiel or Lucifer. So, how should we understand this complex? The Maioral is the Archangel while the King Exu is the Devil, the Lord of the World, of the temporal state. This means that Exu Rei is an office which can be assumed by a handful of the Exus in the upper reaches of the hierarchy. Usually this equates to Exu Mor, Exu Rei das Sete Encruzilhadas or Exu Lucifer. Potentially, Exu Calunga can also assume the supreme crown, but I have never heard of this, though I have heard of a few temples that consider Satanael their Exu Rei and Maioral.

Fontenelle defined Exu Rei as the *Absolute*, the crowned powers of Exu and the sum of all evil. One is warned against working with him in the context of black magic, instead high magic and kabala are advocated. There is a general concern with avoiding the harder and brutal manifestations of these powers considered to be *essential tension* by nature.

Similar ideas are found in the cult of Obeah, as was taught to me through a Trinidadian lineage. Here we find Papa Bones to be the king of the cult and he is, in many ways, similar to Omolu. Papa Bones is often described and depicted as a cosmic skeleton. Papa Bones is also understood to be a trickster spirit, but he also has a darker counterpart, Sasabonsam, a monster from the forests in the kingdom of Ashanti. Sasabonsam and Papa Bones are the malefic and benevolent reflexes of

the same form, and are as such suggestive of the conflict inherent in both Satan and Lucifer that finds resolution in St Michael. A similar dynamic seems to be at play in the mysterious Maioral as well.

There is a conflict, but a dynamic conflict, which is mirrored in the fight between the higher and lower soul attempting to take control of our actions. It is man who instigates the war between Satan and Lucifer. For those who are motivated by satanic impulses, Exu turns into the devil; for those motivated by aspiration to the divine mind, Exu will turn into a powerful guardian and loyal friend, a manifestation of the Absolute. The manifestation is related to the worshipper's heart and soul. As we have seen so far in this grammar, the problem of evil is far more complex than the common distinction of Christianity, which simply separates the infernal and empyrean kingdom. Let us recall that the Bogomil heretics believed that God created Satanael from his shadow. It is important to note that the name of the angel who fell originally had the ending –*el*, signifying his divine status as a son of God. Lucifer, Satanael and Satan are perhaps better viewed as a trifold reflection of the King of Shadows himself. Lucifer represents the Promethean element introduced into creation, the principle of movement, change and wisdom. He is our higher soul, the divine reason or a vehicle for nous connecting us to all things in great harmony. Satanael, on the other hand, represents the bridge towards our lower nature, he is the deity of choice and the challenge that opens the possibility of entering within the kingdom of the emotional and ecstatic life that should ideally be subdued by the faculty of reason. If we allow our emotional life to assume the throne of our being we easily fall into corruption, and instead of being kings and queens of our domain, we enter into slavery and confusion. By crossing the bridge forged by Satanael, we turn ourself into Satan, the exalted perversion of spirit with no recourse to the golden chain or light-seed of divine becoming. In accordance with the *via negativa*, it is easy to become convinced that 'evil' is the absence of God. And truly, we can agree that absence of the light-seed facilitates the corruption of mind, soul and heart, leading to a fall of our own being towards matter, like Satanael when he lost his divine status and fell away from the source.

The term *black magic* has a multitude of understandings and, sure enough, all possible interpretations of black magic can be validated in the realm of Exu, because we have the threefold segmentation of his realm: it both represents a mystery in itself – that we shall, for the time being, leave somewhat concealed – and also, the fall and corruption that man can bring upon himself. If we cannot keep our nature high and our character good in our Promethean pursuits, the balance between the sensual and intellectual world can collapse: we fall into Hell where Satan is the King, and we lose our serenity and mindfulness. Ultimately this leads to activities associated with black magic, in the sense of them being motivated by the corruption of the soul. Such magical acts aim towards manipulating the will of others on the basis of satisfying the hunger and drives of the lower soul. This is negative magic and contradictory to the very essence of Lucifer himself. We must understand that Lucifer does not make choices on behalf of man, he represents an option, like Satan, and it is this paradoxical and intense contradiction that makes Quimbanda a path sharper than any blade. Contrasted with many other paths of magic and evolution, the danger of falling into corruption and insanity is far more prominent.

Calling Lucifer is very different from calling Satan, and Exu Lucifer is of a wholly different spiritual coloration. While Satan is working on our desires, urges and impulses by operating on them in a hidden and perverse manner, Lucifer works on our higher mind. Connecting with this force will often be dangerous for the unprepared mind, due to the immense pressure his nature represents. Even low levels of manifestation always involve obtaining the serenity and purity of all possible forces earlier present in the temple. Everything is cleaned away to make room for just a small amount of this force. A manifestation of the fallen nature is not signified with the Luciferian dignity, which aims at re-embracing the divine fire. Worship at the table of Satan, where all vices and perversions are served in the halls of Hell, is for those who see Exu as the portal to short-term goals and direct all attention to the flesh and their immediate need. By intricate mechanisms, Exu can ignite the fire of the flesh and open up the labyrinths of our own lower soul with the same ease as the doors to Jerusalem on high are flung open for the seeker to see the glory of paradise.

Exu Rei represents the expression of both your higher and lower aspirations to the full extent of their nature, and in this many Seekers go wild or resort to explanations based on biased dualism. This is again related to the reputation of the various grammars of the Arte, such as the *Lemegeton*, ascribed to Solomon, the grimoire ascribed to Honorius, the *Black Pullet* and *Grimorium Verum* which all have a sinister reputation. As the enlightened reader knows, this is far from the truth: here is another challenge for the seeker presented by Hermes Trismegistus himself to sanctify the quest. However, these grammars of the Arte can very well lead one man to the regent of Hell, as they lead another to the King of Knowledge. They simply reveal the plain truth, that man himself is man's greatest enemy. The choice lies with the Pilgrim, not in the thorn-road of which the grimoires are the map. Most assume that the summoner is of a Christian orientation or at least a mystic, since this aspiration opens a dual way between the empyrean and infernal realms, enabling the magus to find balance between the kingdoms. Seen from such a perspective, it is understandable that a Christian-oriented gnosis is often prominent in the grimoires.

Given this we yet again find St Michael the Archangel being the power that contains this dynamic flux and frustration and enables a stable work to be possible with the legions of Hell. In this function he is the tyrant of all crossroads.

Sacred Items: Hyssop, Galbanum, all night blooming flowers, cherry, tobacco, gold, the colours red, black, and white, tridents, diamonds and quartz crystal.

Lucifer: Gold, red, white, roses, lilies, bloodstone.
Satanael: Red, black, gold, mandrake, obsidian.
Synthesis: Crystalline with shades of red, mistletoe, opal.
Satan: Black, asafoetida, henbane, onyx.

Pontos Cantados of Exu Rei

A encruza é de Exu,	The crossroad is of Exu,
Afirmo e não errei (bis)	It is stated and I am not wrong (×2)
Saravá Povo da Quimbanda,	Saravá Quimbanda People,
Saravá nosso Exu Rei. (bis)	Saravá our Exu Rei. (×2)
Sr. Sete meu amigo de alma,	Mr. Sete my soul's friend,
Sr. Sete meu irmão quimbandeiro,	Mr. Sete my quimbandeiro brother,
Gira todo mundo gira	Spin, the whole world spins,
Mas seu Sete é da coroa	But Mr. Sete is from the crown
de Oxalá. (bis)	of Oxalá. (×2)
Sete facas de ponta em cima	Seven pointy knives
de uma mesa,	upon a table,
Sete velas acesa lá na encruzilhada,	Seven lit candles there at the crossroad,
Exu é rei, Exu é rei.	Exu is king, Exu is king.
Exu é rei lá nas Sete Encruzilhadas.	Exu is king there at the 7 Crossroads.
Deu a meia noite,	Midnight arrived,
Quando meu pai chegou (bis)	When my father arrived (×2)
Corregira, vai ficar lá madrugada,	The dance is on, it will be there 'til dawn,
Salve Exu, salve Exu,	Salve Exu, salve Exu,
Rei das Sete Encruzilhadas.	King of the Seven Crossroads.
O meu senhor das armas,	My lord of arms,
Diz que eu não valho nada,	Says I am not worthy,
Oia lá que eu é Exu,	Look there I am Exu,
Rei das Sete Encruzilhadas.	King of the Seven Crossroads.
Oia lá, catira de Umbanda,	Look there, dance of Umbanda,
Espia espia quem	Take a peak, take a peak at who
vem lá!	comes there,
É o supremo rei de Quimbanda,	It is the supreme king of Quimbanda,
Chefe de chefe é Maioral,	Chief of chiefs is Maioral,
Todo povo tá me saravando,	All the people are saluting,
Papai na Umbanda mandou me chamá!	Father in Umbanda told me to call!

Exú Rei é o maioral,
Exú Rei é o maioral,
Ele vem fazer o bem,
E também fazer o mal.

É Mojubá Seu Exú Rei é Mojubá,
É Mojubá,
Seu Tranca Ruas na quimbanda
  é Mojubá,
É Mojubá! Seu Tranca Ruas
  é Mojubá,
É Mojubá,
Sete Tronqueiras na magia
  é Mojubá,
É Mojubá! Sete Tronqueiras
  é Mojubá,
É Mojubá,
E a Pomba Gira na defesa
  é Mojubá,
É Mojubá! Pomba Gira é Mojubá,
É Mojubá.

Exu Rei is the maioral,
Exu Rei is the maioral,
He comes to do good,
And also to do evil.

Is Mojubá, Mr Exu Rei is Mojubá
Is Mojubá,
Mr Tranca Ruas in Quimbanda
  is Mojubá,
Is Mojubá! Mr. Tranca Ruas
  is Mojubá,
Is Mojubá,
Sete Tronqueiras in Magic
  is Mojubá,
Is Mojubá! Sete Tronqueiras
  is Mojubá,
Is Mojubá,
And Pomba Gira in defence
  is Mojubá,
Is Mojubá! Pomba Gira is Mojubá,
Is Mojubá.

The following two pontos can also be used for Exu Mor:

A meia noite na Capela
  Ele é o mal,
Maioral, Maioral, Maioral,
E na entrada do Inferno
  Ele é o mal,
E de pé na Encruzilhada
  Ele é o mal,
Maioral, Maioral, Maioral,
E do alto da Calunga
  Ele é o mal,

At Midnight at the Chapel
  He is Evil,
Maioral, Maioral, Maioral,
At the entrance of Hell
  He is Evil,
Standing at the Crossroad
  He is Evil,
Maioral, Maioral, Maioral,
From the top of the Calunga
  He is Evil,

E de pé no Cemitério	*Standing at the Cementery*
Ele é o mal,	*He is Evil,*
Maioral, Maioral, Maioral,	*Maioral, Maioral, Maioral,*
E pra os inimigos Ele é o mal,	*To his enemies, He is Evil,*
E na Escuridão Ele é o mal,	*And in the Darkness, He is Evil,*
Maioral, Maioral, Maioral.	*Maioral, Maioral, Maioral.*
Voando em duas asas negras,	*Flying on two black wings,*
Voando pelo mundo inteiro,	*Flying through the whole world,*
Voando em duas asas negras,	*Flying on two black wings,*
Voando pelo mundo inteiro,	*Flying through the whole world,*
Na linha de Exu,	*In the line of Exu,*
Seu Exu Rei foi o diabo que	*Mr Exu Rei was the devil*
eu chamei primeiro,	*I called first,*
Na gira de Exu,	*At the dance of Exu,*
Seu Exu Rei foi o diabo que	*Mr Exu Rei was the devil*
eu chamei primeiro.	*I called first.*

Pontos Riscados of Exu Rei

This is a kabalistic ponto of Exu Rei, used in order to facilitate meditative contact with Exu Rei, such as in dreaming. The ponto is adapted from the *Grimorium Verum*.

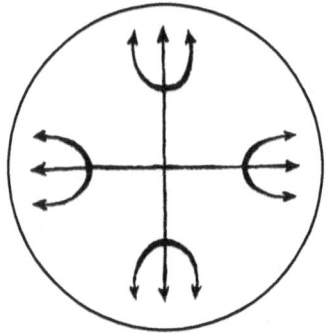

This ponto of Exu Rei is the most simple and useful of the pontos and can be used in a multitude of different ways.

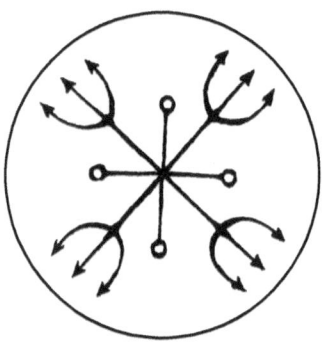

This ponto represents Exu Rei when he takes charge of a situation and can be used in order to dominate a situation, and also to soften difficult possessions.

This ponto is used in order to attract spirits and can also be used in order to empower Exu Rei's presence. It can also serve as a protective talisman when used in the making of patuás and charms.

This ponto is called Ponto Maioral and represents a synthesis of the powers of Quimbanda as reflected within Exu Rei. We have the two swords that denote the equality between the male and female powers, the seven crosses denoting the importance of this number in so many circumstances and the sun of St Michael crowning Exu Rei, denoting that he is overseen by a wise angelic host.

Exu Mor (Belzebub) Lucifer & Asmodeus

Exu Mor presents quite a puzzle, and a multitude of contradictory explanations are given for him, but the simple truth of his origin will help us to understand more of the progeny of the demonic influences in the hierarchies of Quimbanda. His mythical origin can be traced back to the destruction of Solomon's temple, which was constructed on the mountain Mor or Moriah, which is latin for *death*. In the seal of Belzebub we even find the insignia of the pillars of Solomon's temple, a J and a B. It is an adaptation of this seal that is often used as his ponto riscado. These letters are both *Jak-in* and *Boaz* as well as *yud* and *beith*. *Jak* means he will establish, and *bo* means confusion. From the destruction of the temple confusion is established and man is given an opportunity for deliverance, but he is also hurled towards the terrestrial where demonic intellects that attempt to pervert mankind are found. As such, Exu Mor symbolises the house (*beith*) of confusion. Martines de Pasqually says about this that: *The number of confusion of the second column is designated by the binary rank held by the first letter of the word Boaz*. Ultimately the pillar of confusion carried the secrets of Cain's legacy as the pillar of Jakin veiled the secrets of the descendants of Seth. So the mystery of Exu Mor is contained in yet another observation of Pasqually: *Confusion derives from two powers in opposition, to sustain on the one hand, and to liberate on the other*. In this we are also reminded of how Al-Arabi saw Iblis as the power that affirmed the perfection of the Creator's design. We should also mention that the name Beelzebuth or Bael Zebub does not necessarily refer to The Lord of Flying Things, such as flies, but it can also refer to the Lord of Zebub, a place of unknown location, that might describe the location of Mount Mor. It can also mean *beith zebul*, in conformity with what is written in Kings 1 8:13 meaning *the house upon high* which opens up avenues of understanding Exu Mor that harmonise with the confusion arising from dyadic opposition. From this origin Exu Mor represents a profound principle as being the Lord of the House of Confusion. This might be taken as the symbolism of Janus in his capacity of presenting multiple choices for the seeker, and herein is found both his mystery and his danger.

Beelzebub is the second in command in the legions of Quimbanda. This Exu is a high ranking general and king of this realm. He rules the spirits of the streets, and is said to be one of the more aggressive Exus. His prominence amongst the ranks of Exu is probably due to his renown as god of the witches, and also the fame the Kabala achieved amongst students of the occult in the 13th and 14th century. The ten sephirot that express the faces of the godhood also have their dark reflection. Many of these spirits carry clear indications of belonging to Geburah, the sephira of wrath, blood and energy. MacGregor Mathers gives the following hierarchy for the sephirot:

1 · Satan and Moloch
2 · Beelzebub
3 · Lucifuge
4 · Ashtaroth
5 · Asmodeus
6 · Belphegor
7 · Baal
8 · Adramelech
9 · Lilith
10 · Naamah

The interesting point to note here is that most of these deities represent the gods venerated by tribes that were in opposition to what came to be known as the Israelites. Moloch was a Canaanite god of fire. Asmodeus, a Persian spirit with close terrestrial connotations was incorporated in the Jewish myths as an enemy of God. In the case of Belzebub, the probable origin is Bel-se-buth; or ultimately, the great rival of Jahveh, the Moabite god Baal Zebub or simply Baal, who was referred to as the adversary by Hasidic Jews in the 18th century. An argument may be made against Belzebub being a demonic deity presiding over flies; this attribute may arise from confusion with some Mesopotamian fiend. We find the same theme in Belphegor, which is probably a corruption of Baal Peor, a god of licentiousness depicted in a form typical of the ithyphallic Priapus, a proper icon for the God of the Witches. Adramelech is said to be the brother of Asmodeus and his name means King of the Underworld. These few comments are made to remind you, dear reader, of the complexity of the matter at hand.

We also have a famous confession quoted by Richard Cavendish, the monk Jean del Vaux attested, without torture, that he and some other people worshipped Belzebub in 1595 as their Grand Master, which naturally brings to mind the accusations hurled at the Knights of the Temple. It seems that the icon of Belzebub, Lord of Flies, Prince of Seraphim and Daimon of the month of July, in his ambivalence and capacity as a repository of the many gods that opposed Jahveh, can shed even more light on the nature of Quimbanda and especially its relation to European witchcraft practices. Certainly great, arcane teachings related to the practice of the Knights of de Molay can be discovered with this Exu as one's guiding spirit.

But the references do not stop there. If we look at the descriptions given of the infernal council both in de Plancy and also in Haggadic and Talmudic sources Asmodeus and Moloch are both deities that form part of the spiritual substance of Exu Mor. I would even go so far as to state that there is no essential difference between Asmodeus and Exu Mor, but only those which forms of reverence, culture and time have made evident. The Asmodeus connection is interesting in the greater scope of Quimbanda presented in this work because Asmodeus was, as in the legends of Exu Mor, involved in the building of Solomon's temple, and hence the one who would bring about its destruction. Rabbinical sources tell us of a certain Ashmedai, considered to be a fellow of good will, until he became ensnared by Bathsheba, one of Solomon's wives, the one who was consumed by the spirit of Lilith. Ashmedai in the throes of passion became enflamed with the spirit of Asmodeus and here we find the origin of Exu Mor. Another haggadic story tells how Asmodeus was the offspring of Adam and Na'amah. Some rabbinical sources make an equivalence between Asmodeus and Samael, and through this to the serpent in the Garden of Eden, these three being of the same potency. Yet this is not so, as the serpent pertains to a mystery closely related to Exu Mor, namely the mystery of the Dragon Exu. These mysteries are intimately connected, but the one is not the other.

Moloch should also be mentioned, not just because of his fiery tastes, but because his image was composed of seven compartments to receive seven different offerings that were set on fire at the heart of the statue. Moloch, whose name means king, was depicted as a horned bull. The shared sympathy between the goat and the bull in terms of fertility and endurance should be noted. Scrapings of the bones of bulls are a critical and necessary part of his secret. All these forms find their expression in Exu Mor who is basically the erratic and lustful element in Quimbanda, it is the fire of embers drenched in blood and sperm. It is here we find the beginning of ecclesiastical diversity and heresy.

Sacred Items: Old sticks and batons, tridents, goatskin and goat skulls, bull and human bones, absinthe, red wine, tobacco, mandrake and myrrh.

Iconography: He is depicted as a red goat or bull similar to the depiction of Baphomet given by Eliphas Lévi.

Pontos Cantados of Exu Mor

Dentro de uma casa velha,	Inside an old house,
Aonde mora escuridão,	Where darkness lives,
Ô passa um homem sempre em frente,	Oh a man always passes in front,
Mas com seu chapéu na mão,	But with his hat at his hand,
Ô, quem tem asa sempre voa,	Oh, one who has wings always flys,
Ô, que tem fé sempre caminha,	Oh, one who has faith always walks,
Eu não giro na luz não,	I don't spin in the light,
Porque a noite é sempre minha.	'Cause the night is always mine.
Eu andava na beira do trilho,	I was walking at the side of the track,
Firmando o meu ponto	Making my ponto strong
quanto o trem passou,	when the train passed,
Eu ouvi timbalá de martelo	I heard the sound of the hammer
que veio do inferno,	that came from hell,
O Diabo mando,	The Devil has sent,
Exu é do inferno,	Exu is from hell,
O Diabo mandô.	the Devil has sent him.

Foi de baixo da ponte preta,	It was under the black bridge,
ouvi um grito de socorro,	I heard a scream for help,
Não umbanda, nem quimbanda,	Not Umbanda nor Quimbanda,
Magia Negra vem trabalhá,	Black Magic comes to work,
Os olhos desse homem	This man's eyes
tem Magia sim,	have Magic,
Magia negra ele faz,	He does black magic,
Seu Pai é Barrabás,	his father is Barrabas,
Magia negra ele faz,	He does black magic,
Seu Pai é Belzebu,	his father is Belzebu.

Pontos Riscados of Exu Mor

Kabbalistic ponto of Exu Mor.

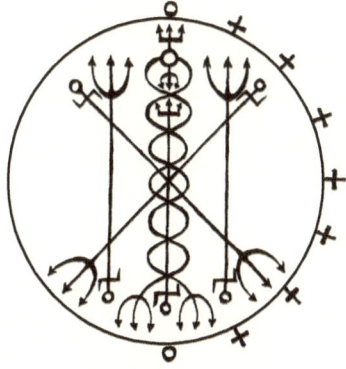 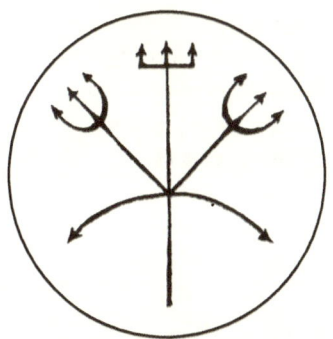

Ponto for manifesting him. Ponto for workings.

Pontos Cantados of Exu Lucifer

Porque pede o mal,	Why are you asking for evil,
Se eu sei fazer o bem,	If I know how to do good,
A escolha da sua vida,	It is the choice of your life,
É você mesmo que tem,	And this is really what you have,
Eu sou o equilíbrio,	I am the equilibrium,
Que apimenta a sua vida,	That spices up your life,
Eu posso até ser,	I can even be
O seu melhor amigo,	your best friend,
Se você acreditar,	If you do believe,
Nas palavras que eu lhe digo,	in the words I am telling you,
Sou o exu Lucifer,	I am Exu Lucifer,
O verdadeiro maioral,	the true Maioral,
Trabalho para o bem,	I work for good,
Mas sei fazer o mal,	but know how to make evil,
A escolha do caminho,	The choice of the path,
É você mesmo quem faz,	is of your own making,
Pois a minha obrigação,	because my obligation is,
É acatar a sua decisão.	to abide by your decision.

Exu Lucifer é menino   *Exu Lucifer is a boy,*
  é falso ate no andar,   *and false even in his steps,*
Exu lucifer é menino,   *Exu Lucifer is a boy,*
  nao promete pra falta,   *promises not to lack,*
Tesoura q corta ouro,   *Scissor that cut gold,*
  nao pode corta metal,   *may not cut metal,*
Cortai nos meus inimigos   *Cut from my enemies*
  a lingua q fala mal,   *their evil tongues.*

Deu Meia Noite,   *It was midnight,*
Deu Meia Noite, (bis)   *It was midnight,* (× 2)
Sete facas encruzadas,   *Seven daggers crossed,*
Em cima de uma mesa,   *On top of the table,*
Quen atirou foi Lucifer,   *He who took the shot was Lucifer,*
Pra mostra que ele é.   *To show Who He is.*

Ponto Riscado of Exu Lucifer

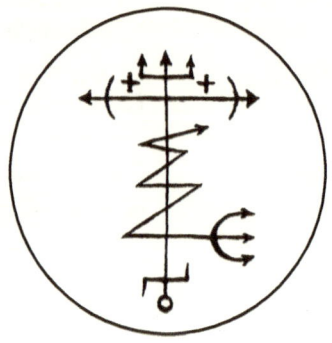

Exu das Duas Cabeças

Duas Cabeças is at times also called Exu Yangi, the laterite rock that is indispensable for making an *igba* of Èsú and the majority of the Exu *assentamentos* in Quimbanda. It is also said that this Exu is a patron of homosexuals, given its androgyne nature, but I find this to be questionable since Quimbanda at large is a cult that takes special interest in all things and people who are liminal in society. For the spirits of Quimbanda it is crucial that one is honest and true to oneself, there is really no favoring of one over another. If we follow the association with Yangi we find that this Exu carries a tremendous transformative and eruptive power and can turn wine into water and sweetness into bitterness with great ease.

This repeats a similar idea that we find in Janus/Bifrons, who is the doorway to the past and the future. It is the caduceus coiling around the central axis. It is seperation and it is God looking back at himself. It follows from this that this Exu is prone to separate as much as to unite, and every offering made for this Exu must be dual, and preferably conflicting. For example, a common gift is to give champagne and cachaça, two things that are not normally consumed together. Or gifts are given which are in marked opposition, like sweet and bitter, spicy and milky and so forth. The workings with this Exu follow this form too, and are used to accomplish radical transformations, literally to turn what is bitter sweet and what is sweet bitter.

We should also take notice that the twain-headedness was not an uncommon feature in European demonology. Baal and Asmodeus along with several other goetic spirits, like the dukes of Venus, Aim and Bim, are spoken of as having multiple heads.

Sacred Items: Laterite, volcanic minerals, everything bittersweet, forked items in general, wormwood and myrrh.

Iconography: A humanoid figure with two heads, at times the body can look like serpents and other times as burning wood. The heads can be of the same sex but a male and a female head are the most common form.

Ponto Cantado of Exu das Duas Cabeças

Ele é homem, ela é mulher,	*He is man, she is woman,*
Tem duas cabeças,	*It has two heads,*
É Exú da fé,	*It is Exú of faith,*
Sua demanda é firme,	*Its work is strong,*
Grande é seu axé,	*Its power is great,*
Saravà Exú das Duas Cabeças,	*Saravá Exú das Duas Cabeças,*
Laro laro laroyé.	*Laro laro laroyé.*

Ponto Riscado of Exu das Duas Cabeças

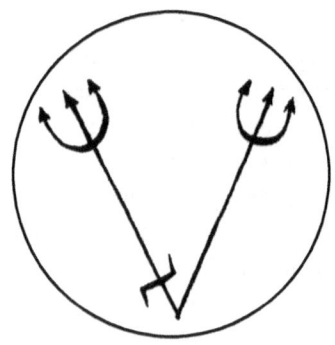

Exu Pomba Gira (Klepoth)

Fontenelle comments in his book about Exu that Klepoth is identified as Pomba Gira, Woman of Seven Husbands, in other words Figuiera do Inferno, the Fig Tree in Hell. He further refers to this Exu as the priestess of the Goat of Mendes and in this we see the intimate relationship this spirit has with Exu Mor and Exu das Duas Cabeças. If we turn to the accounts of Strabo we learn that the Goat of Mendes was the ram god Banebdjed, protector of the soul of Osiris. The fusion of Banebdjed, the ram and the goat, were perhaps because Eliphas Lévi saw a similarity in how the sexual cult around these animals of fertility was conducted. In Mendes the ram was revered as the power of fertility, hence the semen of its priesthood was highly valued. It might be that there is a connection between the lost phallus of Osiris and his soul. Lévi however took the ram and referred to it as the Goat of Mendes, inseminator and fornicator with women. In this he was likely influenced both by the image of the whore riding the Beast in the *Book of Revelation*, as well as the tales told of the practices of witches on the continent paying reverence to a goat with a candle between his horns.

Pomba Gira is the protector of women, a fierce, great adversary. In workings of love and the unjust treatment of women, she is the spirit we call upon. Many are of the opinion that no spell is complete unless Exu Pomba Gira has intervened. As Klephoth she is a serpent's nest and a legion in its own right, a celebration of the female essence and its myriad of reflections. It is the power protected by the spirits of Quimbanda, because it is from her that their power is made possible.

Sacred Items: Champagne, cigarillos, perfume, jewelry, velvet, pearls, Dama de Noite (*Cestrum nocturnum*), Jasmine, Roses and Willows.

Iconography: She is depicted as a free woman, proud of her sensuality and womanhood, usually challengingly dressed in red and black, sometimes showing her breasts.

Pontos Cantados of Exu Pomba Gira

O galo cacarecou,	The rooster sung,
Oh Pomba Gira,	Oh Pomba Gira,
Oh Pomba Gira,	Oh Pomba Gira,
Oh guingangá.	Oh guingangá.
Pomba Gira girá,	Pomba Gira girá,
Pomba Gira gire,	Pomba Gira gire,
Tatáretá Tatáretê,	Tatáretá Tatáretê,
Pomba Gira chega,	Pomba Gira arrives,
Pomba Gira chegou,	Pomba Gira arrived,
Pomba Gira girou,	Pomba Gira spun,
É a muié de Sete Exus,	She is woman of Seven Exus,
Sá Pomba Gira chegou.	Lady Pomba Gira arrived.
Pomba Gira, Pomba Gira,	Pomba Gira, Pomba Gira,
Pomba gira, tatá crué,	Pomba Gira, cruel tatá,
Olha Pomba Gira, Pomba Gira,	Look Pomba Gira, Pomba Gira,
Pomba Gira, tatá crué.	Pomba Gira, cruel tatá.
Tala, Tala-tá na Pomba Gira,	It's there, it's there in Pomba Gira,
Tala, tala, para que não caia,	It's there, it's there so it will not fall,
Tala, Tala-tá na Pomba Gira,	It's there, it's there in Pomba Gira,
Tala, tala para que não caia.	It's there, it's there so it will not fall.

Ponto Riscado of Exu Pomba Gira

Ponto for workings.

Exu Omolu

Nothing created is ever lost in nature. Everything is subject to transformation. Omolu is the keeper of this secret. He is the graveyard dirt where all possible influences from the soul and the sub-terrestrial are parted, brought together again and re-established by the hand of transformation. He is depicted as a red-robed skeleton holding a cutlass and a cross, surrounded by sepulchres and coffins. Omolu is the man at the gate, the torch in the portal, the mirror of what comes after life. He is the cross found planted in the center of the Calunga, to which all veneration is given.

Omolu, Obaluwaye and Soponno are all names of the original Yoruba Orisa that became incorporated in Umbanda/Quimbanda at some point between the last part of the 18th century and the first part of the 19th century. It is reasonable to assume that Omolu found his place within Quimbanda through similar avenues as the Orisa Èsú; by association and potency. Omolu and Obaluwaye means the same, the Lord of Earth but *aiye* which is usually translated as *earth* has a wider connotation and might be better translated as *the field of human activity*, because aiye is really the crossroad where the visible and invisible worlds meet. Death and life merge here constantly. Omolu as brother of Shango and Lord of smallpox and infectious diseases, with mosquitos and ants as his messengers, carries a vibration most accommodating to the nocturnal fire of Quimbanda. In Umbanda, Omolu and Nana Burucu (alternate Yoruba spelling, Nana Buluku) are considered the grandparents of Jesus Christ and parents of Oxalá. In Africa, Omolu is a sort of dread king on the outskirts that one appeases to keep disease away, or summons for war; usually counting on the fact that his active powers create collateral damage. As the Lord of infectious disease he is also capable of miraculous healing. In Umbanda he is syncretised with St Blaise, St Lazarus, St Roque and on rare occasions with St Nicholas. These are seen as various stages of maturity of Exu Omolu. He is also given the form of São Bento, a black-cloaked saint flanked by a raven who has a church dedicated to him in the heart of São Paulo. Heretics and witches were executed outside this church which was built on ground sacred to the Indians.

As mentioned, Omolu is the same as Obaluwaye, but even if there are similarities to be found it is interesting to look somewhat closer at who this spirit really is. The apparent confusion came into being through two avenues: one was the syncretism with the Saints and the other was through Candomblé. In Candomblé there is a tendency to equate Omolu and Obaluwaye, or if there is difference it is one of generation, Omolu being an older representative of Obaluwaye. This is quite correct as the name Omolu means *child of God* and denotes a very immediate descent and relation to God. The cult of Omolu is closely related to the mysteries of death and its transformation, while Obaluwaye is a deity of disease, especially smallpox, cholera and malaria and is the same force working during the daytime. Obaluwaye's reputation as a healer is often preferred over his misanthropic qualities. Certainly they both can heal, but Omolu is more ready to do such things than Obaluwaye.

The power of healing is found in the mystery of St Lazarus, who suffered death and resurrection. This saint has been ascribed to both Obaulwaye and Omolu, and thus represents the magnificent powers and mysteries of Omolu/Obaluwaye. In reality it is Nana Buluku, the mother of Omolu, who represents the power of healing, but this aspect has become quite clouded in the Diaspora in general and Nana Buluku did not make it across to the legions of Quimbanda, although she does have a strong affinity with Pomba Gira Rainha da Calunga. Certainly there is the whole issue of Yoruba influence that should be discussed more fully, but such lengthy discussion of morphology fall outside the practical aims of this work. Another saint syncretised with Omolu is St. Blaise, an Armenian bishop from the fourth century who was chased away from his diocese into the wild hills. When he was finally found he had the gift of communion with beasts as well as the ability to cure in apparently magical ways. He was asked to give up his worship but he refused and was tortured to death, his flesh ripped off with sharp metal tools before he was finally decapitated. This is the legend of Omolu as understood as the Boneherd, the master of the cemetery. One can understand from this that Omolu is the gate to many mysteries concerning the transition from life to death, pain and its enlightenment as well as the price paid for being resolute. Amongst the many kings Omolu demands absolute respect and his subordinates have this same serious atmosphere about them. He is the king of the mystery of Death and he guides the hand that transforms.

Sacred Items: Keys, shrouds, black and white candles, crosses.

Iconography: A skeleton robed in red veils holding a small coffin in his hands, a chain with a cross and a key around his neck.

A multipurpose padé for Omolu

Take a terracotta bowl and cover the base with honey. Then fill the vessel half full with manioc or corn flour and mix well with a bottle of *dendé* (palm oil). Make sure that you mix it only with your left hand. Cover this with *alobaça* (onion rings) and sprinkle with more dendé. You will then make popcorn, but not with salt. You will use sea sand as the 'spice' for this purpose and cover the padé with this. On top of this you will place a slice of raw, unspiced pork.

You can for Omolu, as with many other Exus, use alobaça as a tool for divination – take two onions and cut them in half and utilise them as you would the four shells.

Pontos Cantados for Omolu

O! Saravá, sarava,	O! Saravá, sarava,
O rei Omolu vai chegar,	King Omolu will arrive,
Ele é o rei,	He is the king,
É rei na Quimbanda,	Is king in Quimbanda,
É o Maioral!	He is the maioral!
Tereré, Tereré Omolu,	Tereré, Tereré Omolu,
Ego, ego Omolu,	Ego, ego Omolu,
É de pemba Omolu,	Is of pemba Omolu,
Tereré, Tereré Omolu,	Tereré, Tereré Omolu,
Ego, ego Omolu.	Ego, ego Omolu.

Pontos Riscados for Omolu

This ponto is used for many purposes.

This ponto is used for manifesting his powers and also for works of healing.

The Kingdom of the Crossroads
(Encruzilhadas)

Also called the Kingdom of the Streets, the Kingdom of the Crossroads is ruled by the King and Queen of the Seven Crossroads, syncretised with Ashtaroth who shares features with Exu Rei, as we have already discussed. Ashtaroth in Quimbanda is seen as a composite of the King and the Queen, a merging between Exu das Duas Cabeças and Klepoth. This couple is stern and they are called upon when grave difficulty is experienced, or they arrive in giras and communions to point out errors, usually in quite denigrating and unpleasant ways. A crossroad is a place of power and they can be found everywhere, not only where roads and tracks meet. The tronco is a place of power whether a crossroad or a place of violence or seduction or liminality. In the theology of Quimbanda a crossroad represents opportunity and it is here that flows and blockages are worked. If you seek to open or block hidden and more obscure opportunities Exu Marabô is worked; if the transition of a departed soul is worked then Exu das Almas can be petitioned. As we see from the Exus' assigned rulership of the particular places of power in the kingdom, the Kingdom of the Crossroads holds a most versatile spirit legion.

The People of the Crossroads of the Streets • Exu Tranca Ruas
The People of the Crossroads of the Harp • Exu Sete Encruzilhadas
The People of the Crossroads of the Mound • Exu das Almas
The People of the Crossroads of the Track • Exu Marabô
The People of the Crossroads of the Woods • Exu Tiriri
The People of the Crossroads of the Calunga • Exu Veludo
The People of the Crossroads of the Market Square • Exu Morcego
The People of the Crossroads of Open Spaces • Exu das Sete Gargalhadas
The People of the Crossroads of the Beach • Exu Mirim

Exu Rei das Sete Encruzilhadas (Ashtaroth)
Exu King of the Seven Crossroads

ASHTAROTH is the King of the seven crossroads of power and a mighty general, third in command of the legions of Lucifer. Any road can be closed or opened with the aid of this Exu. This Exu is a gentle spirit, very similar to Lucifer in his ways, and dominates the more aristocratic Exus. We meet him in *Lemegeton* as an infernal duke, and thus he is ascribed to Venus. He is said to be a beautiful angel riding a dragon and commanding vipers. Some sources claim that he is originally a Syrian god, probably because of the connection with Ashtor or Astarte, Venus, or Ishtar. In the Bible she is referred to as a deity worshipped by the Zidonians (Phoenicians). Associated with fertility, she could belong to the Moon, but other factors indicate that she is more connected to Venus. There are many transformative powers found in this royal Exu, who in spite of his aristocratic manners has a most violent temper, not to mention that this Exu is dual-sexed. Ashtaroth, like the King of the Seven Crossroads, will reveal all things past, present and future, and can teach any natural science.

This Exu can also be used in works of clairvoyance and revelation. He is a teacher amongst the Exus. He is also an Exu of amorous affairs and can solve difficulties in any kind of relationship. He can be used to confuse and mislead people and inspire hubris, and thus pave the road to misfortune for the person targeted.

Sacred Items: Serpents, bats, opal, ruby, onyx, meteorite, orchids, cherry and flavoured tobacco, absinth and anis.

Iconography: A handsome winged man dressed in red and gold, holding a serpent and a trident with a dragon lying at his feet.

Pontos Cantados of Exu Rei das Sete Encruzilhadas

Eu levo uma garrafa de marafo,	I bring a bottle of marafo,
E no cruzeiro eu vou	And at the cruzeiro I will
lhe ofertar,	offer it to you,
Eu vou chamar Exu Rei,	I will call Exu Rei,
Ele é o Exu que vai me ajudar,	He is the Exu that will help me,
Olha o coroa dele que brilha,	Look at his crown that shines,
Com a luar,	Under the light of the moon,
Na encruzilhada ele vai trabalhar,	At the crossroad He will work,
Para que seus filhos posso melhorar,	So your children can be better,
Iná, Iná é mojuba	Iná, Iná (fire) is mojuba
Exu Pomba Gira é,	Exu Pomba Gira is,
Iná, Iná é mojuba	Iná, Iná is mojuba
Exu na ponta dos pés.	Exu is tiptoeing.

Eu sou Exu,	I am Exu,
Um Exu fora da lei!	The outlaw Exu!
Ela é a Rainha,	She is Queen,
E eu sou teu Rei,	And I am King,
Eu não agüento esta	I can't bear this
maldita paixão,	cursed passion,
O amor reclama e machuca	Love reclaims and hurts
o coração,	the heart,
E você vive dizendo,	And you keep saying,
Que Exu tem coração,	That Exu has a heart,
Quem sabe um dia possamos	Who knows if one day we can,
junto,	together,
Ver o dia amanhecer,	See the dawn,
Por favor não vai embora,	Please don't go away,
Pois ainda é muito cedo,	'Cause it is too early,
Beba mais um copo,	Drink one more cup,
Para sentir o meu aconchego.	To feel my comfort.

Ponto Riscado of Exu Rei das Sete Encruzilhadas

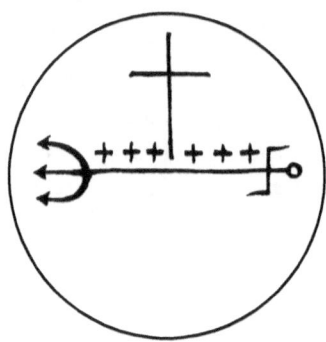

*A Working with Exu Rei das Sete Encruzilhadas
or Exu Sete Encruzilhadas to open the ways*

On the last Friday of the month, for seven months, go to a crossroads at midnight. Before leaving take a bath mixed with cachaça and three of the herbs belonging any of the spirits residing in the Kingdom of the Crossroads. Take to the crossroads a bottle of cachaça, one can of beer, one red candle, one black candle, the ponto of Exu drawn with red pemba on black cloth, a pack of matches and two cigars. Go to the centre, where the roads meet, and pour out the beer saying: *This is for you Exu Porteira so you can open the ways for me and grant me license to work with Exu of the Seven Crossroads. I pray that your machete works with me and helps clear the paths for me.*

Now bow down and say: *I greet you, powers of the Crossroads, please grant me license to work in your kingdom.*

Make a cross-sign with cachaça at the four cardinal points as well as the mid-quarters (making eight points in all), and lastly on yourself. Place the ponto on the crossroad, light the candles, light the cigars and place one on the ponto, pour half the bottle of cachaça around the ponto and speak to Exu. Drink three small sips of the cachaça during your prayers. Then take the box of matches and pull seven of the matches halfway out of the box and close them in this position. Present the matches on the ponto and say: *This fire and flame I offer to you, spirits of the Crossroads, King of the Crossroads, so that all my ways will be opened and all doors previous closed now be open for me. I know your powers and I know you can help. Help me now and I will come back to this crossroad and show my gratitude.*

Promise what you will give to Exu upon completion of your wish and leave the area. It is crucial that you keep your promise. No matter what you do, do not neglect to keep your word. Exu is a spirit of honour and does not like deceit, lies and broken promises.

Exu Tranca Ruas (Tarchimache)
Exu Streetblocker

In many ways he is similar to Ashtaroth, being a reflex of his King, who is third in command in the hierarchy of power, following Belzebub. It is this Exu that gave the spirits of Quimbanda the task of guarding the streets and crossroads of power. This intensely supportive and helpful spirit lives in the streets and crossroads of urban and rural areas alike. The street is conceived of as the rural river, the point of access to the mundane world from the world of spirit. Tranca Ruas is a well-tempered spirit with an immense knowledge, and it is possible to work to establish a contact with him for gaining his favour as a guiding spirit. Since crossroads and streets are everywhere, we will find that this Exu is related to all lines or sites of power in important ways, especially in the line that represents the last crossroads of human life, the Line of the Souls. He is also placed at important junctures in the Line of the Forest and Weeds. He is deeply related to the powers of the waters, especially the Ocean, as well as the gypsies and the line of Harp or Hell. He is related to the Moon, stars and the arte infernal. The various kingdoms he is seen in points out the importance of this spirit and the mystery of the crossroads itself. In one of his pontos it is sung: *He is the*

owner of the Street/Who runs in the streets/Who works with the souls/It is me, Tranca Ruas*. This Exu is an excellent protector of practitioners of Quimbanda, and of gates and doors. Many adherents of this Exu have reported how a fearsome man has made his presence felt by those who approached the house of the devotee with bad intentions. He is also called Lembaré, said to be his original African name carrying the same idea as his Quimbanda name as a spirit of roads and opportunities.

Sacred Items: Trident, sword, iron, hematite, the herb known as Sword of St Jorge, red and white roses or flowers from the street in such colours.

Iconography: A red-hued Exu, kneeling with a trident. He is wearing a leopard skin that covers his head and loins. Sometimes he is depicted with goat's hooves.

Pontos Cantados of Exu Tranca Ruas

Seu Tranca Ruas nos cobre com sua capa,	Mr. Tranca Ruas covers us with his cape,
Quem tá na sua capa não escapa,	The one in his cape can't escape,
Sua capa é uma Cruz de Caridade,	His cape is a Cross of Charity,
Cobre tudo só não cobre a falsidade,	That covers all, but falsity.
O Luar ... Lá no alto da Rua,	The moon shines... There above the Street,
E Ela se foi prá sua Aldeia,	And she went to her village,
Está esperando Tranca Ruas do Luar,	Waiting for Tranca Ruas from the moon,
Ele é filho do Sol ele é filho da Lua.	He is the son of the Sun, He is the son of the Moon.
O sino da Igrejinha faz belém blem blam,	The church bell sounds belém blem blam,
Deu Meia Noite o galo já cantou,	It's midnight and the rooster already sang,
Seu Tranca Ruas que dono da gira,	Mr. Tranca Ruas is the owner of the gira,
E corre gira porque o Rei mandou.	And runs the gira 'cause the King ordered.

Bará Exu, Bará dono da Rua,	*Bará Exu, Bará owner of the street,*
Bará Exu, saravá Seu Tranca Ruas,	*Bará Exu, sarava Mr. Tranca Ruas,*
Tranca Ruas Bará, Bará,	*Tranca Ruas Bará, Bará,*
Exu Bará, Bará, Bará.	*Exu Bará, Bará, Bará.*
Quando o galo canta,	*When the rooster sings,*
As almas se levantam,	*The souls rise,*
E o mar recua,	*And the ocean recoils,*
É quando os anjos do céu	*It is when the angels from heaven*
dizem amém,	*say amén,*
E o pobre do lavrador diz aleluia,	*And the poor farmer says aleluia,*
Diz aleluia, diz aleluia,	*Says Aleluia, says aleluia,*
Seu Tranca Ruas diz aleluia,	*Mr. Tranca Ruas says aleluia,*
Diz aleluia, diz aleluia,	*Says Aleluia, says aleluia,*
Seu Tranca Ruas diz aleluia.	*Mr. Tranca Ruas says aleluia.*
Vem descendo a Lomba,	*He comes from the mound,*
Vem correndo Ruas,	*He runs through the Streets,*
Quem trabalha com as Almas,	*Who works with the Souls,*
É Seu Tranca Ruas.	*It is Mr. Tranca Ruas.*
Tranca, tranca, tranca a Porteira,	*Lock, lock, lock the Gate,*
Para que não entre demanda,	*So that no spells can enter,*
Tranca-rua em minha Tronqueira,	*Tranca Rua in my shrine,*
É trabalhador da Kimbanda.	*He is the worker of Kimbanda.*
É Meia Noite,	*It's Midnight,*
Lá no Céu tá brilhando a Lua,	*In the Sky the moon is shining,*
E no Cruzeiro,	*At the Cruzeiro,*
Tá trabalhando Tranca-rua.	*Tranca Rua is working.*
Tranca Ruas das Almas,	*Tranca Ruas of Souls,*
Mora no alto da Lomba,	*Lives at the top of the mound,*
Onde o galo canta,	*Where the rooster sings,*
Onde as Almas tão de ronda.	*Where the souls are circling around.*

Eu amei alguém,	*I loved someone,*
E esse alguém amou ninguém,	*And this someone loved no one,*
Eu amei o sol, eu amei a lua,	*I loved the sun, I loved the moon,*
O lá na encruzilhada eu amei Tranca Ruas.	*Oh, there at the crossroad I loved Tranca Ruas.*

Pontos Riscados of Exu Tranca Ruas

This is the kabbalistic ponto of Exu Tranca Ruas and can generate a powerful manifestation of this Exu. It is also very good to use as a protection when building macutos.

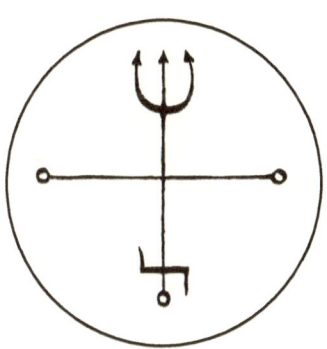

This ponto is the general ponto for calling Tranca Ruas and is used for protection and defence.

This ponto is used when employing Tranca Ruas in works of attack and malefic magic, especially to sabotage the ways of enemies by closing all their opportunities and possibilities
of progress.

This ponto represents Tranca Ruas in connection with Omolu and is a good ponto to use in works of healing and necromancy.

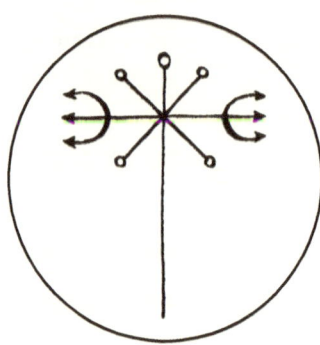

This is the ponto of Tranca Ruas do Cruzeiro that can be used for spiritual elevation and purifications. It is a ponto that repels negativity effectively. One can trace this ponto with white pemba on a banana leaf, call Exu and use the ponto as part of a bath of purification.

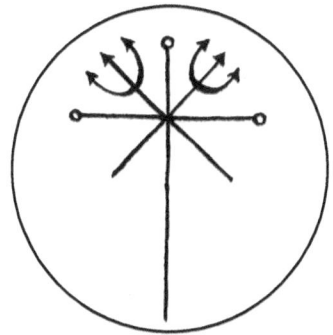 This is the ponto for Tranca Ruas da Encruzilhada (Lembaré) and can be used for opening blockages or creating them.

A working to gain the favor of Exu Tranca Ruas that he might guide you

Take a black cloth of exquisite quality and with red silken thread sew his signature in the centre of it. Place this cloth at a crossroads at midnight, and present four black candles and four red candles at each of the four points. Cover the signature on the cloth with a terracotta bowl, in which you will place *farofa* made with 21 chili peppers and raw beef or the tongue of an ox, which are prepared together with generous amounts of *Ataare* (alligator pepper) that you have chewed yourself. Then take four cigars and cross them, two and two on each side of the offering. Take three more cigars and place them, crossed, in front of the offering. Three small daggers should be present inside the offering. Finally, take seven boxes of matches, placing them around the offering. The boxes should be half open and reveal the red end of the matches. After these preparations, light a charcoal disc and use sulphur and myrrh mixed as an incense to draw forth this spirit. Call him by prayer and song and sacrifice a black cock on the offering. A few drops of the blood should be allowed to fall on the incense. This should be enough to cause possession and the spirit will teach you from this point on. After the work is done, take the cloth with you. It will serve as the vehicle between man and spirit every time you seek out Exu Tranca Ruas' guidance.

Exu das Almas
Exu of the Souls

Burial mounds are haunted by this spirit of newly-made graves who ensures the passage of the deceased one, and is in charge of the communication between the departed one and its family. This Exu is infinitely wise and comforting. Whenever you are at a funeral and feel sudden rushes of compassion, the easing of pangs of grief, or the presence of the departed one, this marks the presence of Exu das Almas. He is also an Exu that is present when corpses are washed and prepared for the journey to the other side. This Exu loves water, white and the number nine. An effective working when one seeks to ease passing, or to facilitate communication is to make a circle of nine white candles on the mound shortly after the funeral. In the centre you will place a piece of black cloth on which his ponto has been drawn with white pemba. On this give an offering of water, bread and a cigar, then ask him for solace and to open the doors of communication. This being done, be attentive as you softly sing his ponto. He dresses like an undertaker, black suit, white shirt; he holds lilies and tridents in his hands.

Sacred Items: White pemba, lilies, beeswax, honey, tridents and black and white cloth.

Iconography: A well-dressed undertaker holding in his left hand nine lilies and in his right nine black and white candles.

Ponto Cantado of Exu das Almas

La no cruzeiro da lomba, At the mound's cross,
Vem a trabalhar, He comes to work,
Com velas de sebo, With candles of lard,
E água pra limpar. And water to clean.

Ponto Riscado of Exu das Almas

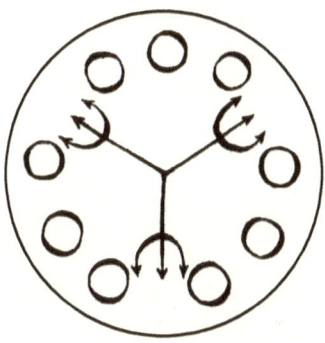

Exu Marabô (Put Satanakia)

A GREAT HEALING EXU with a preference for fine wines and cigars. It is said that this Exu speaks and writes French fluently and is an all-round gentle and wise spirit of an aristocratic bent. He is followed by a crow that protects him fiercely. Absinthe, chartreuse, port and red wine are to his liking. He dwells at the crossroads and in temples decorated to his glory. His pontos cantados refer to him as *ganga*, which reveals a deep connection with the Bantu faith and suggests that he is one of the older Exus. Some have suggested that his name means *the Exu who protects his people*, but it is likely that his name is derived from the Marabô of Ghana and Sierra Leone, a sorcerer or a Ganga. There might also be a connection here with the Sufi *silsila* known as Marabout.

Marabó is related to crossroads, and takes a particular interest in errant people and pilgrims, hence his domain in the kingdom is of the tracks. Given his old and wise stature, he is well equipped to give good advice and possessions tend to be of a gentle and clearly articulated type, but this is not always the case. There is a potential for almost all Exus to become enraged and uncontrollable and so it is with Exu Marabô. He prefers to challenge people coming to him directly, rather than using foul language. He is an aristocrat in every sense and can often be perceived to have a hot effect on women, stimulating their senses and sexual desire. It is not uncommon to apply this Exu in works for the restoration of male libido and potency.

Amongst the daimonic spirits of the West he is said to be related to Put Satanakia, linking this Exu to the realm of Solomonic magic, in particular the *Armadel* and *Lemegeton*.

His domain is largely that of occult inspiration and the giving of wisdom, especially concerning stellar mysteries and works of the crossroad and the crow.

Sacred Items: Iron, castor seeds and oil, any kind of quartz, especially those made yellow by sulphur. The colours red, black, and yellow.

Iconography: A bald but bearded dark skinned deity of a heavy build. His red cape forms into wings around him. He is armed with sword and chalice and guided by the crow.

Pontos Cantados of Exu Marabô

Eu tá, eu tai,
Quem foi que me chamo,
Eu é Exu! Eu é Exu!
Exu Marabô! Exu Marabô!

I am here, I am here,
Who called me,
I am Exu, I am Exu!
Exu Marabô! Exu Marabô!

Eu fui no mato gangá, apanhar cipó,
Eu vi um bicho gangá, de um olho só,
O Exu gangá, o Exu gangá
   é Marabô.

I went to the woods, gangá, to get liana,
I saw a beast, gangá, with only one eye,
The Exu gangá, The Exu gangá
   is Marabô.

Ele vem de longe mas chega aqui,
E quando vê alguém lhe chamar,
Vem salvando toda a encruza,
Já chegou Seu Marabô.

He comes from far but comes here,
And when he sees someone calling him,
He comes saluting all at the crossroad,
Mr. Marabô already came.

Poeira, poeira,	*Dust, dust,*
Poeira de Exu Marabô poeira,	*Dust of Exu Marabô dust,*
Poeira de Exu Marabô, poeira,	*Dust of Exu Marabô dust,*
Poeira da encruzilhada,	*Dust of the crossroad,*
Poeira, poeira.	*Dust, dust.*
Quem nunca viu,	*Who never saw,*
Venha ver,	*Come to see,*
Marabô na encruza,	*Marabô at the crossroad,*
É de quengueré.	*Is of quengueré.*
Ele é Marabô Toquinho,	*He is Marabô Little Stump,*
Dono do canto da rua,	*Owner of the corner of the street,*
Ele quando pega a demanda,	*When he gets the work,*
É sempre Ogum que manda,	*It is always Ogun that orders,*
Pedaço por pedacinho. (bis)	*Piece by piece.* (twice)

Pontos Riscados of Exu Marabô

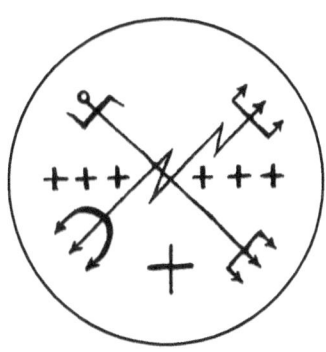

This ponto is the most common one and can be used when calling upon him.

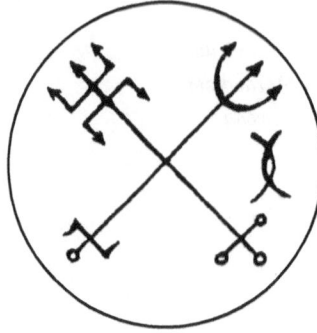

This ponto can be used when his presence needs to be strengthened and he is called upon in order to solve very delicate situations.

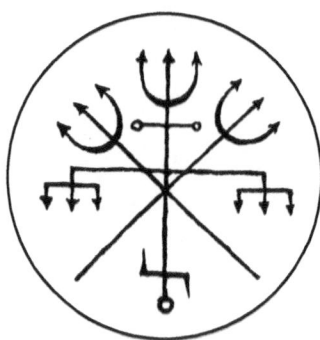

This ponto is used in works of domination.

This ponto is used in order to exorcise possessions and to neutralise negative energies.

A Working

To call him, offer the seeds of the castor plant, seven in all, wrapped in a silk cloth. This you should present to him at a crossroad, giving also the gift of seven feathers of the crow. This should be given on his signature written with yellow flour (flour mixed with sulphur) on the dirt. Call him with the following words:

O Exu gangá, o exu gangá é Marabô
Marabô is in the crossroad
O Exu gangá, o exu gangá é Marabô
He is coming to my aid
O Exu gangá, o exu gangá é Marabô
Eeee Exu gangá ooooo
Maraboooo

Then state your desire, which you write down with dove's blood on parchment and present with his gifts. State your request seven times for seven nights. On the seventh night you will go back to that same spot and pour red wine on it, thanking him for granting your desire. If the desire has not been granted, you will tell him so by lighting two black candles and again calling him to your aid, this time asking him to come to you in dreams.

To make his descent in dream possible, draw up the preceding signature with the intention clear in your mind, and put it under your pillow. Pray for him to meet you in the land of dreams to tell you what you need to know. Beside your bed place a chalice of absinthe as a present, or a chalice of wormwood tea mixed with strong liquor, with his signature drawn under and inside the chalice. By this formula he will come and he will teach you.

Exu Tiriri (Fleruty)

A POWERFUL CURADOR who excels in works of cleansing. He is often accompanied by a Pomba Gira. He is also good to use for divination and has a great understanding and compassion for human misery. He is however quite stern and demanding of his mediums and is a more rash energy, often identified as an Ogun-like fire. As such it is important to be diligent when he is worked as he has a reputation for being punitive if details are overlooked. He is said to be of a black hue and has unpleasant features, but is gentlemanly in all his ways. He is a womanizer and a great mediator between the various kingdoms of power. He can be applied effectively in works concerning relationships, either clandestine ones, or for those suffering from problems or external abuse and oppression. This is perhaps connected to a legend which tells that Tiriri had an incarnation in Ireland, where he seduced the daughter of a wealthy man, who despised him as a womaniser and made sure that he suffered for conquering his daughter. All kinds of torture were inflicted upon the handsome womaniser until he finally died from the abuse. Accordingly, he can be used with great efficiency in works of destruction, especially in cases of abuse. In powerful workings he often brings with him his ally Exu Tranca Ruas, especially workings for bringing ruin to the lives of people. It is also important to point out that this Exu may find its origin in Oyo state, Nigeria, given the prominence of this Exu in traditional houses of Orixa worship in Bahia with roots in Oyo state. His name might also be from Tupi Guarani where the name refers to *a bird that makes noise*, a bird of the marshes. Others say it is a reference to the violently invasive weed known as *tiririca*, or goat's beard (*Cyperus rotundus*) with its razor-sharp leaves. This weed can be shaped into brushes and used for calling upon Exu Tiriri.

Exu Tiriri is a carefree and gentle spirit, who usually manifests calmly but with the temperament of a warrior; he is one of the most forceful and enigmatic protectors amongst the legions of Hell. He is an Exu who can manifest in very different ways and his preferences can vary quite significantly. He accepts peppered cachaça as much as beer, and rustic cigars as much as smooth cigarettes.

Sacred Items: Pemba, roses, cachaça, guns, iron, tiririca.

Iconography: A young clean-shaven Exu with big ears and crippled arms, a sinister smile and deformed legs. He is a red-skinned Exu.

Pontos Cantados of Exu Tiriri

Exu Tiriri Bará,
Bará Exu Tiriri,
Salve o Povo de Aruanda,
Exu Venceu demanda,
Exu Tiriri Bará.

O sino da igrejinha faz
  belém blem blem,
Exu na Encruzilhada,
É Rei, é Capitão,
Exu Tiriri,
Trabalhador da Encruzilhada,
Toma conta, presta conta,
No romper da madrugada.

Corre, corre, corre gira,
Corre, corre toda Encruza,
Quem trabalha no Cruzeiro,
Demanda não recusa.

Ele é... Tiriri Bará!...
Ele é... Tiriri Bará!...

Laroiê Exu ê Cuba ô,
Ê mojubá é,
Laroiê Exu Tiriri Lonan.
Quer te pegar,
Olha moça que gosta de samba,
Olha o moço que quer batucar,
Arué, arué, arué,
Arué, arué, arué.

Exu Tiriri Bará,
Bará Exu Tiriri,
Hail to People of Aruanda,
Exu won the magical combat,
Exu Tiriri Bará.

The church bell sounds
  belém blem blem,
Exu at the Crossroad,
Is King, is Captain,
Exu Tiriri,
Worker of the Crossroad,
Takes care and reports,
At the break of the dawn.

Runs, runs, runs gira,
Runs, runs all crossroads,
Who works at the Cruzeiro,
Never refuses spells.

He is...Tiriri Bará!...
He is... Tiriri Bará!...

Laroiê Exu ê Cuba ô,
Ê mojubá é,
Laroiê Exu Tiriri Lonan.
It wants to get you,
Look the girl that likes samba,
Look the boy who wants to play drums,
Arué, arué, arué,
Arué, arué, arué.

Pontos Riscados of Exu Tiriri

Kabbalistic ponto.

This ponto is effective when fumigations & purifications are needed. It effectively repels any kind of negativity. Simply light a red candle on top of this ponto drawn on virgin paper on Friday night and pray to Exu Tiriri to remove obsessive spirits and negativity. The next night add the ponto to incense and fumigate the house.

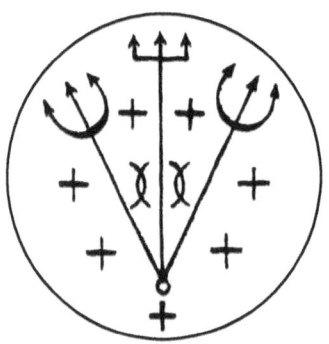

This ponto is for Exu Tiriri do Cruzeiro and is used in specific workings concerning the cemetery.

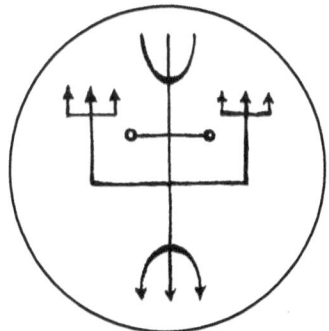

This ponto is for Exu Tiriri da Calunga and is used in works of vengeance and revenge.

Exu Veludo (Sagathana)
Exu Velvet

Exu Veludo is the immediate assistant of Ashtaroth and a powerful spirit, his goat foot indicating a strong connection with the otherworld. He is depicted as a gentleman with a dark blue cape, always in good humour and high spirits. He is polite and well spoken, a genius in languages and linguistics. He is also a powerful protector of women, especially against male hostility. This connection stems from his relationship with Pomba Gira Rainha da Calunga, a solemn and powerful queen of mature age that Exu Veludo protects with great vigour, as well as the legions of nymph-like vampires under her command. Several legends say that this Exu came from the Orient and spoke Swahili. Other stories say that he was an Arabic emir who was murdered somewhere along the coast of Brazil and yet others say he was a Malé (an Exu directly related to the Muslim communities in Rio de Janeiro and Salvador in the 18th century). Naturally, he might have held all these three incarnations and more besides. He is intimately connected to the Mossorubi line, but represents more the mysteries of prayer and trance that we encounter in some Sufi *silsilas*.

He dresses in velvet clothes and wears a turban and delights in costly garments and jewellery. He takes a special delight in women of Arabic descent or women attracted to Arabic customs and disciplines. He can as such be seen as an Exu that bridges the kingdom of Quimbanda into

the mysteries of Islam and Sufism. He is also known under the name Elumbandé and has a strong relationship with oxen.

Sacred Items: Velvet, turbans, Arabic knives, tridents and daggers.

Iconography: A red skinned Exu with a black or blue velvet cape, dressed like an Arabic nobleman.

Pontos Cantados of Exu Veludo

Comigo ninguém pode,	*Nobody can get me,*
Mais eu pode com tudo,	*But I can get it all,*
Na minha Encruzilhada,	*At my crossroad,*
Eu me chamo Exu Veludo.	*I am called Exu Veludo.*
Auê Veludo...	*Auê Veludo...*
Seu cabrito deu um berro,	*Your goat screamed,*
Rebentou cerca de arame,	*Broke the iron fence,*
Estourou portão de ferro.	*Broke the iron gate.*
Vence demanda,	*Wins the spell,*
Quebra tudo,	*Breaks it all,*
É meu Compadre,	*He is my trusted one,*
Exu Veludo,	*Exu Veludo,*
Elumbandé, Elumbandé Exu,	*Elumbandé, Elumbandé Exu,*
Exu, Exu, Veludo.	*Exu, Exu, Veludo.*
Exu pode com fogo,	*Exu can deal with fire,*
Ele pode com tudo,	*He can deal with everything,*
Saravá Exu veludo,	*Saravá Exu veludo,*
Quem demanda comigo,	*Whoever sends spells to me,*
Não chove miúdo,	*Is not raining dew,*
Saravá Exu veludo.	*Saravá Exu veludo.*
Descarrega, Seu Veludo,	*Discharge, Mr. Veludo,*
Leva o que tem que levar, (bis)	*Take whatever you have to take,* (×2)
Com sua força bendita,	*With your blessed strength,*
Leva o mal pra o fundo do mar.	*Take the evil to the deep of the ocean.*

Pontos Riscados of Exu Veludo

This ponto can be used in order to appeal to Exu Veludo in order to combat negativity.

This ponto can be used in works of seduction, love and domination.

A Working to defeat abusive men

If a woman is harassed by a man, she can appeal to Exu Veludo to hinder the abuser in the following way. At the edge of a river make a crossroads with stones from the river, with a circle of stones in the middle. Throw some cachaça to the four gates of the crossroads and greet the powers of the crossroads. In the middle of the circle, draw the ponto for domination and place a fine piece of dark blue velvet on the ponto.

Light two candles, one black and one red, and pour some fine liquor, such as amaretto, and some strong cachaça around the ponto. On the velvet place seven red chili peppers and a small dagger. Pray to Exu in your own words, asking that he take the dagger and the velvet, so he can in silence and glory smash your abuser. Finally, light a cigar for him and leave it with the dagger. Leave the place and do not return for three nights.

Exu Morcego (Guland)
Exu Bat

Exu morcego possesses the mystery of vampirism and is truly legion as he is a network of allied creatures and hidden agents in the world of night. This Exu has the power to cause incurable illness and insanity in those we make the target of his workings. He is an aristocratic and wise spirit, one of the older Exus. The stories repeatedly state that he was burned, like St Cyprian, and his presence often comes with the smell of burnt flesh or sulphur. The many legends alternate between speaking of him being condemned for witchcraft and sorcery or alchemy; commonly he is considered a master of both arts. He is intimately related to the power of prayer. Workings with him involve bats and domestic animals, like dogs, cats, pigs and so forth. He is amongst the more powerful and intelligent of the sorcerous spirits of Quimbanda. He works in the kingdom of Calunga and the Crossroads and also works in the kingdom of Souls where he takes care of the souls of those who committed suicide. Exu Morcego is also said to play a part in the equilibrium of the cosmos. In order to work with this Exu, one uses black candles for malefic workings and red candles for benevolent workings. He gives and takes with equal ease. He is fond of absinthe, any kind of tobacco, wine and whiskey. Some say that Count Dracula, as immortalised by Bram Stoker, was a manifestation of this Exu, or at least he was the force which inspired Stoker. It is said that Exu Morcego is the hidden point of power in the Brotherhood of the Black Lily, a secret cult dedicated to the mysteries of Nosferatus and the undead.

The arcana of Exu Morcego is vast and complex and there are three particular arts ascribed to him, these being alchemy, skinleaping/shapeshifting and a particular sexual mystery encoded in Quimbanda that is lodged at the heart of Morcego's skinleaping power.

He is also one of the powers who know the methods of using the kiumbas in safe and structured ways. He is especially good in breaking down dependency on drugs and alcohol. He is of course an effective spirit to use in workings for countering any form of vampirism. When coming down in the terreiro he can jokingly flash his claws to people and often has savage fits where he brutally or laughingly demonstrates a cruel disregard for living beings. Yet mostly he behaves like a gentleman, albeit with a vein of cruelty running through him.

Sacred Items: Dried bats, iron, diamond, toads, lodestone, spider's web.

Iconography: A proud red-hued spirit with a serpent's tail and prominent batwings, carrying a trident.

Pontos Cantados of Exu Morcego

Ó meu senhor das almas,
Só voa quem tem asa,
Olha que sou o exu Morcego,
Sou um dos reis na encruzilhada.

Oh my lord of souls,
Who flies only because of the wings,
Look I am Exu Morcego,
I am one of the kings at the crossroad.

Seu terno branco, sua bengala. (bis)
Na encruzilhada, quiri quiri quiri,
Exu Morcego dá risadas. (bis)

His white suit, his cane. (×2)
At the crossroad, quiri, quiri, quiri,
Exu Morcego laughs. (×2)

Exu Morcego, ele é homem é,
Exu Morcego, ele é homem é,
Exu Morcego, ele é homem é,
Na gira da Quimbanda
é homem é. (bis)

Exu Morcego, he is a man,
Exu Morcego, he is a man,
Exu Morcego, he is a man,
At the gira of Quimbanda,
he is a man. (×2)

Exu Morcego	*Exu Morcego,*
O céu escureceu,	*The sky grew dark,*
Exu bateu asas na calunga, (bis)	*Exu flapped his wings at the calunga,* (×2)
Voou, voou,	*Flew, flew,*
Exu Morcego saravou. (bis)	*Exu Morcego saravou.* (×2)
Estava amanhecendo,	*The dawn was arriving,*
Vi um morcego no ar,	*I saw a bat in the air,*
Pedi a proteção,	*I asked protection,*
De nosso Pai Lúcifer.	*Of our Father Lucifer.*

Pontos Riscados of Exu Morcego

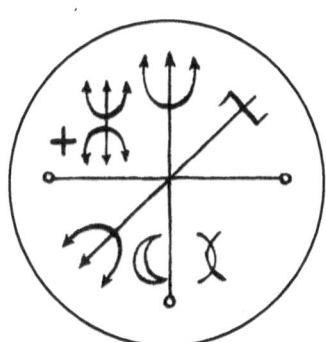

This ponto is used when one seeks to combat dependencies and the effects of vampire attacks.

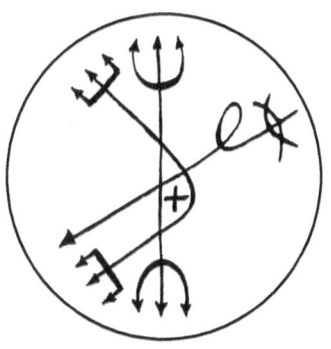

This ponto is used when one want to call upon this Exu, and also in works of attack and combat.

A Working to remove the effects of vampirism

When you feel fatigued for no reason, when spirits of the night are haunting you and succubi or incubi do not leave you alone, you can perform this ritual in order to restore the natural equilibrium and send the malignant spirits back to their source. The ritual is performed on Monday night, in the Great Hour. Take with you manioc flour, matches, seven red candles and seven black candles, a picture of the victim, three good cigars, a mirror, black cloth, red pemba, dendê, red wine, Untie All powder and Exu oil. Place the cloth on the crossroads, mark the eight corners of the cloth with Exu oil, anoint the candles and arrange them around it. Ask the license of the powers of the crossroads to work there and light the candles. Mix the flour and dendê into a pudding and place it on the plate. Set the picture of the afflicted one on the pudding and light a cigar. Fumigate the area with the cigar. Pour wine over the picture saying: *Exu Morcego, cleanse my blood from all impurities and take away the spirits tormenting my peace and soul. Send the spirits back to my offenders.* Place the mirror over the picture, facing upwards, and pour the rest of the wine over the mirror saying: *May the blood of my enemies be infected with ghosts and nightmares, may my suffering be their suffering.* Sing to Exu and leave the crossroads taking three steps backward, then turn around and do not look back. Upon arriving home, take a bath with sea salt.

Exu das Sete Gargalhadas
Exu of the Seven Laughters

AN EXU SO OMNIPRESENT in Quimbanda that it is easy to diminish his value. He comes in the laughter commonly announcing the arrival of Exu in the terreiro or in the medium. Some say this Exu fell from the stars and is the same as Exu Sete Estrelhas (Exu of the Seven Stars). These stars are Ursa Minor and as such this Exu brings the possibility for the reign of Quimbanda to unfold upon Earth by virtue of its connection with Polaris. This is a lascivious Exu who is said to walk with the Pomba Giras of the brothel, and so he is found in any brothel or tavern where the atmosphere is soaked in joy and hedonism. This Exu can be used in works of reconciliation and naturally to bring joy to situations of grief and sadness. This Exu is not occupied with human despair and trouble; rather he finds delight in overriding sad states with a joyous attitude towards life, and in this is found his remedy. Some also say that this Exu is a patron of standup comedians, which is interesting considering the at times hilarious but sharp observations he has on the world and the human condition.

Sacred Items: Wine, beer, flowers, incense, tridents.

Iconography: He often dresses in multicolored vestments cloaked in a black and silver cape wearing a top hat and holding a glass of wine and a trident.

Pontos Cantados of Exu das Sete Gargalhadas

Passei pela encruza a meia noite,
Um assobio ouvi e gritei,
Saravá todo povo da encruza,
Sete Gargalhadas nesta hora
   me valei.

I passed by the crossroad at midnight,
I heard a whistle and I screamed,
Saravá, all people of the crossroad,
Sete Gargalhadas in this hour,
   save me.

Quem pensa que o céu é perto,
Nas nuvens não vai chegar,
Exu Gargalhada está rindo,
Do tombo que vai levar,
Quem pensa que o céu é perto.
Nas nuvens não vai subir,
Exu Gargalhada está rindo,
Do tombo que vai cair,
Ri quá, quá, quá, (bis)
Ai que linda risada que Exu vai dar,
Oh que linda risada,
Ri, quá, quá.

Who thinks the heaven is near,
And the clouds will not arrive,
Exu Gargalhada is laughing,
About the fall,
At the one that thinks the heaven is near.
And the clouds will not lift,
Exu Gargalhada is laughing,
About the fall,
Laughs quá, quá, quá, (×2)
Oh a beautiful laugh Exu will have,
Oh beautiful laugh,
Laughs, quá, quá.

Ponto Riscado of Exu das Sete Gargalhadas

Exu Mirim (Serguthy)
Exu Child

Mirim is a tupi word meaning child, or to be more precise, pre-pubescent. This Exu favours mothers and children. He is said to be eager to help the quimbandeiro when they work love-bindings and works of havoc. He resides at the sides of highways and main roads where he is found accompanied by children that are prone to cause discord and mischief. In Umbanda he is related to the mysteries of the *eres* and Ibeji, children and twins responsible for movement in creation by virtue of their chaotic transformative quality. He can be found residing close to the shrines of Cosmas and Damian, and some say these powers are identical.

This Exu is a legion by himself, as he interacts with all kingdoms and Exus as their childish mirror. He can give good fortune to marginalised people and is especially protective toward those suffering social difficulties. However, since he has the temperament of a child he can easily behave obnoxiously and likes to play pranks. He has manifestations related to, for instance, Exu Caveira, in which he takes care of the affairs of children that have been abducted. When he works with Exus like Zé Pelintra he tends to induce drug dependencies and vices.

Mirim is said to come in 49 variations, this is because most Exus are followed by a *mirim*. For instance Exu Caveira is frequently accompanied by Exu Mirim Caveirinha (Little One of the Skull) who at times does good service for Exu Caveira, but other times is an intrusion that makes you lose focus in your ritual work. When this happens it is good to provide a coca-cola and a handful of sweets on his ponto with a pink and black candle to turn this force into something helpful in your working rather than a hindrance. We find the same with magical expert Exu Capa Preta whose mirim is considered a most vengeful spirit.

It should also be mentioned that Exu Mirim is a great reconciliator and is apt at dissolving misunderstandings. He is equally good at creating confusion as he is in opening the roads for prosperity. He takes a particular interest in people who have suffered a bad fate. Finally we should remember that it is important to be careful with this Exu if one has children at home, as this Exu loves to inspire children to mischief.

Sacred Items: Guaraná, sweet liquors, coca cola, cigarettes and sweets, red, blue and black candles, flowers and toys.

Iconography: His form is often of a small Exu or a child holding a trident, but his manifestations are so varied that it is impossible to give a single form of this Exu.

Pontos Cantados of Exu Mirim

Exu Mirim é meu Exu de fé!
Exu Mirim é pequeno
   na Quimbanda!
Exu Mirim saravando a encruza,
Exu Mirim vencendo suas demandas.

Exu Mirim is my Exu of faith!
Exu Mirim is the little one
   in Quimbanda!
Exu Mirim saluting at the crossroad,
Exu Mirim winning your spells.

Exu Mirim é um Exu formoso!
Ele é Exu de fé!
Tem um pai e tem um mano,
Esse mano é Lúcifer!

Exu Mirim is a handsome Exu!
He is Exu of faith!
He has a father and a brother,
This brother is Lucifer!

Exu é Malelê, é laroyê,	Exu is Malelê, is laroyê,
Povo da Rua é Malelê,	People of the Streets are Malelé,
É Exu Malelê,	Exu is Malelé,
É Exu Malelê.	Exu is Malelé.
Exu Caveirinha,	Exu Caveirinha,
Venha trabalhar,	Come to work,
Levanta dessa tumba,	Rise from this grave,
Faz pedra rolar,	Make the rock roll,
Na mão esquerda a foice,	At the left hand the sickle,
Na cinta o punhal,	At the belt the dagger,
Não sai da linha, mano,	Don't get out of line brother,
Pra não se dar mal.	Then you can't get in trouble.
Mas ele é amigo do Capeta, (bis)	But he is a friend of the Devil, (×2)
Vamos todos saravá,	Let's all saravá,
Capinha Preta.	Little Capa Preta.

Pontos Riscados of Exu Mirim

Ponto of Exu Mirim to be used in works of attraction and legal difficulties.

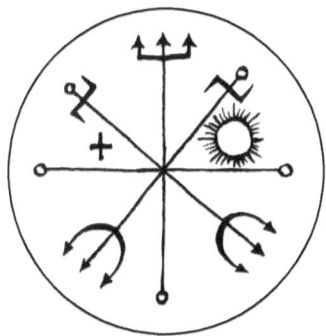

Ponto of Exu Mirim to manifest his power to work good as well as evil.

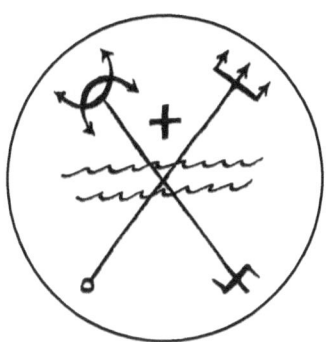

Ponto of Exu Mirim to be used when one is in need of protection.

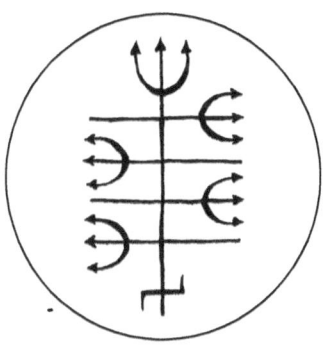

Ponto of Exu Malandrino to be used when working with Zé Pelintra or to bring malefica upon one's enemies.

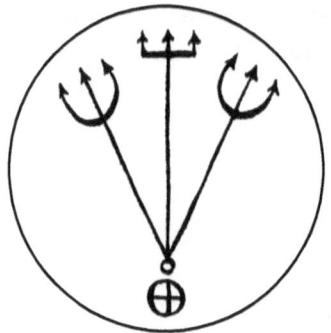

Ponto of Exu Menino to be used in any kind of work.

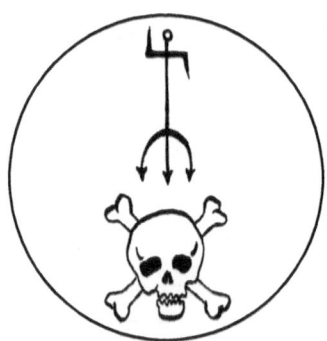

Ponto riscado of Exu Caveirinha to be used when one needs protection against deadly spells.

Ponto of Exu Caveirinha to be used to call upon his intersection in the Kingdom of Souls and the cemetery.

The Kingdom of the Cross
(Cruzeiro)

RULED BY Exu Rei dos Sete Cruzeiros and Pomba Gira Rainha dos Sete Cruzeiros. The Cruzeiro refers to the central cross in the cemetery, where Omolu dwells, but it has also become a reference to the act of crossing from one state to another or from one place to another. As such this kingdom ensures the transition from bad to good and vice versa. It is the kingdom of transformation in all forms and is particularly active in liminal states, whether an eclipse or twilight, whether in nature or in one's life. Hence the idea of the cross also means a turning point, and a place for decision and chance. The king of this kingdom is close to Exu Veludo, given the protective support he gives to the Queen of the Cruzeiro who is at times identified as the same as Pomba Gira Rainha da Calunga. This is not so, they are sisters yet distinct, even if they come down in very much similar ways, that is, sudden, stern and direct. Theirs is the solemnity of active grave mounds. This couple are great conciliators in disputes of all kinds, but in particular they are guardians of marriages, oaths and pacts. This Queen pays obeisance to Pomba Gira Rainha de Sete Encruzilhadas and it is said that Exu Mor has endowed this couple with unique powers and that he is their Maioral. One works with the king of this kingdom by using the pontos of Exu Rei and Exu Mor together with those of Exu Sete Cruzeiros, as these potencies are what makes this Exu a king in this kingdom.

The People of the Cross of the Street · Exu Tranca Tudo
The People of the Cross in the Market Square · Exu Quirombô
The People of the Cross in the Harp · Exu Sete Cruzeiros
The People of the Cross of the Woods · Exu Mangueira
The People of the Cross in the Calunga · Exu Kaminaloá
The People of the Cross of the Souls · Exu Sete Cruzes
The People of the Cross in the Open Spaces · Exu Sete Portas
The People of the Cross of the Beach · Exu Meia Noite
The People of the Cross of the Ocean · Exu Calunga

Exu Tranca Tudo (Frutimiere)
Exu Lock All

An Exu whose name means *lock everything* or *lock all* preserves vast sexual arcana, and is the patron of sexual orgies and banquets. As the name indicates he can block everything, good or bad. He is a spirit which is indifferent to morals and ethics and takes special delight in eruptive sexual behaviour and orgies. It is said that one of his incarnations was as the Marquis de Sade, and that his first incarnation on Earth was as a devotee of Dionysus. He can be used in workings where a stillness of mind or situation is needed, and he is effective in workings where lawsuits are concerned as he is reputed to make any charge against good people disappear in the machinery of the justice system, especially in cases of serious charges. There is a particular sexual arcana tied to this Exu that involves the use of intoxication and orgy to accomplish one's goals. The working involves submission of one participant who is used as a scapegoat for what one needs to lock down. In this process the person accepting this role will be restrained physically as the Exu is called into the vessel of flesh. The vessel is then fed champagne, hot herbs and cachaça upon the flesh as it is from here Exu will feed. The spirit presence is expelled by sea salt and water. The procedure is radical and passions must at all times be kept in control by the Tatá and those attending the working. A softer version is to offer up fatty foods, especially pork loin and ribs together with a padé and work this on a cloth of black silk accompanied by multicoloured candles, seven in number.

Sacred Items: Keys, handcuffs, cords, trident, whips, leather, cigars.

Iconography: He is an red skinned Exu, bald and with a Roman style cape. He holds a baton and a trident and a skull rests at his side

Pontos Cantados of Exu Tranca Tudo

Ele é Exu formoso,	*He is a handsome Exu,*
Sua capa de veludo, (bis)	*His cape of velvet,* (×2)
É, é, é, povo de Ganga,	*He is, he is, he is, of the people of Ganga,*
Vai chegar Seu Tranca Tudo.	*Mr Tranca Tudo will arrive.*
Trancou, trancou, ele vem tramcar,	*Locked, locked, he comes to lock,*
Trancou, trancou, ele vem pra trabalhar,	*Locked, locked, He comes to work,*
Sua Quimbanda é muito forte,	*His Quimbanda is too strong,*
Mas seu ponto é miúdo,	*But his ponto is small,*
Ele sabe sempre o que faz,	*He always knows what to do,*
Saravá seu Tranca Tudo. (bis)	*Saravá Mr. Tranca Tudo.* (×2)
Bacanal, oi bacanal,	*Bacchanal, oi bacchanal,*
Não vivo sem você,	*I can't live without you,*
Vou pedir Exu Tranca Tudo,	*I will ask Exu Tranca Tudo,*
Pra me favorecê.	*To favour me.*

Pontos Riscados of Exu Tranca Tudo

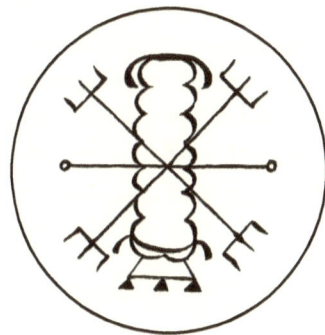
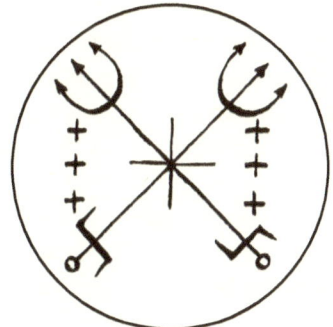

A Working to block an enemy or a negative situation

This working can be used against any kind of adversary attempting to damage your possibility of progress, or who is disturbing and annoying you. The work should be done on a Monday under a waning moon when night is falling. Place a glass of cachaça on his ponto marked on black cloth. Under the glass write down the name of the person in question. Now place three red and three black candles around the cloth. In a container mix the powders of Tranca Tudo, black pepper and red chili together with Exu powder. Sing the ponto while shaking the contents and make a circle around the glass with the powder. Anoint the four corners of the cloth with Exu oil and place them in the cachaça. Tell Exu why you came to him and fumigate with arruda (rue), myrrh and chili. Then take some of the powder and scatter it around the crossroads in a counter-clockwise direction and make a packet with the glass, name and powders. Take the packet to a tree and ask license of the tree to bury the packet there. Take three steps backward cursing your enemy in the name of Exu, turn around and do not look back. Leave the candles burning at the site and upon completion of the request go back to the same spot and offer seven candles, a bottle of cachaça and some fine cigars.

Exu Quirombò

IF THERE IS AN EXU WE CAN CONSIDER PERVERSE, it is this one. It is common in Umbanda and Quimbanda to hear the expression that one has Exu or Pomba Gira *walking in front of a person*. This means that this spiritual energy is clouding the vision people have of you and the response of the world becomes wicked. This Exu often has a hand in such situations, especially if they lead to situations of an erotic nature. This Exu leads people into compromising situations and is reputed to be responsible in cases where people have ended up in drug addiction and prostitution for no good reason.

This Exu is at times confused with Mirim, but this childish and innocent look is most likely borrowed from demonological representations of Lucifer, who is also depicted as an innocent youth. This Exu has an intimate connection with the kiumbas and might be seen as a king of kiumbas considering how he ignites obsessions in people and can inspire people to debauchery and carelessness.

Even for the mediums that handle this energy, caution is advised, as this is clearly one of the more wilder and untamed forms of Exu. He can be used in works to provoke passion, but this often leads to obsessions. He is a mystery unto himself and can with great benefit be worked as a dark mirror of your own soul in rites of communion.

Sacred Items: Cigarettes, tridents, opium, cannabis, roses, silk, vipers, all things erotic.

Iconography: A youthful spirit dressed in bohemian extravagance holding a bottle of absinthe, a rose and a trident.

Ponto Cantado of Exu Quirombô

Quem matou, quem matou,	*Who killed, who killed,*
Quem matou a cainana, (bis)	*Who killed was a serpent,* (×2)
Foi Exu Quirombô,	*It was Exu Quirombô,*
Que ganhou sua demanda. (bis)	*Who broke down your spell.* (×2)

Ponto Riscado of Exu Quirimbô

Ponto for use in works of domination and igniting obsession.

Ponto for protection and to ignite stability.

Exu Sete Cruzeiros
Exu of the Seven Crossings

WITH SIMILAR POWERS TO THE King and Queen of the kingdom this Exu is used in works of reconciliation and attraction. He is also considered a sort of director of wayward souls roaming the cemetery and can be used as an intermediary for the ease or use of these spirits. He can be used as a spiritual power to witness pacts and to seal workings done with the residents of the Campo Santo. This Exu often works with Exu Veludo, Exu Morcego and Exu Asa Negra and whilst the king is occupied with the reconciliation of lovers, this Exu is more focused on the attraction and desire between people. He is a fierce protector of women and steps up to defend women who are looked down upon because of their lustful ways and brings praise to strong women with a playful sexuality.

Sacred Items: Champagne, whiskey, cachaça, velvet, silk, tridents, daggers.

Iconography: A handsome Exu elegantly dressed in red and black, often with a panama hat, holding a bottle of champagne dressed in silk ribbons, and holding a dagger.

Pontos Cantados of Exu Sete Cruzeiros

Pomba Gira chegou no reino,	Pomba Gira arrived at the realm,
Pomba Gira no reino chegou,	Pomba Gira at the realm arrived,
Ela viu seus sete homens,	She saw her seven men,
Só, não viu Seu Sete Cruzeiros,	But not Mr. Sete Cruzeiros,
Ela sacudiu os ombros,	She shook her shoulders,
Ela se balanceou,	She shook herself,
Voltou para encruzilhada,	She went back to the crossroad,
Sete Cruzeiros ela buscou.	She sought Sete Cruzeiros.
Corre, corre, Cruzeiros,	Run, run, Cruzeiros,
Sete Cruzeiros já chegou,	Sete Cruzeiros already arrived,
Na porta do cemitério ouvi uma gargalhada,	At the gate of the cementery I heard a laugh,
Sete Cruzeiros já chegou.	Sete Cruzeiros already arrived.

Ponto Riscado of Exu Sete Cruzeiros

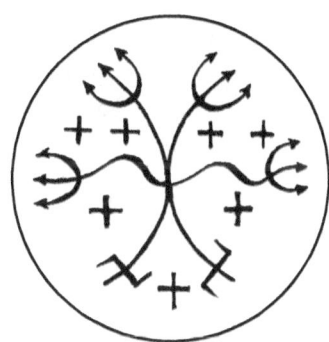

Exu Mangueira (Agalierap)
Exu of the Mango Tree

An aristocratic exu quite similar to Marabô. As his name indicates, he resides by the mango tree and leaves or bark of this tree are sacred to him, as are the fruits. The tree itself can be used as an object of adoration and one's work can be done at its foot. In many things his preference is the same as that of Marabô. His ability to cure is seen by some as greater even than that of Marabô, due to his fierce temperament and ruthless defence of his worshippers. However, the similarities between Exu Mangueira and Exu Marabô are so great that one can easily confuse one with the other. Mangueira tends to be less eloquent than Marabô and we should turn to his daimonic correspondence to draw the distinction between these two Exus more sharply. Agalierap is a demon-king of Hebrew origin and we find him mentioned in *Le Véritable Dragon Rouge* as an important servant of Lucifer, commander of the second Hell and a spirit who gives knowledge across time, revealing that which is hidden. He is good for works where you desire to sow discord amongst men and he knows the virtues of plants and minerals. This Exu possesses the secrets of the woodland as they take the shape of trees in general and working with this Exu will bring forth host upon host of Exus with a deep connection to trees. The mango tree is an essential component in spirit vessels and can be considered the woodland guardian of the cult. A temple/terreiro dedicated to the spirits of Quimbanda should have a mango tree in close proximity.

Sacred Items: Trident, sword, mango, fig, absinthe, red wine, cachaça, tobacco.

Iconography: A strong man with red hue and a prominent moustache, armed with sword and trident.

Pontos Cantados of Exu Mangueira

Exu ganhou garrafa de marafo,	Exu gained a bottle of marafo,
E levou na capela pra benzer!	And brought it to the chapel to bless it!
Seu Mangueira correu e gritou:	Mr. Mangueira ran and screamed,
Na batina do padre tem dendê!	In the priest's cassock there is palm oil!
Tem dendê, na batina do padre tem dendê! (×4)	There is palm oil, in the priest's cassock there is palm oil! (×4)
Viva as almas!	Hail to the souls!
Viva a coroa e a fé	Hail to the crown and faith
(ô viva as almas!)	(hail the souls!)
Viva exu das almas!	Hail Exu of Souls!
Ele é Seu Mangueira de fé!	He is Mr. Mangueira of faith!
(ô viva as almas!)	(hail the souls!)
Exu trabalha de pé,	Exu works standing,
Não se senta na cadeira!	He doesn't sit in the chair!
Gosta de beber marafo,	He likes to drink marafo,
De brincar com o seu garfo!	And to play with his fork!
Saravá Exu Mangueira! (bis)	Saravá Exu Mangueira! (×2)
O sino da igreja,	The church bell,
Faz belém-blém-blém,	Sounds Belém-blém-blém,
Exu na encruzilhada,	Exu at the crossroad,
É Rei, é capitão.	Is King, is captain.
Exu Mangueira,	Exu Mangueira,
Trabalhador na encruzilhada,	Worker at the crossroad,
Toma conta, presta conta,	Takes care and reports,
Ao romper da madrugada.	At the break of dawn.

Pontos Riscados of Exu Mangueira

A ponto used to bring him down in the temple.

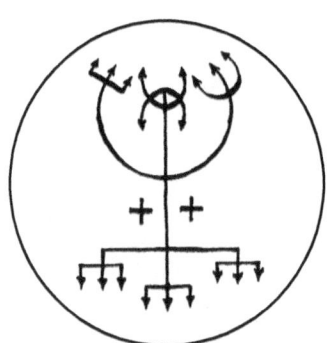

This ponto is used in works of attraction and seduction.

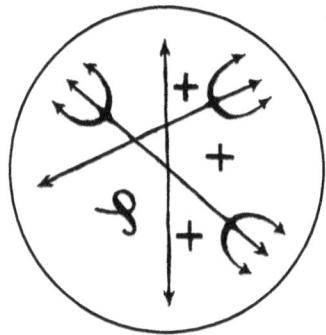

This ponto can be used in order to fortify his presence.

This ponto can be used when one want to work on issues of prosperity and material fortune.

A Working to bring forth favours

As a servant of Lucifer and the closest companion of Marabô, one calls him by presenting a mango wrapped in a black cloth together with a blonde beer at the crossroads. His signature should be drawn in the sand using a stick from the mango tree. Repeatedly draw his signature, while calling him in the following way:

Exu Mangueira, gangá auê,
Eee Exu Mangueira aiá,
As I call you come to my aid.

Pour some beer on his signature from time to time and you will surely feel a mighty presence arriving at your circle.

Exu Kaminaloá
(Tharithimas)

Working together with Exu Mangueira he is said to be one of the six most powerful Exus. He is also the Chief of the lines of Exus known as Mossorubi. He is a black man, crowned with feathers and pierced through his lips, nose and ears with heavy rings. His specialty is provoking mental disorders. He can also arrive accompanied by Exu Ganga/Exu Mulambo, suggesting a common African origin by virtue of both being Ganga that is sorcerer and healer. His distinctively Indian features are more the consequence of adopting their arts than being an Indian himself. As such, this Exu represents the meeting point between the indigenous practices of Brazil and the arts of the African witches in such practices as catimbó and the cult of Caboclo. We find in the genuine cults dedicated to Caboclos in Brazil that people of different nations upon their merging with the cult are considered Caboclos and encantados. Exu Kaminaloá represents this kind of mystery and is clearly a power that can open new avenues in what seems fixed. He is a constant reminder that nothing is carved in stone when it comes to Quimbanda. He is usually found in the cemetery and the woods but is a spirit that likes to manifest in uncommon environments and can be as equally worked in the forest as in the cemetery. Exu Kaminaloá prefers strong tobacco to fine ones. He is a ruddy spirit, infinitely wise and old and it is suggested that he has a deep connection with the pretos velhos, if not in fact being one himself. When he comes down he prefers to be seated, like many pretos velhos.

Sacred Items: Feathers, metal rings, jewels, trident, tobacco plants, cachaça, ayahuasca.

Iconography: An Exu looking like a black hued Caboclo with many tribal piercings holding a cigar and a trident.

Pontos Cantados of Exu Kaminaloá

Exu foi batizado,
E recebeu a sua cruz,
Na falange de Dom Miguel,
Kaminaloá nos defende, nos conduz.

Exu was baptized,
And received his cross,
Amidst the the legions of St Michael,
Kaminaloá defends us and guides us.

Exu formoso assim eu nunca vi
Kaminaloá é cheio de luz,
Na linha de Mossurubi.

A handsome Exu like him I never saw,
Kaminaloá is full of light,
In the line of Mossurubi.

Pontos Riscados of Exu Kaminaloá

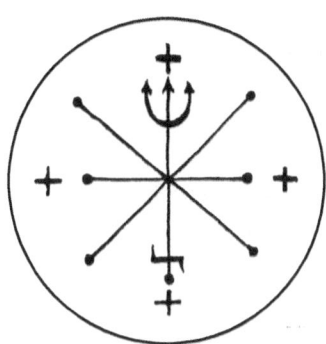

Ponto of Exu Kaminaloá to be used in works of attack and defence.

Ponto of Exu Kaminaloá for use in any kind of work and for the manifestation of his power.

A Working to ignite mental disorder and insanity in a person

It is necessary to warn against the consequences of such rituals as this, as the damage done is usually permanent.

This ritual is done on a Friday at midnight under a waning moon. You will need a pot with a lid, cachaça, animal bones, peppermint oil, mercury, dendê, Exu oil, chili pepper, alligator pepper, Punish powder, Confusion powder, powdered charcoal, Attraction powder, a volt (that is, an item belonging to the person), the name of the person written with red pemba on black cloth, a cigar and candles. You need to bathe before and after the ritual. It is also important to ask protection from one's guardian angel or perfect nature, one's daimon or patron spirit, or your ancestors before proceeding with the ritual. At midnight go to the cemetery, do not enter but lurk somewhere quiet near its walls. Ask license of the spirit to work there and spread the black cloth on the ground. Mark with red pemba the ponto of Exu and sing the ponto cantado. Place the pot over the ponto and put the volt inside the pot, together with the name, covering it with powders, chili, mercury and peppermint. Dress seven black candles with Exu oil and light them. Light the cigar and fumigate the area and the insides of the pot and close it. Then intone: *Exu Kaminaloá, I greet you and your powers and I ask that you enter the mind of NN to confuse him and to destroy his sanity. Make him mad and insane, make him totally lose control.*

Take seven steps backwards, turn around, and leave. When the target has been affected, return and make ebo to Exu, in order that the insanity will not touch you.

Exu das Sete Cruzes (Mersilde)
Exu of the Seven Crosses

An Exu who likes to work by himself and even if his domain is solely the cemetery, he has no humble relationship with the Lord of the Cemetery, Omolu. He is considered to be an independent spirit. He causes unnatural deaths, like suicide, and murderous crimes of passion and jealousy. It is said that this Exu was present at the sufferings of Jesus Christ. Some even say that it was this Exu forcing the hand of chance to set in motion the suffering and transition of Jesus, being the spirit that inspired Judas Iscariot. Exu das Sete Cruzes possesses the power of the transportation of dead bodies and it might be this Exu who took away the body of Jesus and also that of Moses when the adversary attempted to take possession of it. The spirits of his fold represent forces that can be highly disruptive, and he holds great sway over kiumbas. His kabalistic signature, which is essentially the seal of the demon Mersilde, speaks of the bitter draught that sent Socrates to his death, and bears a gravestone and seven crosses, which hint at his deeper mystery and magic. His is the work of a poisoner of soul, spirit and body. When this Exu comes down in giras it is often to make corrections and it is important to pay attention to all he says, because he does not repeat himself and important counsel is usually given in between distractions and observations that at the time seem odd. He is an ambiguous ally and needs to be pampered when worked with.

Sacred Items: Tombstones, cords, heart, brain, lungs, graveyard dust, bones, wormwood and all bitter herbs.

Iconography: He wears black trousers, has fangs and prominent horns. Often he is said to be flanked by vampires in the cemetery. He carries a trident and his special site is a tomb inscribed with seven crosses.

Pontos Cantados of Exu das Sete Cruzes

Sete Cruzes no Inferno,	Seven Crosses in Hell,
Não promete pra não faltar, (bis)	He can't promise so it will not lack, (×2)
Quando pega uma demanda,	When He gets a spell,
Vitória ele tem pra dar,	Victory He has to give,
Ele é Exu que vence missão,	He is Exu that wins his missions,
E não escolhe ocasião.	He doesn't choose the opportunity.
Seu Sete Cruzes no Cruzeiro,	Mr Sete Cruzes at the Cruzeiro,
Está para nos ajudar,	Is here to help us,
Seu marafo e seu dendê,	His marafo and his palm oil,
Ele gosta de cuidar.	He likes to take care.
Exu das Sete Cruzes,	Exu of Seven Crosses,
Das Sete Cruzes ele é!	From Seven Crosses He is!
Carrega as Sete Cruzes,	He carries the seven crosses,
Pro compadre Lucifer.	And brings them to Lucifer.

Pontos Riscados of Exu das Sete Cruzes

Ponto to bring down this Exu.

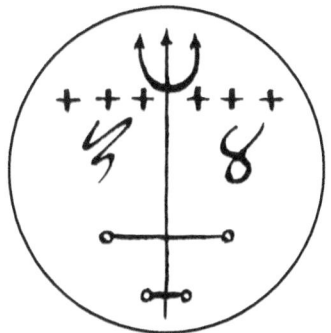 Ponto used in works of protection and defence.

A Working to defeat one's enemies

The work presented here is of an extremely dangerous nature so care and purity of soul should be observed.

Exu Sete Cruzes is drawn to the souls of people about to die by their own hand, by murder or any kind of unnatural death. He is also drawn to people marked by an unstable and aggressive disposition. The usual pattern is that the victim falls into a deep depression; all of his or her instabilities and bad behaviours are reflected within their soul. This will in many cases lead to suicide or withdrawal into isolation from the world of men, often because of some dreadful accident that it precipitates. This Exu lives in the cemetery, but can also be called in other desolate places. The spell is best done in the graveyard: a tombstone or something similar is a necessity. Of course, if spirit dictates other forms than this formula, one is well advised to follow the inspiration of spirit itself. You will need the following:

Sulphur
Gunpowder
7 nails
Pepper
Efun
Blackthorn, three staves, about 30 cm long each

Ivy
Graveyard dirt
Red and black thread
Heart of an animal
Castor oil
A Poisonous or bitter substance
A broken cup or glass that can still hold liquid
Vodka (or similar)
3 cigars
7 candles
Black and red cloth
The name of the offender
A hammer

Call Exu Rei and Exu Pomba Gira by drawing and singing their pontos. Light the sulphur incense and then the candles. Present offerings in the form of three chili peppers and pour some vodka on each ponto (you might want to use wine for Pomba Gira). Then make a third ponto between them, which is the ponto of Exu das Sete Cruzes. On the upper part of the ponto of Sete Cruzes place the black cloth, and on the lower part place the red one. The cloth should not cover the ponto, just touch its perimeter. The circles can be drawn with corn flour, ordinary flour or efun. On each piece of cloth, make a small mound of graveyard earth and place a lit cigar on top. Now call forth the Exu of the Seven Crosses in the following way – mark seven crosses on a tombstone in the cemetery while reciting this call:

> First cross: *Owner of the Seven Crosses I call you.*
> Second Cross: *Come to my aid in my hour of need.*
> Third Cross: *As you did with the Lord, do unto my enemies.*
> Fourth Cross: *Owner of the Seven Crosses I call you.*
> Fifth Cross: *Let my enemies taste your bitterness.*
> Sixth Cross: *I leave my enemies in your hands.*
> Seventh Cross: *May I walk as your ally in this night of retribution.*
> Amen.

When this is done, present him the following items: the pieces of wood, the heart, the nails, thread, the broken cup filled with poison or bitter substance, castor oil and the name of the offender.

Oh Exu of the Seven Crosses,
I know your might and your fright,
Please let my enemy, (name so and so)
Know the awesome powers you have,
I present here for you the heart of my enemy.

Write the name of the enemy seven times in a crossed pattern on the piece of paper i.e. each time you write the name, the names should cross each other. Place it inside the heart. Then take the three pieces of Blackthorn and tie the heart between them with Ivy and thread. Present the heart to the ponto again and state your desire:

This bitter draught I give my enemy to drink.
(Pour the bitter substance on the heart)
This oil I give to weaken his life.
(Pour castor oil on the heart)
These nails I give so he can be taken away.
(Present the nails to the ponto and spray with vodka and tobacco smoke.)

Sing his ponto, which is:

Exu Saravá aué. Exu Saravá euá.
Seven Crosses is coming through the Night!
He is coming to take my enemies away!
Exu ha! aué! Exu he! euá!

When you feel that Exu das Sete Cruzes is present, take the hammer and focus intensely on the desire as each nail is driven into the heart. See vividly in your mind's eye how your enemy is gasping for air and how his chest is burning with pain. When finished, leave the heart in the center of the ponto and light a circle of gunpowder around the spell (not on it) and see how Exu comes to claim the heart as the gunpowder is burned up. This being done, cover the heart in the cloth and bury it beside the ponto. Give a final libation of vodka and thank the spirits for their aid.

After the working you should clean yourself with running water, washing the skin, especially the hands, feet and face with lavender and/or laurel. Pay attention to any dreams which occur.

Exu Sete Portas (Surgat)
Exu of the Seven Doors

Exu of the seven doors unlocks any door. He can discover hidden treasures. He is a guardian of thieves and is said to be the protector of the African heritage we find in Quimbanda. Whenever we are confronted with a hindrance to opportunities, this Exu can be appealed to. His mysteries are vast, and he can be taken on as a teacher of the Art of Exu given his enormous knowledge of the cult. He is usually placated to open doors, opportunities and closed roads, but his mystery is shared with Exu das Sete Gargalhadas. There is a stellar mystery at his root, as he is related to the constellation of the Pleiades and is the sum total of the seven planets amongst the Exus. Naturally, this Exu can be quite aloof and enigmatic, and is always a softly spoken gentleman. He is a teaching spirit and the doors he prefers to open are the doors of the soul and perception. This Exu is always present in giras when the door is placated and venerated. In doing this, the gira makes itself open to whatever stellar influence is needed for the telluric work being done.

Sacred Items: Keys, locks, chains, doorknobs, aromatic tobacco, nutmeg, anis, sacred books.

Iconography: He carries a trident, wears only a pair of red trousers and bears a scroll marked with seven church doors.

Ponto Cantado of Exu Sete Portas

A porta estava fechada,	*The door was closed,*
Não havia como abrir,	*There was no way to open,*
Pedí a Exu das Sete Portas,	*I asked Exu of the Seven Doors,*
Que abrisse pra mim.	*To open this for me.*

Ponto Riscado of Exu Sete Portas

Exu Meia Noite (Hael)
Midnight Exu

Midnight Exu is especially active in the Hour of Power, when the church bell strikes midnight, and for the 49 minutes before and after midnight. In addition, he is found at the 'real' midnight, when vesper is rising. He is well versed in all kinds of magic and was said to be the tutor of the Antiochian priest St Cyprian, who was reputed to have converted to the Church in order to carry on with his dark practices without disturbance. The grimoire bearing the name of St Cyprian is said to have been inspired by Midnight Exu.

Another story tells that he was a baron, well versed in astrology and the magical arts, coming from Portugal to Santos, Brazil who later moved to Minas Gerais, Brazil where he fell in love with a fourteen year old girl. He married her, but on the wedding night she didn't bleed and so he suspected her of not being a virgin. He expelled her from his house and killed her family. Later he received news that she had given birth to his son and he took her back, regretting his unjust acts. The child died and so they tried again. Another child was born, who also died – and so did she. This was a devastating blow for the repentant nobleman and he become, like Faust, haunted by a dark shadow that was slowly killing him and upon death he became an Exu full of regret, but also charity. Other legends tell that he was a priest and mirror those of St Cyprian which has lead to a thorough identification with this Exu and the Saint of Necromancers.

This Exu is a gentleman, and he is serious in all his dealings. He is depicted with one goat foot and one human foot, denoting his position on the threshold between the worlds. He is said to have eyes of fire and to inspire fear in people when he comes down. His form fits very well with the idea of Satanas and he can bestow the powers of hygromanteia and astral magic.

Midnight Exu has seven legions with their generals under his command, ending with Exu Curadôr. This speaks of his excellence in healing and alchemy, but the knowledge of divination, tarot, the mysteries of Kabala and astrological magic are also a part of his domain. One can say that Midnight Exu is the spirit who today moves people with an inclination toward medieval magic. The fruits of his inspiration can be seen in the works of Eliphas Lévi and how the ideas of high magic influenced Quimbanda.

The deepest part of his mystery is related to the death of Jesus Christ, the Son of God and the exact moment on the Holy Friday when Jesus gave up his breath and the veil in the temple was rent asunder. In this instant Midnight Exu assumed his power and from this were established the 40 days of Lent when the spirits of Quimbanda are free to roam the world. Midnight Exu ensured a sharing of the divine powers amongst the legions and this gave the Exus their particular specialities and locations in the kingdoms. This thread stretches from Longinus to Nicodemus to St Cyprian, mediated by Judas Iscariot. Midnight Exu is all about balance, he is the feather point of the scale, the night that casts the longest shadow.

Sacred Items: Tridents, old books, bells, rosaries.

Iconography: A bearded Exu with a tail and one goat foot and one human foot. He is elegantly dressed with a black cape, holding a trident.

Pontos Cantados of Exu Meia Noite

Exu da Meia Noite,
Exu da Encruzilhada,
Salve o povo de Arruanda,
Sem Exu não se faz nada.

Exu da Meia Noite,
Exu of the Crossroad,
Hail to the People of Arruanda,
Without Exu one does nothing.

Você que tem guia,
Você que tem coroa,
Você que é um Exu da hora boa,
A hora boa é....
A Hora Grande,
Elumbandé Meia Noite!
Elumbandé meu Senhor!

You that has a guide,
You that has a crown,
You that are an Exu of good time,
The good time is...
The Great Hour,
Elumbandé Meia Noite!
Elumbandé my Lord!

Boa Noite Moço, Boa Noite Moça,
Sete Cruzes acabou de chegar;
Boa Noite Moço, Boa Noite Moça,
Meia Noite acabou de chegar.
Ele vem, da sua Calunga,
Tocando zabumba,
Ele vem trabalhar;
Ele vem, das Sete Catacumbas,
Fazendo macumba,
Só prá te ajudar.
Boa Noite Moço, Boa Noite Moça...

Good Night boy, Good Night girl,
Sete Cruzes just arrived,
Good Night boy, Good Night girl,
Meia Noite just arrived,
He comes from his Calunga,
Playing drums,
He comes to work,
He comes from seven mounds,
Making macumba,
Just to help you out.
Good night boy, Good night girl...

Pontos Riscados of Exu Meia Noite

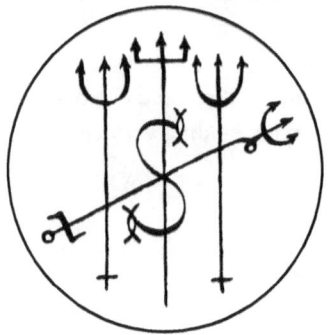

Ponto riscado of Exu Meia Noite used for protection.

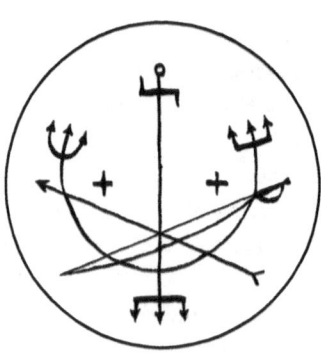

Ponto used to manifest his power, and in works of attack.

Here are a few spells from the book of St Cyprian, said to be reminiscent of the magic he was taught under Exu Meia Noite, which are given in order to illustrate his mysteries.

The Work of the Black Cat Bone

This work must be done on the half moon or even better on the night of Holy Friday. Go to a river, making sure that you are alone, and fill an iron cauldron with water from the river. Make sure that the moon is reflected in the water, then add seeds and twigs of willow and lilies to the water and make a fire of willow and other lunar woods. When the water is boiling put the black cat into the water alive and boil it until the meat is loosened from its bones. Then take a linen cloth upon which the ponto of Exu Meia Noite has been drawn and strain the bones through it. You can now attain the bone of power or the bone of invisibility. The bone of invisibility is found by placing each bone in turn in your mouth as you look into a mirror; when your image fades or blurs the correct bone is in your mouth and will be taken for safekeeping and proper use. To gain the bone of power you need to throw all the bones into the water whilst singing the ponto of Exu Mea Noite having a black candle lit at your back and observe closely, as one bone will go against the current. Seize this bone and wrap it in the cloth and do not let it leave your sight for three days and nights, because in these days and nights Exu Meia Noite will come to try and take the bone away from you. Whatever you do, do not lose the bone, it must be kept as your sign of triumph. This being done, Exu Meia Noite will grant you the powers to direct his legions.

A Working to petition demonic aid for wreaking vengeance

To wreak vengeance on an enemy, you should proceed in this way: take a black cat and, after tieing its paws with a cord of tiririca (*Cyperus rotundus*) take it to a crossroads at night and say: *I, NN, on behalf of*

Almighty God, the Most Holy Cyprian and Exu Meia Noite order the demon to appear here under the blessed yoke of obedience and superior laws. Lucifer, Satan, I order you to go into the body of this person that I want to do evil to, and do not leave until I order so, and help me with anything I ask you to during my life, (here you state your demanda in fiery and lamenting fashion). *Oh great Lucifer, emperor of all that is Hell, I seize you and tie you to the body of* (say the name of the enemy), *just as I have seized this cat. After you do everything that I want, I offer you this cat; I will bring it here when everything is ready.*

After the demon does what has been asked, you should go to the place where he was summoned and say twice: *Lucifer, Lucifer, here you have what I promised.* With these words, release the cat.

How to make a pact with a demon and create a little devil

Write on virgin paper in your own blood: *I, with the blood from my little finger, write this to Lucifer, so that he will do everything I want in life, and if this does not happen, I will no longer belong to him* – then sign your name.

Write the same words on a black hen's egg which has been fertilised by a black cock. Puncture a hole in the egg and let a drop of blood from the little finger of your right hand drop into it. Wrap the egg in cotton and black silk together with silver dust and place it under the black hen. From this egg will be born a little devil which should be kept inside a silver box with silver powder. Every Saturday feed the box blood from the little finger on your right hand so the little devil can drink the blood and grow strong. As the little devil grows in the blood bond with you, so will your magical abilities grow stronger and stronger.

Exu Calunga
Syrach · Gnomo · Calunginha

One of the epithets of this Exu is the Crossroad at the Bottom of the Ocean. As Exu Calunga, he is first and foremost an Exu of the Cemetery and his place amongst the hierarchies as the bridge between the greater chiefs and the lesser chiefs indicates his liminal domain, as well as the importance of the underworld and realm of earth elementals amongst the Exus. Calunga sometimes appears as a dwarf-like creature, which explains the name Gnomo. His relation to the depths of the Ocean links him with the powers of mermaids and sirens, and sailors who died at sea and have entered his legions. The depths of the ocean represent mystery and secrecy, and in the case of Calunga they are intertwined with death. Exu Calunga is mostly used in works dealing with dead sailors and spirits of the ocean, both in works of great healing and to create emotional disturbance in the victims of his rage. He is also found within the earth of the cemetery and is thus the mysterious axis that connects those who died at sea with the kingdom of Omolu.

There is more to this mystery, some of which I have discussed in *Pomba Gira and the Quimbanda of Mbùmba Nzila* where the relationships between Exu Calunga, Syrach and Scirlin are related to Klepoth and Venus in the form of Pomba Gira. If we continue on this avenue we will see that Syrach, or rather A'arab Zaraq, is the Archduke of the Venusion order of Shades and husks (klepoths) with Ashtaroth being perhaps the most noteworthy in the ranks. A'arab Zaraq is commonly translated as *Ravens of Dispersion* and is born from a volcano pregnant with fire. It we superimpose this imagery upon Exu Calunga, we see a volcano erupting in the depths of the ancestral waters releasing memory and elementals, spirits and forms, that brings heat to our blood and emotions, which constantly threaten with the powers of fear and dispersion. A'arab Zaraq is found stirring the darker strains in the sephirah and makes beauty and passion run out of control. As such it is a particular fire, the fire from the heart, whose mystical power is seen burning in the Lord crucified. The heart of Christ in flames and thorns is a most proper sign for the particular quality of Exu Calunga. He is the basin of blood overflowing in red rivers of power and memory.

Sacred Items: Sea sand, shells from the ocean, poisonous sea fish and thorny plants.

Iconography: He is a red skinned spirit with small features. His gaze is sharp and his horns small but thick. He seems to be poised in a way that threatens imminent attack.

Pontos Cantados of Exu Calunga

Eu tô te chamando ô Calunga,
Pra você vir trabalhar,
Quando eu te vejo, ô Calunga,
Vejo também a sereia do mar.
Eu tô te chamando ô Calunga,
Pra você vir trabalhar,
Quando eu te vejo ô Calunga,
Vejo também a sereia do mar.
Eu tô te chamando ô Calunga,
Pra você vir trabalhar,
Chega também a sereia
   do mar.

I am calling you oh Calunga,
So you are coming to work,
When I see you, oh Calunga,
I also see the mermaid from the sea.
I am calling you oh Calunga,
So you are coming to work,
When I see you, oh Calunga,
I also see the mermaid from the sea.
I am calling you oh Calunga,
So you are coming to work,
And who also arrives is the mermaid
   from the sea.

Rodeia, rodeia,
Rodeia, meu Santo Antônio rodeia (bis)
Meu Santo Antônio pequenino,
Amansador de burro brabo,
Que mexe com Seu Calunga,
Tá mexendo com o diabo,
rodeia, rodeia Exu rodeia.

Spin, spin,
Spin, my Saint Anthony spin (×2)
My little Saint Anthony.
Tamer of the stubborn donkey,
Who messes with Mr. Calunga,
Is messing with the devil,
Spin, spin Exu, spin.

Exu é cainana,
Quem te mandou, cainana,
Foi exu cainana,
É meu protetor, cainana,
Ele é quem me livra, cainana,
De todo horror, cainana.
Exu cainana. (bis)

Exu is cainana, (a viper)
Who sent you, cainana,
It was Exu cainana,
Is my protector, cainana,
He is the one that sets me free, cainana,
From all horror, cainana,
Exu cainana. (×2)

Pontos Riscados of Exu Calunga

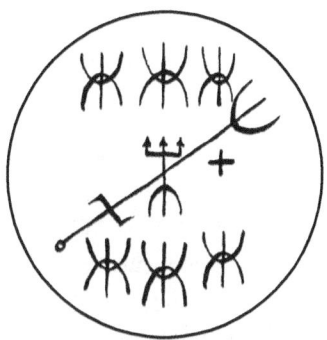

This is the ponto that calls down the power of this Exu.

Kabalistic ponto for general use.

The Kingdom of the Woods (Matas)

Rulership of this kingdom is given to Exu Rei das Matas and Pomba Gira Rainha das Matas. They govern all the Greenwood except for what grows in the Cemetery, which carries a different quality and vibration all together. This kingdom guards places of power in nature, the flowers, waters, trees and stones. Caboclos and Indians abound in this realm and the kingdom has an affinity with trance states where connections are made with the many spirits of nature. Consequently we have Exu Pantera Negra being active in this kingdom. The king of this realm is worked through his many Exus, in particular Exu das Matas. The king himself is a more lofty yet omnipresent spirit who shapeshifts amongst the trees and plants. This kingdom holds the secrets of cures, healing and sorcerous transmutation.

The People of the Trees • Exu Quebra Galho
The People of the Parks • Exu Sete Sombras
The People of the Woods at the Beach • Exu das Matas
The People of the Meadows • Exu das Campinas
The People of the Highlands • Exu Serra Negra
The People of the Mines • Exu das Sete Pedras
The People of the Snakes • Exu Sete Cobras
The People of the Flowers • Exu do Cheiro
The People of the Plough • Exu Arranca Tôco

Exu Quebra Galho (Frimost)
Exu Branchbreaker

BRANCHBREAKER is a slang term referring to giving or receiving small favors. In the broken branches of the lonely trees and in the silence of the dark fields at night we will find this Exu and here he assumes his power. He is said to lead women astray into perversity and he is good to use for breaking up relationships in the most catastrophic manner. He can inspire women to leave their home for no good reason, except to seek out carnal pleasures. He is a great patron of illicit and clandestine sexual relationships. He is an Exu of the forest and wild, uncultivated regions. He can also be asked to intervene in unhealthy relationships, but one needs to exercise great care, since he is particularly fond of twisting the minds of women. He often works with Exu Pagão and can be worked very well with Exu Morcego and Maria Mulambo. Beneath this savage activity when this Exu is well worked and seated, an infinitely wise and clerical Exu with a long history within the Church is revealed, and it is said that he even had stigmata as a consequence of being a follower of the holy St Francis of Assisi. It is probably his ecstatic inclinations that have given him his erratic reputation, and it is possible to mediate these two forms through what is offered to him.

Sacred Items: Perfumes, gunpowder, tree branches full of shoots, cherry, grapes, oils, candles, whiskey, white wine.

Iconography: He is depicted in the form of a proud and strong Tatá Ganga dressed in a priest's vestment holding a trident and a cross.

Ponto Cantado of Exu Quebra Galho

Ouvi um ruído na mata,	*I heard a noise in the Woods,*
Não sei o que será,	*I didn't know what it was,*
Pra mim é o Quebra Galho,	*To me it was Quebra Galho,*
Que veio trabaiá,	*That came to work,*
Quem matou, quem matou.	*Who killed, who killed.*

Ponto Riscado of Exu Quebra Galho

A Working to break up an unhealthy relationship

Go to the forest, and light one red and two black candles. Make two dolls of dry weeds. Inside the dolls place seven strips of paper with the names of the couple you wish to separate. Tie the dolls with a black cord and place them on a plate. On one doll put perfume mixed with pepper, and on the other cachaça mixed with Diavolo powder. Draw the ponto of Exu Quebra Galho on a piece of black cloth and wrap the two dolls in the cloth. Sprinkle Domination powder on the package and call upon Exu to cause the one to dominate the other, the other to dominate the first, and to bring an end to their relationship. Open the pack, and cut the black cord with which the dolls are tied with a knife; force and intent are important. Pour cachaça around the place, leave a cigar and burn the dolls. Leave the place while the dolls are burning, thanking the powers of the forest for their assistance. When you return home, take a bath in coconut-water, basil and sea salt and forget about the working.

Exu Sete Sombras (Morail)
Exu Seven Shadows

*S*EVEN SHADOWS possesses the power to make a person invisible. He is very much connected to the earth. Worms and ants are sacred to him. He can be used in workings where certain matters need to be veiled in secrecy. He is one of the more obscure Exus and his energy is difficult to direct. Legend tells us that this Exu was chained in a cave in Hell by his master Exu Lucifer and in workings with him Exu Lucifer (as Exu Rei) must be brought in as a controlling force. His offerings should be placed close to anthills when the star of Vesper is rising. The ants are his messengers and anthills can be worked in various ways at night to bring forth this Exu. He is reputed to bring nightmares and constant paranoia in his victims and can be used in workings where one seeks to reveal dark secrets. In such cases he is worked in shady places in a park close to the victim's house.

Sacred Items: Worms, ants, tridents, twilight, desolate parks.

Iconography: A red and black skinned figure carrying a trident, having both hands chained to the ground whilst he himself is obscured by the shadows, in this way many phenomena will appear in front of him.

Ponto Cantado of Exu Sete Sombras

Eu vi um formigueiro,	I saw an anthill,
Fui ver se estava lá,	I went to see if it was there,
Encontrei Exu das 7 Sombras,	I found Exu das 7 Sombras,
E pedi pra me ajudar.	I asked him to help me out.

Ponto Riscado of Exu Sete Sombras

Exu das Matas (Hicpacth)
Exu of the Woods

Where the weeds grow high we find this Exu of the fields, these are as suitable a place to find him as in the woods. He is said to be very good at bringing back lost loved-ones. He ignites a form of obsession in the person one desires to have back. This Exu is a hunter and knows the secrets of the woods; he is a concentration of all the powers of the wild regions and the woods, and is as such a good healer and medicine-man. This Exu is one of the untamed, wild Exus, a common feature of all beings related to the woods. One needs to be of a courageous nature to work with these spirits as they will relentlessly test your bravery. In the past the candidate presented for initiation would have to confront this terrible force alone in the woods, solely guided by a single candle where Exu das Matas, or rather his king, would come down upon the seeker and inflame him or her with the healing powers of the woods. This mystery is still present in Quimbanda, either in this form or by the dreaming encounter with the greenwood through jurema and ayahuasca.

Sacred Items: Bugs, cachaça, tobacco, any apparatus for pulverising leaves, sticks of wood.

Iconography: A mature black man dressed in worn red and green pants and a simple white shirt, a medicine bag hanging over his shoulders, and a laurel staff and a trident in his hands.

Pontos Cantados of Exu Das Matas

Exu das Matas é,	*Exu das Matas is,*
Exu das Matas é,	*Exu das Matas is,*
Exu das Matas é meu senhor,	*Exu das Matas is my lord,*
Exu das Matas é,	*Exu das Matas is,*
Eu vi um clarão nas matas,	*I saw a flash in the woods,*
E pensava que era dia,	*I thought it was day,*
Era o Exu das Matas que fazia sua magia.	*It was Exu das Matas who was doing his magic.*
Estava perdido na mata,	*I was lost in the woods,*
Na mata fui encontrado,	*In the woods I was found,*
O caminho foi aberto,	*The way was opened,*
Pelo Exu das Matas.	*By Exu das Matas.*

Ponto Riscado of Exu Das Matas

A Working for the return of a lover or companion

This work has to be done in the forest, close to a riverbank. On Monday, in the twilight, recall the loved one you wish to see again. Mark with white pemba the ponto of this Exu on a red cloth. Put the cloth on the ground, light seven candles anointed with Exu oil around it, greet the powers of the wood and place on the ponto a picture or an item belonging to the person you want to return. On a virgin plate, mix manioc flour and dende into a pudding. Present the plate on top of the picture and pour Come To Me powder, Lodestone powder and place seven coins on the flour. Sing to Exu and pray to Exu and finally place seven flowers of millefoil on the plate, pouring a bottle of sweet red wine over the offering while repeating your desire. Leave the place by taking three steps backwards, then turn around and do not look back. When the person you desire has returned, go back to the same place and repeat the same procedure but in thanksgiving.

Exu das Campinas
Exu of the Meadows

A THOUGHTFUL SPIRIT that oversees the realm of calmative plants at night and is said to empower the dew with his powers as it forms on certain plants. In particular rue, valerian and chamomile are sacred to him, rue being so sacred that some call him Exu Arruda (Exu of the Rue). This Exu walks amongst Caboclos and alchemists. He is an Exu of the springtime. He is a patron of curandeiros and folk healers and is an Exu used for facilitating plant communication. He is a great healer of erratic passions and even more so of cures of the body. Some say he was once a great hunter, but he gave this up and now only eats plants and smaller animals, like quails and rodents, hence these animals are particularly sacred to him. His workings should be done in the plains, preferably close to ant hills as his loyal assistant is Exu Formiga (Exu of the Ants), who some say is identical to Exu Tranca Tudo, and Exu Sete Sombras.

Sacred Items: Eggs, meadow flowers, tobacco, rue.
Iconography: A black man with a white beard and hair, dressed in worn-out clothes of linen carrying a medicine bag, a trident and a knife.

Ponto Cantado of Exu das Campinas

Campinero é reré.	*Dweller in the fields is reré.*
Campinero á, (bis)	*Dweller in the fields*, (×2)
Saravá Exù das Campinas,	*Saravá Exù das Campinas,*
Laroyé emojubà.	*Laroyé emojubà.*

Ponto Riscado of Exu das Campinas

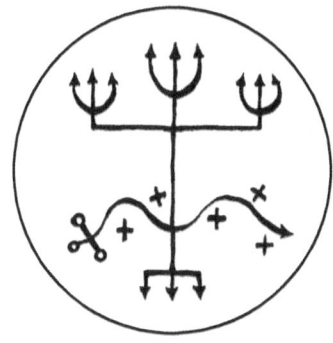

Exu Serra Negra
Exu of the Black Highlands

EXU SERRA NEGRA comes as a powerful Caboclo Quimbanderio who is an avenue of catimbó in Quimbanda. He is the power of earthquakes. He is considered a destroyer of cities and is greatly concerned with the dignity of the forest in the highlands and because of this some say he walks with Curupira, the guardian of the forest. Curupira is said to be a dwarfish black being with hairs of flame and backward pointing feet, a merciless and cruel spirit that enjoys feeding on human flesh. Consequently this is a serious Exu that often brings dread to the terreiros and temples, as his energy is so massive and overwhelming. Often tremors announce his arrival. He loves raw tobacco and oak-flavored cachaça. He speaks little, and commonly restricts himself to short affirmations to questions. He can be a great source of stability in complicated situations and some say he brings peace to those overcome by urban stress. He is also close to the spirit known as Tabatinga, seen as the master of sinister Catimbó practitioners, often said to be the *king of the smoke at the left*.

Sacred Items: Rocks and stones in their raw form, tobacco, black feathers, majestic trees, nuts, tridents, burning logs.

Iconography: A young strong Caboclo, dressed in green and red holding a pipe and a trident.

Ponto Cantado of Exu Serra Negra

No alto da serra (bis)	On the top of the hill, (×2)
Era rei Tiriri ô ganga ...	It was king Tiriri ô ganga...
Saravá seu Serra Negra,	Saravá Mr. Serra Negra,
Sála muganga ê sála ...	Sála muganga ê sála...
O Exu Serra Negra chegou, chegou!	Exu Serra Negra arrived, arrived!

Ponto Riscado of Exu Serra Negra

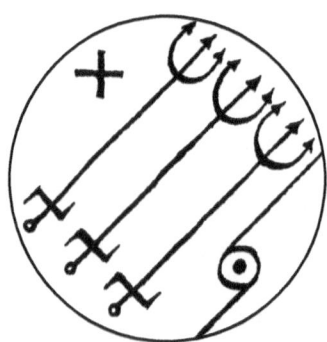

Exu das Sete Pedras (Humots)
Exu of the Seven Stones

His work is related to stones, precious and otherwise. He is a great alchemist and can teach this science. His knowledge of physics and chemistry makes him an expert in divination. He is said to work through any form of oracle, be it shells, bones or cards and has a vast astrological knowledge. This Exu is not particularly useful in works of attack, but rather defence, as his temperament is not aggressive but serene, albeit protective. We turn to this Exu to gain insight into problems and situations, and to ask him for advice, especially when situations or people have fallen apart for no good reason. He is also said to be good at detecting secret manuscripts and occult texts. Legend tells that he used to live in the state of Minas Gerais and that St Anthony of Padua can be used as his mask. He is said to work closely and well with Exu Meia Noite.

Sacred Items: Chemicals, stones, cowries, tarot cards.
Iconography: A well-dressed Exu surrounded by all kinds of stones.

Pontos Cantados of Exu das Sete Pedras

Seu Sete Pedras,	Mr. Sete Pedras,
livra os caminhos que passo,	free the paths for me,
Seu Sete Pedras,	Mr. Sete Pedras,
livra os caminhos que passo,	free the paths for me,
Quando ando com Sete Pedras, (bis)	When I walk with Sete Pedras, (×2)
Meus caminhos não têm embaraço.	My ways have no obstacles.
Peguei na ponta do lápis,	I got hold of the tip of the pencil,
Comecei a rabiscar,	I started to scribble,
Sete Pedras estava junto,	Seven Rocks came to me,
E veio me ensinar.	And came to teach me.

Ponto Riscado of Exu das Sete Pedras

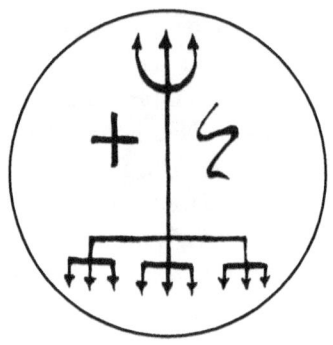

Exu Sete Cobras
Exu of the Seven Vipers

VIPERS ARE THE FORM that Sete Cobras comes as, in particular the Coral snake, the Surucucu, Cascavel (rattlesnake) and Jararaca. The Viper Exu's temperament correlates with the specific type of viper he comes as, and we should tread carefully in his presence. It is common to ask for his aid when we are already working with another Exu in this kingdom, as Exu Sete Cobras can be unpredictable. He loves lemon trees and bamboo groves and his workings are better done here than in any other place. He is usually applied in offensive works and to cause an environment or relationship to become poisoned and sicken.

Sacred Items: Rats, small birds, feathers, eggs, snakeskin, vertebrae, tridents, cognac, cachaça.

Iconography: He is depicted as an erect snake in black and red with traces of green, composed and ready to strike.

A Working of poisoning

To make a situation sick and poisonous you will make a powder consisting of feces of dog and cat that are mixed with the powders of bat, dried nettles and iron filings. To this is added the head of a viper and the powder is placed upon his ponto written in black on a green cloth. A life force offering such as a chicken or any kind of rodent is given and the sacrifice being done, the carcass is filled with eggs and one bottle of cachaça is poured over it. You then take the powder and leave the sacrifice on the ponto flanked by three green and four black candles and seven cigars. This powder can be sprinkled in the room of the one whom you seeks to offend, or at their door or gate. But beware, even though a tireless worker this Exu can also easily turn upon his own.

Ponto Cantado of Exu Sete Cobras

Eu vi um cobra no mato,
Que falou com mim,
Exu Cobra se chamou,
Laro laro laroyé.

I saw a snake in the woods,
That spoke with me,
Exu Cobra called himself,
Laro laro laroyé.

Ponto Riscado of Exu Sete Cobras

Exu do Cheiro (Aglasis)
Exu of the Scent

DIRECTLY UNDER the command of Exu Caveira, he is in a category of his own. He is to be found where flowers are in abundance. His offerings are incense and essences of flowers. One should avoid presenting him cachaça, and if it is done, it must be an aromatic variety; he prefers sweet fruity wines. In many ways, he resembles a Bacchus from Hell thriving upon beauty and sweetness in all forms. His rituals are done solely by using flowers and plants, and bestow the gift of communion with plants and flowers. He appears as a nude white man, and from the scent that comes with him one knows whether he has good or bad intentions. This fragrant character needs to be replicated in the terreiro as well. If this Exu is being called to make despacho, one needs to fill the room with sweet scents, if the opposite is the case, one fills the room with the smell of foul flowers. Daisies, sunflower and cloves are especially sacred to him. Perfumes made under his supervision will have an extraordinarily magnetic effect that will be in accord with the desire given to the perfume or oil.

Sacred Items: Clove, cinnamon, flowers, perfumes, sulphur, wine.

Iconography: A light skinned man with reddish hue, often nude, holding a trident and an orchid.

Ponto Cantado of Exu do Cheiro

Ele vem das flores,
Co coroco co,
Ele é Seu Cheiroso,
E seu cheiro tem axé.

He comes from flowers,
Co coroco co,
He is the Scented One,
His smell has power.

Canta o galo no terreiro,
O meu chefe é maioral,
Flor do mato não tem cheiro,
Quando Exu vem trabalhar,

The rooster sings in the terreiro,
My boss is the Maioral,
Flower from the woods have no smell,
When Exu comes to work,

Eu me chamo Exu do Cheiro,	*I am called Exu do Cheiro,*
Giro o toco num girá,	*I spin the trunk in a gira,*
O meu chefe do terreiro,	*My boss of the terreiro*
é Exu Rei Mairoal	*is Exu Rei Maioral.*

Ponto Riscado of Exu do Cheiro

Exu Arranca Toco (Minoson)
Exu Trunk Puller

INTIMATELY LINKED to the Caboclo of the same name this Exu's power is in open fields and secluded pastures. He has the power of domination and is deeply connected to the spirits of the earth. It is said that he can bring great wealth, inspire the discovery of great treasures and grant good fortune in gambling. The wealth he bestows can also be of a non-material quality and he is a difficult spirit to understand. He works both in the kingdom of the woods and the souls, and is a close ally of Omolu. He is reputed to work both good and evil with great ease and is well versed in the use of herbs. He knows the secret of magical intoxication and holds a particular affinity with the Jurema and Manaca (*Brunfelisa uniflora*). He is said to be close to Lucifer, but without a desire to reign, which might explain why this Exu is so mysterious, or rather not as tangible as many other Exus. He removes obstacles swiftly and almost unnoticeably, no matter how severe they might be. He manifests in the form of a Caboclo, often with lamenting cries and is said to guard unmarked graves in the woods. His favourite offerings are fennel and wormwood which can be steeped in cognac and given together with cigars and candles.

Sacred Items: Feathers, dry wood, roots, tridents, raw tobacco.

Iconography: An Exu that looks like a Caboclo, with a red and green cape, holding a trident.

Ponto Cantado of Exu Arranca Toco

Oi lá nas matas tem,	Ah, there in the woods,
eu vou mandar buscar,	I will ask to bring something,
Oi lá nas matas tem,	Ah, there in the woods,
Eu vou mandar buscar,	I will ask to bring something,
Arranca Toco que chegou pra trabalhar.	Arranca Toco arrived to work.
Sou eu sou eu sou eu nao falo que não,	I am, I am, I am, I don't say I am not,
Sou exu arranca toco,	I am Exu Arranca Toco,
Moro nas mata virgem,	I live in the virgin woods,
Sou eu sou eu sou eu nao falo não,	I am, I am, I am, I don't say I am not,
Exu arranca toco,	Exu Arranca Toco,
Que chegou aqui neste gonga,	That arrived here in this shrine,
Vou dar minha gargalhada,	I will give my laugh,
Mas não pensem que eu sou louco,	But don't you think I am crazy,
Eu sou forte na encruza,	I am strong at the crossroad,
Me chamam ArrancaToco,	They call me Arranca Toco,
Barauê,barauá,	Barauê, barauá,
Arranca Toco vai chegar	Arranca Toco will arrive.

Ponto Riscado of Exu Arranca Toco

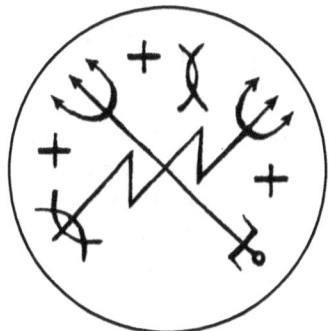

The Kingdom of the Cemetery (Calunga)

RULERSHIP OF THE CEMETERY is given to Exu Rei das Sete Calungas and Pomba Gira Rainha das Sete Calungas (or the King and Queen of the Cemetery). The King of the Calunga is close to Omolu and some say they are identical. The King of the Calunga rules this kingdom with his Queen. They are serene, solemn and majestic spirits that serve as stabilising forces for all forms of spiritual presence in the boneyard. It is common to refer to this kingdom as the *Calunga pequeña*, or *the little Calunga* whilst the ocean is considered the greater Calunga in memory of the African wisdom that sunk to the Cruzeiro at the bottom of the ocean during the Atlantic crossing. In this kingdom we find the mystery of death broken up into various fields of activity, each with a unique power that guards the secrets of the Calunga as revealed in its alternate name of Campo Santo, or Holy Field. But this Holy Field is similar to Campostella, or field of stars. The Calunga is the kingdom where stars die and are brought back to shine. Here we find spirits of comfort and prayer, but also fiery and turbulent spirits who roam the Cemetery, as do several winged Exus lurking in high places.

The People of the Cemetery Gate · Exu Porteira
The People of the Graves · Exu Sete Tumbas
The People of the Catacombs · Exu Sete Catacumbas
The People of the Cremation Oven · Exu Brasa
The People of the Death's Head · Exu Caveira
The People of the Cemetery Greenwood · Exu do Cemetério
The People of the Grave Mound · Exu Corcunda
The People of the Pits · Exu Sete Covas
The People of Mirongas and Shadows · Exu Capa Preta (Exu Mironga)

Exu Porteira
Exu of the Door/Gate

He stands at the gate of the Campo Santo and before we enter the realm of Death we must pay him a tribute, as we would do with any spirit in the position of Charon. Three coins and some tobacco is a proper gift to give him for allowing us to use the cemetery. Naturally a greater offering can be made, the coins and tobacco are the bare minimum.

It is this Exu who guards the door of the temple and terreiro when a gira is performed. He is the spirit who welcomes and denies visible and invisible visitors. He is the confidant of Omolu and Exu Caveira. He is frequently said to be an Exu loved by Ogum who in Umbanda tends to hold his position as doorkeeper. This Exu is revered because of his cunning and strength, and he has a stellar connection, both with the constellation of Orion and with the Crow that rides on the back of Hydra. We can appeal to this Exu when we want to dispel unwanted situations, influences and people. He is reputed to work fast and to have a particular affinity with St. Expedite. Some use this saint as a mask for him, which might explain the association with the constellation Corvus, the Crow. Since he is the Exu that guards the passage of spirits he is one of the Quimbanda Exus that perhaps comes closest to the Yoruba Èsú. As with Exu das Sete Gargalhadas, this Exu is constantly present in the giras, but his influence is so broad that it is often overlooked. There is however treasure upon treasure to be gained from cultivating a relationship with this Exu.

Sacred Items: Crosses, coins, door hinges and keys.

Iconography: He is depicted as a bald man with a goatee, dressed in a red suit, having gold coins for eyes and holding a whip and a trident.

Ponto Cantado of Exu Porteira

Portão de ferro,	Iron Gates.
Cadeado de madeira,	Locks of Wood,
Na porta do Cemitério,	At the Cemetery door,
Onde mora Exu Porteira.	Where Exu Porteira lives.

Ponto Riscado of Exu Porteira

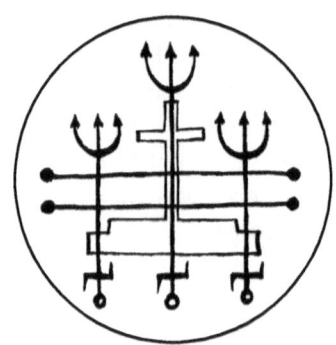

Exu Sete Tumbas
Exu of Seven Tombs

One of the quieter exus, he is given to all kinds of malefic and shady works. When we send legions of dead souls to attack someone this Exu is quite happy to execute our wish and is a willing aid in works like Dead Man's Box. He appears like a black Freemason, his clothes torn and dirty, often with a greyish powder covering him, this being the ashes from the crematorium. He works with woods and waters and it is with these he performs his mysterious acts. These are not common waters, but the waters from rotting corpses, the waters used to wash corpses and the muddy liquid that seeps out of decaying graves. Likewise his works are with rotting woods and this category includes bones, especially porous ones, as well as coffin parts and roots in the process of rotting under the action of corpse fluids. Some say that this Exu has the ability to resurrect the dead for a little while by using a white shroud washed in herbs like levante and anis with his ponto drawn upon it. This cloth is then spread out on the tomb and the soul is called to take shape within the shroud. It is also possible to make a doll filled with items from the tomb, worked with and placed under the shroud and fed absinthe, tobacco and gunpowder to aid in the resurrection. He is an uncanny fusion of Preto Velho, Freemason and Necromancer.

Sacred Items: Black and white candles, crosses, coffins, gunpowder, waters and bones.

Iconography: An old black Freemason in ragged and torn clothes carrying a coffin and a trident.

Ponto Cantado of Exu Sete Tumbas

Na setima tumba do Cemitério,	*At the seventh tomb of the cemetery,*
Seu Sete Tumbas gemeu,	*Mr. Sete Tumbas groans,*
Saravou sua encruza,	*Salutes his crossroad,*
E levou o mal que é meu.	*And takes the evil that is mine.*

Ponto Riscado of Exu Sete Tumbas

Exu Sete Catacumbas
Exu of Seven Catacombs/Mausoleums

Usually draped in a thick black cape, this Exu is young, strong and warrior-like. He has a great love for fine cigars, knives, swords and peppers of all kinds. He is skull-faced, either partially or completely, and is found at mausoleums, where urns are buried and in family graves. He is often depicted as standing on a mound of skulls and bones in memory of his patronage of mass graves. This Exu is very protective of his mediums and is interested in the medium's well being. He is calm and wise, but can be easily agitated to indulge in strife and war. He is resorted to in magical combat and in court cases.

If one seeks to call the attention of this Exu to a person or a group of people you can go to the Calunga, pay the doorman and enter. Upon entering you count to seven from the first mausoleum in a straight line. This will be your curse track. At the first mausoleum or catacomb (also cemented and tile-decorated graves can be used with good result) leave a black candle on which you have written the name of your enemy. Along with this leave a dish of vinegar and cognac where you place the name or picture of your enemy. Walk to the next tomb and offer another black candle and a dish of cognac and a cigar, continue this sequence until the seventh mausoleum. On the seventh you present his ponto written with red pemba on black cloth and in the middle place a glass of cognac crossed with three lit cigars and light four black candles, one in each quarter. Call him and tell him that you have shown him the path to your enemy, who will now be his enemy. Tap the mausoleum three times with your left palm on the side where the candles point the track towards the target. When Exu arrives for your enemy, offer him vinegar with his favorite drink and he will create disturbance and strife. This work being done to your satisfaction, this Exu needs to be given a black rooster, seven cigars and three bottles of cognac.

Sacred Items: Gunpowder, black silk, tridents, cigar, cognac, obsidian.
Iconography: A tall handsome and strong Exu covered in a black cape holding a trident and a sword.

Ponto Cantado of Exu Sete Catacumbas

No corredor do inferno,	*In the corridor of hell,*
Eu vi Sete Catacumbas,	*I saw Sete Catacumbas,*
Girava num pé só,	*He was spinning on one foot,*
Pulando pelas macumbas.	*Jumping over the macumbas.*

Pontos Riscados of Exu Sete Catacumbas

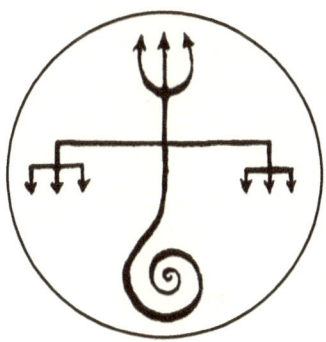

Ponto for bringing him into manifestation.

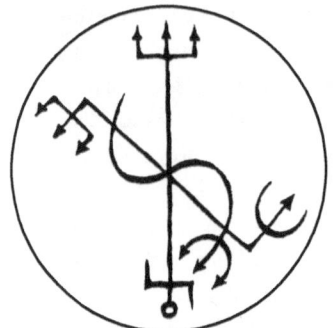

Ponto for use in workings.

Exu Brasa (Haristum)
Exu Burning Coal

Exu Brasa is an eternal fire, a fire that is impossible to extinguish. This is his element and he can be seen as a close relative of the djinn of the Arabian deserts. When he comes down in possession his medium can handle fire and burning coals without being burned. He provokes fires, both physical ones and the fire within men causing passion or rage. When you want to call him, a fire should be lit with coal and wood. He brings the smell of sulphur and cigars with him.

He is said to work in mysterious ways and the solution he gives to a request might be surprising. He resides in the fires of the crematorium; he can bring total destruction and annihilation to persons and situations and is considered merciless. He bears some relation with Exu das Duas Cabeças, given his ambivalent nature. He is one of the Exus that has more familiarity with the Western infernal hierarchies and does tend to come with a distinctively demonic aura around him. This Exu also has a relationship with one of the more profound mysteries of Quimbanda by being tied to the Dragon Exu. He is a deformed Exu, often showing himself as a dwarf-like being. When this form appears he is called Brasinha and is manifesting his Mirim form.

Sacred Items: Peppers mixed with cachaça should be prepared to awaken this spirit. Fire, burning coals, gunpowder, snakes, salamanders and hawks.

Iconography: He is usually depicted with a large head and small horns, fangs and a diabolic grin, standing with one foot in a fire. But he can also appear as a slim man draped in red silk standing in a cauldron of fire and coals.

Ponto Cantado of Exu Brasa

Ai, ai, ai,	*Ai, ai, ai,*
Valei-me Sete Diabos (bis)	Help me Seven Devils, (×2)
Valei-me Sete Diabos (bis)	Help me Seven Devils, (×2)
Exu Brasa é um Diabo.	Exu Brasa is a Devil.

Ponto Riscado of Exu Brasa

Exu Caveira (Sergulath)
Exu Skull

Exu skull is Omolu's right arm and Exu Midnight his left. Exu Caveira is the general of seven legions of Exus, each with their own warlord. Exu Caveira knows the art of war and is a master in planning attacks that bring the enemy to their knees. He defeats all adversaries. It is this Exu who presides over the vigil the Quimbandeiro does in the Calunga and is accordingly a vehicle for an important power that needs to be transmitted to the Tatá to gain the license to work with these spirits. He manifests in the sense of fear and watchfulness of the cemetery after midnight. He is always symbolised by skulls, candles and tridents. Whenever work is done in the cemetery, you need to pay him due respect. This is often done by lighting a black candle on the third grave on the left side of the cemetery. Knock three times on the grave and place the candle, then ask him license to use his kingdom. He supervises the ascent of spirits and souls at the cemetery and thus serves a crucial function in the kingdom of Exu. He is also known to be a very good spirit to approach in problem solving of any kind and is far more concerned with matters of elevation and health than his fearful form suggests.

It is important to mention here João Caveira (John Skull), said to be deeply related to the spirits of the line of Souls and the pretos velhos. Whilst Exu Caveira works in the colours of red black and yellow, this Exu works in black and yellow and is the spirit responsible for executing the workings of Exu Caveira. Legend has it that he was a German or French feudal lord, who despite being of a righteous disposition acted against the voices in his heart and began to abuse his people, turning them into slaves and confiscating their property. Upon his death, he refused to pass over and decided to stay with the lord of the cemetery to help him in his work to repent for his evil deeds on earth. He looks much like Exu Caveira though younger in appearance and holding a skull rather than a trident.

Sacred Items: He loves raw beef or pork drenched in vinegar, which together with seven black candles and absinthe can be presented to him in the cemetery to obtain his favour. He loves skulls, bones and black cloth.

Iconography: He is usually depicted as a tall man, with one goat foot and one human foot, a tail and a cape, holding a trident with a skull resting at his feet.

Pontos Cantados of Exu Caveira

No portão do cemitério
　tem uma corujinha,
Quando o defunto passa ela dá
　uma risadinha,
São sete, sete, sete,
　são sete caveirinha,
Eu vou chamar Caveira pra dançar
　na Nossa Linha.

At the cemetery gate
　there is a little owl,
When the dead one passes it gives
　a little laugh,
There are seven, seven, seven,
　there are seven little skulls,
I will call Caveira to dance
　in our line.

Se matar um boi leve na porteira,
Coma a carne toda e deixe
　os osso pro Caveira,
É poeira, é poeira,
Olha mosca varejeira,
　salve Exu Caveira,
Roeu osso a carne
　não tem mais,
Vai lá no cemitério ver o que
　o Caveira faz.

If you kill a bull bring it to the gate,
Eat all the meat and leave the bones to
　Caveira,
It's dust, it's dust,
Look the blowfly,
　salute Exu Caveira,
He nibbled the bone,
　there is no more flesh,
Go there to the cementery to see what
　Caveira does.

Pontos Riscados of Exu Caveira

Ponto for protection and defence.

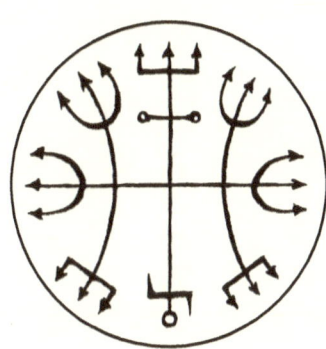

Ponto for the removal of blockages and obstacles.

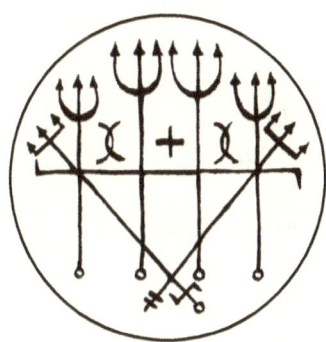

Ponto for protection & calling this Exu.

Ponto for domination works.

Kabalistic ponto.

Ponto Cantado of Exu João Caveira

Moço, vou lhe apresentar,	Boy, I will present you,
Um espírito de luz, pra te ajudar,	To a spirit of light to help you,
Ele é Exu João Caveira,	He is Exu João Caveira,
Ele é filho de Omolu,	He is Omolu's son,
Quem quiser falar com ele,	Who wants to speak with him,
Laroiê Exu.	Laroiê Exu.

Ponto Riscado of João Caveira

Exu do Cemitério (Coquinho do Inferno)(Frucissiere)
Exu of the Cemetery

Exu do Cemitério rules all new epidemics that appear on the face of the planet. The Black Death, Ebola and AIDS are all illnesses signifying the presence of this Exu. He is also the one who possesses the knowledge of curing what cannot be cured. The spirits who have died in agony by such causes are guided by him after their death. The processions of suffering souls that at times are seen in the cemetery are also guided by him. Legend tells that he had several incarnations as a doctor and a surgeon and some say that Dr Mengele was under the influence of this Exu.

The workings with this Exu should be done in the cemetery. He always appears in a cape with red and black stripes. He is a close companion of Exu Tiriri and Exus such as Sete Catacumbas and the entire host of Omolu. He can also be worked with Exu Morcego and Exus related to the Woods and wild places. His workings are particularly dangerous and located within the realm of aggressive magic.

Sacred Iems: Needles, spiders, snakes, trident, poisonous mushrooms.

Iconography: Full beard, red skinned, fanged, carrying a femur and a skull.

The Working of the Spider

This working requires that you obtain a large tarantula and kill it slowly with a knife dedicated to this Exu. The spider is then opened and a piece of snakeskin with the name of the target written upon it placed inside together with a poison of some kind, though preferably mushrooms. Seven needles are then inserted in the spider. This should be done at the darkest corner of the cemetery at midnight, where only the light of a single black candle will guide the working. The work is done on a black cloth on which his ponto has been drawn. This being done the Exu is called to witness your act and you state in a fiery lament your desire. A black rooster is given upon the working's completion together with a bottle of whiskey poured over the working. These forms of workings will affect the victim with mysterious diseases and kiumbas revel in such workings.

Ponto Cantado of Exu do Cemitério

Coquinho do Inferno	*Little coconut from hell,*
Arrebenta Mirombo,	*Breaks Mirombo, (sorcery)*
São da Linha de Congo,	*They are from the line of Congo,*
São Calunga de Quilombo.	*They are Calunga of the Quilombo.*

Ponto Riscado of Exu do Cemitério

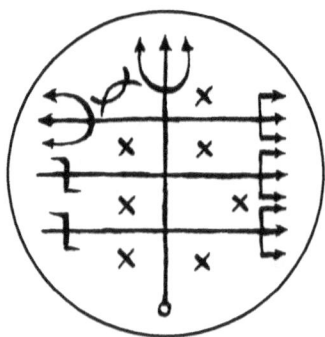

Exu Corcunda
Hunchback Exu

Like Quasimodo of Notre Dame, this Exu is a hunchback. It is said that this Exu can be used in works of depression and to overcome low self-esteem given his interest in helping people who suffer from a lack of acceptance in society because of their deformities. He is said to be a good-humored Exu that one should not cross lest he bring calamity upon the offender, and at times he provokes accidents that cause disfigurement. This Exu is mostly active in the time between the death of an individual and when the earth covers them. It is said that he eases the confusion of the departed one and makes the newly dead at ease with their changed condition. He can be a great aid for anyone suffering social stigma and brings clarity to minds confused by the veil of death.

Sacred Items: White wine, cigars, red cloth and veils.

Iconography: He is a dwarflike hunchback, deformed and dressed in red, carrying a cross and a trident.

Ponto Cantado of Exu Corcunda

Vem, vem Seu Corcunda,	*Come, come Mr. Corcunda,*
Vem trabalhar,	*Come to work,*
Vem, vem, vem Seu Corcunda,	*Come, come Mr. Corcunda,*
Seus filhos ajudar,	*Come to help your children out,*
Exu Corcunda mora na Calunga,	*Exu Corcunda lives in the Calunga,*
Vem de ai seu gargalhar. (bis)	*It is from there his laugh comes.* (×2)

Ponto Riscado of Exu Corcunda

Exu Sete Covas
Exu of the Seven Graves

Exu sete covas is dressed all in black and is very loyal to Omolu. Omolu considers him a kind of guardian of the earth itself. Legend tells that this Exu was created by Omolu himself breathing death upon a gathering of earths from the cemetery that were buried in an empty grave covered with a black cloth for three nights during an eclipse. He is a serious Exu who loves cigars, whiskey and cachaça, but he also has a playful side as he can at times change the graves around and create confusion and turbulence in the cemetery itself. He is a protector of women and can be used by women who have been wronged to inflict harm upon their oppressors.

He dwells at vacant graves, and the moments when a corpse is removed to make place for another marks his sacred time where he sustains the vibrations of the earth and mound, and is an agent of renewal in the cemetery. It is said that this Exu can be called upon to bring people to an early grave, since he is the master of the empty grave, but his preference is for works of healing and bringing love to women in distress. The empty grave can be worked by marking his ponto with bonedust and digging a hole in the centre of it. In this hole the name of the target is given on seven different pieces of cloth tied together. The cloth is fed cachaça and generous amounts of vinegar and raw tobacco whilst the Exu is called. Seven black candles are placed around the hole and three tridents or knives are used to stab the bundle of cloth in the hole. Four of the black candles are then broken and given to the hole. The hole is then covered with earth and three pigeons are offered.

Sacred Items: Mounds of earth, tridents, cigars, whiskey, cachaça.

Iconography: A tall serious Exu, red skinned and dressed all in black with a white veil around his waist, holding a shovel and a trident.

Pontos Cantados of Exu Sete Covas

Ele é Exu pagão,	He is a pagan Exu,
Não tem quem obedecer, (bis)	He has no one to obey, (×2)
Pra ele só interessa,	He is only interested,
Qualquer demandas vencer,	To win any magical combat,
Se o Exu é bom, ele vence demanda,	If the Exu is good, he wins spells,
Seu Sete Covas é rei na Quimbanda.	Mr. Sete Covas is king in Quimbanda.
Eu não tenho patrão,	I have no boss,
Calunga foi quem me criou,	Calunga created me,
Meu nome é Sete Covas,	My name is Sete Covas,
Minha quimbanda eu já louvou.	My kimbanda I already praised.

Ponto Riscado of Exu Sete Covas

Exu Capa Preta (Musisin)
Exu of the Black Cape

He comes with a feeling of great fear. This Exu is analytical by nature and always seeks out the characteristics and constitution of those who call him with great diligence. No secrets remain hidden from his interrogating gaze. He is said to be an adept of Vodou, is of African origin and has a vampiric disposition. When he comes down he tends to bite those he speaks with before he gives counsel in a whispering, murmuring way. He prefers to be seated and he appears to be constantly chilled to the bone.

Exu Capa Preta is often said to be the chief of the terreiro due to his affinity with and precision in the arts of black magic and sorcery. He is reputed to work both good and evil, but his preferences lie more on the evil side. He delights in sowing discord, creating confusion and engaging people in vendetta and assault. His primary colour is black. He prefers his meat raw and it should be pork. He likes cachaça and whiskey, wine and honey. He smokes cigars and cigarettes and his offerings are made in the cemetery. He is to be found both in the graveyard, as well as in the temples of Quimbanda. When he comes down and takes possession he inspires confidence and safety in an eerie way. Big red and black candles, guns and daggers are amongst his favourite symbols. He walks in the company of Tranca Ruas, Meia Noite, Sete Catacumbas, the Caveiras, Calungas and Sete Cruzes. He has a 'shade' living in the cemetery known as Exu Capa Preta da Encruzilhada, who is an elegant, eloquent and well dressed Exu, aristocratic in his manners, who enjoys fine cognac and liquor as well as cachaça together with red roses. He is said to walk with Pomba Gira das Sete Capas who is the same as Pomba Gira Sete Saias, a gypsy Pomba Gira whom he protects fiercely, as he also does with Pomba Gira Menina. It is said that he was the Exu that inspired people like Goethe and Novalis, some legends tell of him having several incarnations in Germany either as a priest or as a successful trader. In both cases he met his end because of his interest in the occult. It is under the eyes of Capa Preta as a witness that any successful pact is made, be it with other Exus or *kiumbas*.

Sacred Items: Trident, alcohol, sweet liquor, cigar, cigarillos.
Iconography: A spirit with fangs, covered with a black cape, seated on the ground.

Pontos Cantados of Exu Capa Preta

Se sua Capa é Preta,
A minha é encarnada,
Me empresta sua Capa,
para eu passar na encruzilhada.

If your Cape is Black,
Mine is red,
Lend me your Cape,
So I can pass at the crossroad.

Quando passar em uma encruzilhada,
Peça ago e firma a cabeça,
Pois ali é o reino de seu
   Capa Preta.

When you pass a crossroad,
Ask permission and make your head strong,
'Cause there you find the kingdom
   of Capa Preta.

Com faca de dois gumes,
Não convém brincar,
É o Exu da Capa Preta,
Vamos respeitar.

With a double-edged knife,
It is not appropriate to play,
It's Exu da Capa Preta,
Let's respect him.

Pontos Riscados of Exu Capa Preta

This ponto invigorates this Exu.

Ponto to be used when he is seated or called down.

Ponto used for workings.

A Working to tie up hostile tongues

The time for this ritual is Saturday night, with the moon waning and preferably at the Great Hour. You will need the following items:

Eight black candles
A tongue
Needles and spikes
White, black and red thread
Seven (or three) different types of pepper
The name of the offender written on seven pieces of virgin paper

(the names should be written twice on each paper crossing each other, as a crossroad)
A piece of raw pork
Cachaça or whiskey
Cigars
A piece of red cloth
Black Pemba
Gunpowder
Two plates
A knife
Mironga Capa Preta*

*This powder can be made by the Tatá and consist of silver filings, copper filings, folha de fogo, nettles, and ashes from mahogany, oak and mango wood. It should all be burned together on his ponto drawn with red pemba on black cloth. Let the powder rest with Capa Preta for seven days making sure that candles are burned all the time and his absinthe and red wine changed every day.

Go to the cemetery and there, at a crossroads, place the cloth and draw the ponto on it with the pemba. Ask Exu Caveira, Tatá Caveira, Sete Caveiras and João Caveira for permission to make this macumba in their kingdom and pour some cachaça to each of the four corners of the crossroad. Light one black candle on the tomb to your left in respect of Exu Caveira. Then light the other seven candles around the cloth and call upon Exu Capa Preta. In the centre of the cloth set one plate, and on this plate present the tongue saying: *Exu Capa Preta, it is me (NN) who has come to the realm of night with my distress. My enemy (NN) is using his tongue to take me down. So I have come here to ask you to take him down and tie up his tongue so he will not speak ill of me again.*

Put the raw pork on another plate and pour some cachaça on it, placing it on the upper side of the tongue and state that this is your gift to him, and that you hope he will delight in this gift so much that he will give you the one gift in return you have asked for. Light a cigar and place it on the plate together with the pork. Cut a hole in the tongue with the knife and fill it with peppers (these peppers should have been mashed to a paste beforehand) with focused aggression. Visualise your enemy as his or her tongue is set on fire as you insert the pieces of paper with his or her name one by one, stating your wish seven times, once for each piece of paper you are putting inside the tongue. Take the threads and wrap them tightly around the tongue. Pour the powders over the tongue and say: *I dominate you, I rebel against you. Your tongue is in my claws and you will never again speak ill of me. You will only know confusion and turmoil, may your wicked tongue lead you to your tomb.*

Then take the nails and use the hammer to drive them through the tongue with great force and anger. Drive the knife previously used through the tongue as well, and place it on the central plate. Continue to sing for Exu Capa Preta, smoke a cigar and drink with him, let ecstasy and anger drive you through this stage and saturate the spell with these emotions, and leave them with the offerings. Finally, you will pour gunpowder over them and ignite the powder. With the ignition, exit the cemetery quickly without looking back and avoiding the smoke touching you.

The Kingdom of the Souls (Almas)

Ruled by exu rei das almas and Pomba Gira Rainha das Almas who are also known as the King and Queen of the Mound (Lomba) because they tend to gravitate to elevated places in the cemetery. The King of Souls is however Omolu with his Queen of the Calunga who works in the kingdom of Souls. We also find these Exus in hospitals, morgues and at wakes. This kingdom is about the grief and sorrow of the transition into death, but also finding clarity in these matters. This kingdom is responsible for the elevation and transition of spirits and communication between the worlds. This kingdom can be worked in order to understand what seems alien for us as much as for aiding us in making sense of any kind of confusion. It is a generous kingdom, mostly serene, but of course with the occasional erratic potencies that are needed in order to generate movement in the kingdom.

The People of the Souls of the Mound · Exu Sete Lombas
The People of the Souls in Captivity · Exu Pemba
The People of the Souls of the Wake · Exu Marabá
The People of the Souls in Hospitals · Exu Curadôr
The People of the Souls at the Beach · Exu Gira Mundo
The People of the Souls at Churches · Exu Nove Luzes
The People of the Souls in the Thicket · Exu das Sete Montanhas
The People of the Souls in the Calunga · Exu Tatá Caveira
The People of the Souls of the Orient · Exu Sete Poeiras

Exu Sete Lombas
Exu of the Seven Burial Mounds

*S*ETE LOMBAS IS SAID TO BE the same as Exu Asa Negra (Exu Black Wings) because they share the same dwelling place. They both thrive at the highest points in the cemetery but whilst Asa Negra is of a more wicked disposition, Sete Lombas is more occupied with healing anxiety and curing insanity, states which Asa Negra is more prone to ignite in people. They are both connected with the vulture and in charge of the purification of corpses and rotten flesh. Sete Lombas is a quiet Exu, as is Asa Negra, but their auras are markedly different. Sete Lombas arrives in serenity whilst the aura of Asa Negra is more agitated. Sete Lombas and Asa Negra are both well-versed in exorcism and are excellent aids for dispelling kiumbas and clinging ghosts.

Sete Lombas is a winged Exu, but like Asa Negra they are vulture wings and not bat wings he possesses. Like the vulture, this Exu cleans up spiritual residues both at the cemetery and also in the confused souls of those mourning their loved ones.

Sacred Items: Vulture feathers, whiskey, cigar, feathers, terracotta jars, snakes and bones.

Iconography: A bird-like Exu, sometimes with wings (in Asa Negra's case, always with wings) dressed in black, dark blue and with traces of bone and red.

Ponto Cantado of Exu Sete Lombas

No cruzeiro, na lomba,	At the cemetery cross, at the mound,
Eu vi um homem gargalhar,	I saw a man laughing,
É o Exu Sete Lombas,	It is Exu Sete Lombas,
Que eu chamo para trabalhar. (bis)	That I call to work. (×2)

Ponto Riscado of Exu Sete Lombas

Ponto Cantado of Exu Asa Negra

Exu Asa Negra que por deus foi desprezado,	Exu Black Wing who by god was despised,
Foi na encruzilhada que ele fez o seu reinado.	It was in the crossroad he made his kingdom.
Agora eu quero ver na força quem pode mais,	Now I want to see by strength who can do the most,
Se é a força divina ou a de Satanás.	If it is the powers divine or those of Satanas.

Ponto Riscado of Exu Asa Negra

Exu Pemba (Brulefer)

As the name suggests, he often uses the sacred chalk, *pemba*, to work his magic. This indicates that his field of activity is related to automatic writing and drawing as well as all things related to signatures and encrypting, sigils and signs, colour and the script itself. He uses all kinds of powders to draw sigils and signs to accomplish his ends. He delights in clandestine love affairs and is a harbinger of venereal disease. He is said to be very capable of releasing imprisoned spirits and people. Like John Skull, this Exu is often used to inspire misery and tragedy. His rites are easy yet dangerous, and he always accomplishes his mission. He is a loyal Exu, who can be quite demanding when he returns to take his payment for works done. Like Tatá Caveira, he has obsessive tendencies and likes to go out on missions. When making pemba it is always a good idea to add the ashes of his ponto to the mixture. The ashes of his ponto can also be used to make a special ink. This ink is made by steeping the ashes in a virgin cup placed on a red cloth marked with his ponto and offering upon it one pigeon and two quails. To the blood and ashes must be added snake, either in the form of ashes, or its oil. This product can then be added to any ink or used as it is in any suitable combination for the purpose of writing. The ink is used for writing down wishes, always on black or white cotton cloth that is stored in a jar, either of brass or terracotta. The jar must be washed beforehand in cachaça and passed through fire. The wishes will remain in the pot for seven days, ensuring that candles are burned and the wishes repeated every day. On the seventh day the wishes are burned and the ashes placed in the jar. When the wish is fulfilled a dove is given to the vessel and communion with Exu is performed together with whiskey or red wine, and tobacco.

Sacred Items: Pemba, dove's blood, ink, pens and pencils, papyrus.

Iconography: A red-hued and black-robed Exu holding a trident and pencil.

Pontos Cantados of Exu Pemba

Exu Pemba é homem forte,	*Exu Pemba is a strong man,*
Promete pra no faltar,	*He promises to not lack anything,*
Quando corre pela encruza,	*When He runs through the crossroad,*
Nossa demanda vem buscar,	*He comes to take our request,*
Ele é Exu da promissão,	*He is Exu of the promise,*
Ele sempre cumpre sua missão. (bis)	*He always fulfills his mission.* (×2)
Pia cobra no cercado,	*Snakes threaten at the fence,*
Quando Exu vem trabalha,	*When Exu comes to work,*
Salve Exu da Pemba Preta,	*Salve Exu da Pemba Preta,*
Que tá aqui pra demandá.	*Who is here to work.*

Ponto Riscado of Exu Pemba

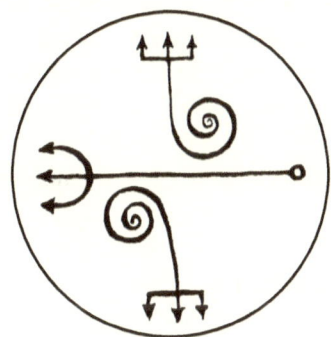

Exu Marabá (Huictigaras)

Serene seeming, but in spite of this tranquil appearance he is a warlord and expert in the techniques of war. He provokes insomnia and insecurity in one's enemies. Like Capa Preta he sees deeply into people and realises their secrets, but he rarely speaks them. He shows many faces depending on the cycles of the earth and the moon. He kills those standing in his way and is considered to be useful only for those who can control their feelings and stand firm in his presence. He is reputed to be merciless and vengeful and can come in dreams and bring nightmares and destruction, insomnia and death. He is also to be found at wakes for the dead and works closely with Exu Kaminaloá, both being capable of helping and abusing any soul. This Exu is strongly connected to the moon and some refer to him as a *half moon Exu*, indicating his volatility and changeability. His power of igniting insecurity comes from this lunar connection. Works with him should observe the traditional qualities of the moon where the waxing moon is good for increase, waning moon for decrease, full moon for fortune and the black moon for destruction and renewal.

Sacred Items: Iron, graveyard dust, castor seeds and oil, any kind of quartz, especially those made yellow by sulphur, the colours red, black and yellow.

Iconography: An Exu in a Roman military uniform, carrying a sword and a trident.

Ponto Cantado of Exu Marabá

Ele provoca o sono,	*He provokes sleep,*
Ele pode matar,	*He can kill,*
Ele é Exu Marabá,	*He is Exu Marabá,*
Que veio trabalhar.	*That came to work.*

Ponto Riscado of Exu Marabá

Exu Curadôr (Heramæl)
Exu Healer

Exu Curadôr is in a class of his own and takes orders directly from Midnight Exu. He is a true medicine man and a great healer often appearing as a Preto Velho, smoking his pipe dressed in simple clothes of white and red. He knows the properties of all plants and works both with herbal cures, and the use of poisons, even on a homeopathic level. Especially sacred to him is urtiga (nettle) which he uses to heal and harm. It is important that one is pure of intent and pure of soul when working with this spirit. Exu Curadôr is well versed in arts of the green kingdom from all over the world. He knows how to prepare herbs that heal and herbs that kill, making him an expert in the kingdom of Osanyin. In fact, nearly all of his legends tell that he was an Osanyista, a devotee of the Yoruba Irunmole of plants, the doctor of Ifá. In the same manner this Exu is also a spirit doctor, and a root doctor, who knows every affliction of the human body and their cures. Curadôr is not only the awareness of plants, he is a plant which heals with one hand and kills with the other.

He can be given cigars and cachaça mixed with honey as offerings. The pipe filled with nettle and datura can be used for mounting his mediums, the pipe is in general the greatest vehicle for summoning him. He looks like a Preto Velho, but his eyes shift from red to green, and because of this some say he was an African shaman and witch. He always carries a bag to collect his herbs and smoking blends and at times he is seen with his companion Pomba Gira Curadôr, a mistress of seduction and sensual gastronomy. This Exu is a calm, yet hot spirit. His name, Curadôr, harks back to the tradition of curandeiros in Brazil. Originally these were wise men and women of African ancestry who knew how to use herbs for ill and good. They could also control animals and were said to possess such insight in nature that they were able to dominate birds and reptiles. Over time these mysteries were fused with European knowledge, but whether the origins were Christian or African, the herb work remained the vehicle of healing. This Exu drinks cachaça mixed with honey and/or spices and herbs. His spells are simple and powerful and often consist of cigars, candles and herbal waters. His gifts are the knowledge of the greenwood and its ability to cure and kill.

Sacred Items: Pipe, spices, herbs, honey, bees, cachaça, coffee, tobacco.

Iconography: A red skinned Exu dressed in a green cape with white and red borders holding a trident and a pipe. Sometimes he appears like a Preto Velho.

Pontos Cantados of Exu Curadôr

Em terreiro de Umbanda,
Exu vem saravá,
Se Preto Velho é doto,
Eu é Exu Curadôr.

In the terreiro of Umbanda,
Exu comes to salute,
If Old Black is a doctor,
I am Exu that heals and cures.

Boa noite, meu senhor,
Exu no reino chegou,
Vamos louvar nossa Quimbanda,
Viva Exu que é Curadôr!

Good night my lord,
Exu at the kingdom has arrived,
Let's praise our Quimbanda,
Hail Exu that is the Healer!

Pontos Riscados of Exu Curadôr

Kabalistic ponto. This is Meia Noite's ponto, which can be used in workings with this Exu.

A Working to cure illness
(this working can also be done with Exu João Caveira)

At the foot of a Cross, place seven crosses in the shape of a cross. On the other side of the cross, make another cross on the ground with seven white roses. Trace the ponto of Exu Meia Noite on the front side and of Heramael on the reverse. Then recite the following prayer seven times with absolute faith and determination: *Exu Curadôr, I ask for your great powers to assist me in the healing and curing of (NN). This is my prayer and I ask that you bestow me this power.*

Then burn the ponto to ashes and apply to the afflicted one, whilst singing the ponto of Exu Curadôr.

The same outline can be used if one desires to open a passageway for a disincarnate spirit to come down in order to enter into communion with you. The ponto of Exu Curadôr is not used, only that of Midnight Exu. The ponto should be traced with white flour and three red roses placed inside the ponto whilst one calls the name of the spirit that communion is sought with.

Exu Gira Mundo (Segal)
Exu Worldturner

GIRA MUNDO IS NOT CONFINED to one given site of power but to the whole world. He is a creative Exu that often inspires those who turn to him in unusual and stimulating ways. For this Exu a road, track or situation is never truly blocked, he always finds a way, often with unexpected events and situations arising, along with the solution.

He tends to induce obsession in the target when used in works of attack or protection and this can at times cause unpredictable outcomes. There is a risk that the bond of obsession actually falls upon the enemy of your enemy – namely, yourself.

He can create a sudden and unexpected turn of events and change bad into good and good into bad. It is difficult to direct this Exu to a given goal; his nature seems to be much more to shake up situations and open opportunities, especially for those of an adventurous spirit. He is assigned the task of collecting wayward souls from all over the world and is said to have had several incarnations as an Nganga or Kongolese medicine man. He is closely related to Exu Calunga as his throne is at the shores of the mighty waters, and is excellent in workings of necromancy, as well as in works of elevation and purification. Some say this Exu was the one that guided the mission of St John the Baptist, a mission that changed the Western world as Christianity spread across the globe.

Sacred Items: Whiskey, cigars, cachaça, quarts, charcoal, swords.

Iconography: A stout spirit in blue and red carrying a trident and holding the world in his hand.

Pontos Cantados of Exu Gira Mundo

É giré, o girá,	*É giré, o girá,*
Gira Mundo vai chegar,	Gira Mundo will arrive,
É giré, o girá,	*É giré, o girá,*
Lá pra o fundo do mar,	To the depths of the ocean,
É giré, o girá,	*É giré, o girá,*

Eu quero vê corré,	*I want to see it running,*
Eu quero vê balançá,	*I want to see it shaking,*
Chegô Exu Gira Mundo,	*Exu Gira Mundo has arrived,*
Que vem trabalha.	*The one that came to work.*
Gira Mundo trabalha,	*Gira Mundo works,*
Das Almas, com sua falange,	*From Souls, with his legion,*
Vai trabalhar,	*He will work,*
* trabalho da Calunga,*	* works of the Calunga,*
As Almas estremeceu,	*The Souls He has shaken up,*
Gira Mundo rei do mundo,	*Gira Mundo, king of the world,*
Pra salvar filhos de fé,	*To save his children of faith,*
Gira mundo, rei do mundo,	*Gira Mundo, king of the world,*
Pra salvar filhos de fé,	*To save his children of faith,*
Gira Mundo rei do mundo,	*Gira Mundo, king of the world,*
Pra salvar filhos de fé.	*To save his children of faith.*
Giró, giró, giro,	*Spin, spin, spin,*
Exu Gira Mundo,	*Exu Gira Mundo,*
Giró, giró, Pomba Gira,	*Spin, spin, Pomba Gira,*
Vence demandas,	*Wins magical combats,*
O reino da linda,	*The kingdom of the beauty,*
* saravá Quimbanda.*	* saravá Quimbanda.*

Pontos Riscados of Exu Gira Mundo

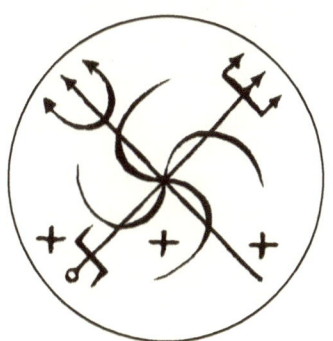

Ponto for general workings.

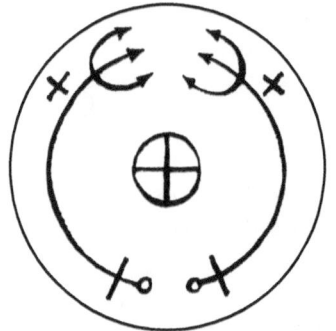

This ponto is used to cause turbulence, or to stop it.

Exu Nove Luzes
Exu of the Nine Lights

Exu Nove Luzes is the power of prayer and vigil, in particular, the novena and Masses said for the dead. He is an ecclesiastical Exu. This Exu presides over the magical lamps in Quimbanda and their oils. It is said that this Exu frequents purgatory, where he prays for his legions. He is ascribed tremendous power as a necromancer and some say that he was taught by the prophet Elijah in the ways of prophecy, death and resurrection. He is a demanding Exu and pays little or no attention to people who are unable to perform a dedicated practice over time, especially reciting novenas. The novena for St Cyprian, St Anthony, St Expedite, St Bento, St John the Baptist or the prophet Elijah himself marks the beginning of a working relationship with this Exu.

When he is worked, his ponto must be drawn with black pemba on white cloth and nine white candles must be placed in a circular fashion around the ponto. Here we can offer bread, water containing pennyroyal, calendula and wormwood, together with absinthe or red wine. In the midst of this a glass of good quality olive oil can be placed and the same herbs as used in the water are then steeped in the oil. This oil can then be used to feed oil lamps dedicated to this Exu. This simple lamp serves to shine upon you when the various novenas are said, and can also be used in works of death, both to say Masses for the dead on behalf of someone living, and to feed prayers of elevation with light.

Sacred Items: Church regalia, bread, wine, whiskey, absinthe, tridents, oils, candles, fire, embers, veils.

Iconography: He dresses like a country priest, always in black with a cross in one hand and candles in the other.

Ponto Cantado of Exu Nove Luzes

Na treva da vida,	*In the darkness of life,*
Eu chamo vocè,	*I call you,*
Saravá Seu Nove Luzes,	*Saravá Mr. Nove Luzes,*
Meu Exu da fé.	*My Exu of faith.*

Exu das Sete Montanhas (Elelogap)
Exu of the Seven Mountains

FOUND IN HIGH PLACES and residing by springs, caves and any cavity in a tree or stone is this remote and reclusive Exu, who is close to the Caboclos. He is associated with wind and putrefaction and loves the darkness of the woods, especially where pines grow abundantly. He knows the secrets of the mountains and what lies hidden within them. His clothing is black and muddy. He is reputed to elevate one's being, a beneficial side-effect when this Exu is used in despachos. He is a clever warrior, more like a sniper than anything else. He is a mellow loner that prefers the company of beautiful women over men, and is a great defender of them. His areas of expertise are court cases and problems with justice. When he is engaged in such works on honourable premises he strikes with a sudden and heavy hand.

Sacred Items: Daggers, pebbles, caverns, tridents, cachaça, tobacco, water mixed with sulphur and earth.

Iconography: An amphibian Exu dressed in black Indian clothing, partly covered with mud, holding three arrows and a trident.

Ponto Cantado of Exu das Sete Montanhas

No alto das sete serras,	*On the top of seven hills,*
Eu botei minha campana,	*I placed my bell,*
Saravá minha Quimbanda,	*Saravá my Quimbanda,*
Chegou Exu Sete Montanhas.	*Exu Sete Montanhas has arrived.*

Ponto Riscado of Exu das Sete Montanhas

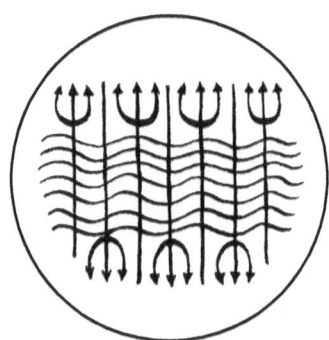

Exu Tatá Caveira (Proculo)
Exu Tatá Skull

Said to be of a Roman Egyptian origin, from around 600 BCE, this Exu was originally named Proclus. It is said he was a good person, a clever and strategic warrior, popular in his district. He was, however, in love with a girl whose father was reluctant to give his daughter to a soldier and demanded that he should acquire wealth and prestige before being given her hand. He started to work his way up and after many years, he owned half the district and was a politician of renown. However, he had a brother, a sinister and sly creature who happened to be a good friend of the girl's father, and the night before Proclus was going to ask for the girl's hand his brother bought the girl. Proclus was greatly saddened, whilst the girl accepted her fate. Shortly afterwards, enemy nations attacked the little city at the Nile River, raped the women, and killed the children. They burned Proclus and many of his loyal comrades. Some say that the 49 men who were burned in this attack formed the basis of the 49 legions of Quimbanda. However, the pain of fire was nothing compared to the pain of betrayal by his brother and so he transcended to the ranks of an Exu. He is said to be an extremely loyal Exu, almost to the point of obsession, and is equally reputed to be ruthlessly unforgiving if crossed. He is depicted in a black cape and skullfaced. He is referred to as a Tatá, meaning that he is an expert in the art of Quimbanda and the mysteries of the soul and cemetery. He is said to be an ambivalent spirit with a quite sadistic side to him, inspiring people to commit crimes and murder. He is also reputed to control drugs and narcotic substances, usually using them towards malefic ends. He provokes dreams of death and can inspire the ruin of man by haunting him in dreams and stoking his desire for drugs. He is a merciless spirit and bonds with him are very difficult to undo. In works of treason and betrayal he is a very eager and efficient spirit to ally with. He likes whiskey, absinthe, dry wine and fine tobacco. He is also said to *grab the horse from the earth* meaning that the medium will experience a vortex of energy rising from the earth and taking hold, which often forces them to lie prostrate on the ground. Possessions with this Exu are rare, as they also are with Omolu.

Sacred Items: Anis, tobacco, graveyard dirt, skulls, tridents, exclusive wines and drinks.

Iconography: An Exu robed in a black cape with red lining, skull faced and pale.

Pontos Cantados of Exu Tatá Caveira

Portão de ferro,	Iron Gate,
Cadeado de madeira,	Wooden locker,
Na porta do cemitério,	At the cemetery's door,
Eu vou chamar Tatá Caveira.	I will call Tatá Caveira..
Calunga, Calunga,	Calunga, Calunga,
Calunga do mar,	Calunga of the sea,
Meu povo é da Calunga,	My people are of Calunga,
Se for vem trabalhar,	If it is so, come to work,
Cemitério pegou fogo,	The cemetery is on fire,
Defunto deu na carreira,	Dead ones running away,
Eu tô chamando, tô chamando,	I am calling, I am calling,
Seu Exu Tatá Caveira.	Mr. Exu Tatá Caveira
Um pombo preto voou da mata,	A black pigeon flew from the woods,
Voou e pousou lá na pedreira,	It flew and landed there at the quarry,
Onde os Exus se reúnem,	Where Exus are gathered,
Mas o reino é de Tatá Caveira.	But the kingdom is of Tatá Caveira.
Eu fico no portão,	I stay at the gate,
Do meu cemitério,	Of my cemetery,
Presto conta e tomo conta,	I take care and report,
Na porteira do inferno.	At the gates of hell.
Quando eu chego ao cemitério,	When I arrive at the cemetery,
Peço licença para entrar,	I ask permission to enter,
Bato com meu pé esquerdo,	I stamp with my left foot,
Pra depois eu saravá,	Then later I salute,

Mais eu saravo Omolu;
Omolu!
Tatá Caveira também,
Assim faço a "obrigação,"
Para o povo do além.

Tatá Caveira gira,
Com o sol e com a lua,
Gira pelo mundo inteiro,
Omolu me coroou...
E Oxalá me iluminou.

Tatá Caveira chegou no Reino,
Ele chegou pra demandar,
Eu vim buscar quem não presta,
É pra Calunga que eu vai levar.

E lá vai seu Tatá Caveira,
Na porta do Cemitério,
Ele vai lá pra bem longe!
Para as catacumbas do Inferno.

But I salute Omolu,
Omolu!
And also Tatá Caveira,
It is like this I do my "obligation,"
To the people from the beyond.

Tatá Caveira spins,
With Sun and Moon,
Spins in the whole world.
Omolu has crowned me,
And Oxalá illuminated me.

Tatá Caveira arrived at the kingdom,
He came to work,
I came here to take what is not good,
It is to Calunga I will take it.

There goes Mr. Tatá Caveira,
At the cemetery's gate,
He goes there, far away!
To the catacombs of Hell.

Pontos Riscados of Tatá Caveira

Ponto for protection.

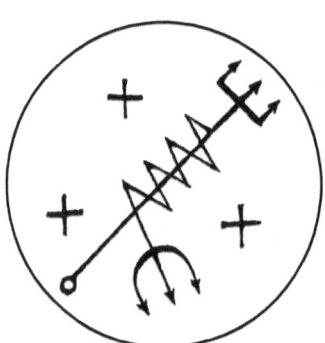

Ponto for attack and defence.

Ponto firmeza, to solidfy his presence.

Exu Sete Poeiras (Silcharde)
Exu of the Seven Dusts

SETE POEIRAS is winged, which means he is considered to be of a more volatile and dangerous nature than many others. He is also an Exu of the streets, but whereas Tranca Ruas moves openly, this Exu walks in the shadows and flies in the dark. He works with opening roads and finding ways. He can serve as a compass to find your way when you are lost, and can also be a guiding spirit of great significance. He is an Exu of transformation into beast-forms and atavisms, and knows the secrets of shapeshifting; as such he is related to the woods and to the Caboclos.

He can stir the bestial urges in people and can cause lycanthropic transformations to occur. When directed against enemies he will relentlessly torment the enemy by night and stir the bestial impulses to such an extent that the victim loses self-control and brings misfortune upon himself. It is possible to work with this Exu on the third night before and after the full moon in order to leave the body in the form of a beast, usually as a dog or wolf (a magical powder is prepared and soaked in oil or cream and applied to the body). It is important that the ponto is drawn upon the body and the bed sheet as well as under the bed in this work. A glass of ayahuasca or jurema together with a glass of absinthe and three red candles should be present whilst his pontos are used.

The mirongas of Quimbanda, the secret of magical powders, rests with this Exu. He rules the people of the Orient, which means he has a strong inclination towards Eastern medicine and alchemy, and can be applied when making alchemical salts and stones of a beastly orientation.

Sacred Items: Earth and dust, crossroads and stones from streets that carry a dark atmosphere.

Iconography: A red-hued spirit dressed in black with red wings, carrying a trident and a small pouch of powders.

Pontos Cantados of Exu Sete Poeiras

Sou pequeno de Angola,	*I am the little one from Angola,*
Porém já sei escrever,	*But I already know how to write,*
Sete Poeiras na Quimbanda,	*Sete Poeiras in Quimbanda,*
Também já sabe ler,	*Also I know how to read,*
Ele é Exu, é um curador,	*He is Exu, He is a healer,*
Ele é Exu, é um vencedor. (bis)	*He is Exu, He is a winner.* (×2)
Quando bateu meia-noite,	*When midnight arrived,*
Que o galo cocoricou ou!	*And the rooster sang,*
Na virada lá na serra,	*In the curve of the Hill,*
Sete Poeira chegou, ou!	*Sete Poeiras arrived!*

Ponto Riscado of Exu Sete Poeiras

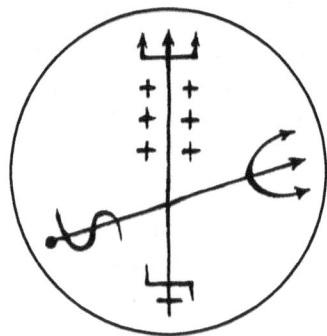

The Kingdom of the Harp (Lira)

Lira is ruled by Exu Rei das Sete Liras and Pomba Gira Rainha de Candomblé (Rainha das Marias), better known as Exu Lucifer and Pomba Gira Maria Padilha (though some say that Pomba Gira Rainha de Candomble and Pomba Gira Maria Padilha are the same). The Exus that work here are involved in art, music, and poetry. But it is also the Kingdom of the Marketplace at night and places of power in the cities, in particular their nightlife. Here we find bohemians, poets, hustlers, pimps, prostitutes and scoundrels. It is a pulsating and dangerous kingdom of gypsies, artists, ecstasy, revelry and creative intoxication. Exu Lucifer is king of this realm, because this kingdom is the world of men.

The People of Hell · Exu dos Infernos
The People of the Cabaret · Exu do Cabaré
The People of the Harp · Exu Sete Liras
The Roma People (Gypsies) · Exu Cigano
The People of the Orient · Exu Pagão
The People who Hustle · Exu Zé Pelintra
The People of the Dumpster · Exu Ganga
The People of the Moonlight · Exu Malé
The People of Trade and Commerce · Exu Chama Dinheiro

Exu dos Infernos
Exu of the many Hells

Exu dos infernos is controversial in particular because he has been given the seal of the mercurial president Avnas known as a night demon in *Lemegeton*. His image is said to be that of a fire that turns into a man, a proper icon of Hell personified. Like Avnas himself, this Exu is said to teach astrology, the liberal arts, to provide familiars, to open roads towards good fortune or lead people to hidden treasures. This Exu is said to be the King of Lost Souls and some say that he takes an especial interest in those lost souls that turn into revenants and ghosts, and teaches them. Some say he takes an interest in suicides, and is a spirit who can incubate suicidal thoughts in people. So this Exu, being the King of the people in the many Hells, tends to take on qualities similar to Hades and Pluto.

Sacred Items: Mercury, black silk, tridents, shrouds, champagne and bitter drinks like fernet branca and jägermeister.

Iconography: A boned Exu, pale faced with dark rings around his eyes wearing a black furry cape, a top hat and holding a trident in one hand and living fire in the other.

Ponto Cantado of Exu dos Infernos

Ara oro rá,	*Ara oro rá,*
Exu dos Infernos emojibá,	*Exu dos Infernos emojibá,*
Ara oro rá,	*Ara oro rá,*
Exu dos Infernos vem pra trabalhá.	*Exu dos Infernos came to work.*

Ponto Riscado of Exu dos Infernos

Exu do Cabaré
Exu of the Cabaret

Exu do cabaré is the companion of Pomba Gira Dama da Noite. It is said that this Exu is like a tricky nightclub owner who is always looking for the advantage in any situation. As such, this Exu is a spirit for opportunists. In his realm we find all forms of taverns and brothels and places of entertainment, be they striptease joints or burlesque shows, but always with a seedy feel. He likes cognac and cachaça and smokes cigars. Razors and daggers are never far from him. He can be called upon to create havoc and to protect clandestine and shady enterprises. He will then veil the business and guide his people to constantly get the upper hand in every negotiation and deal. Caution should be demonstrated, as this Exu tends to sadistically denigrate the opponent or partner, so he is a tricky spirit though he can be placated with cigars, silk ribbons and cognac. A simple trick to invite him to partake in a business meeting is to draw his ponto under two bottles of cognac. One of the bottles is brought to the meeting to be enjoyed between those involved, the other one is left upon a red silk cloth, tied in black silk ribbons flanked by three red, three black and one dark blue candle. A fine cigar is lit and placed on top of the open bottle. Upon completion of the meeting you draw his ponto in a fireplace and cover it with coals and set it on fire. His ponto is sung and the cognac slowly poured on the flames. A red rooster should then be given together with seven razors, all should be burned on the fire.

Sacred Items: cognac, chamapgne, razors, fur, wolves, fine clothing, burning embers.

Iconography: A handsome Exu with black eyes, dressed in a red suit with wolf fur draped around his neck, holding a champagne glass and a dagger.

Ponto Cantado of Exu do Cabaré

É alegria, alegria, compadre,	It's joy, joy, my sworn one,
Vem Exu com sua compadre,	Here comes Exu with his [female] sworn one,
Vem trabalhando na linha da fé,	Here He comes working in the line of faith,
Oi saravamos Exu do Cabaré.	Hi, we salute Exu do Cabaré.

Ponto Riscado of Exu do Cabaré

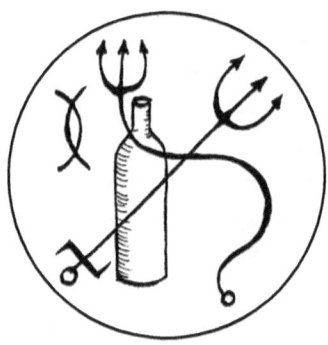

Exu Sete Liras
Exu of the Seven Harps

SETE LIRAS IS THE IMPULSE of Quimbanda we find in all forms of music. He is an Exu that oversees the artistic expressions of the mysteries of Quimbanda, whether in the traditional pontos and their developments, or modern compositions and performances that draw our thoughts to Exu and Pomba Gira. Clearly, this is an Exu of great influence, and is perhaps best seen as having the characteristics of a muse of inspiration. This Exu is a great facilitator of success, and worked with as a spirit guide he can open the roads towards prosperity. He loves cigarillos and has a preoccupation with material cost, in the sense of wanting what is most expensive in terms of fine wines and cloth. If I were to name a famous person to express this Exu, it would be Oscar Wilde. This Exu is clearly a bit on the dandyish side, but a tremendous source of inspiration. This Exu is the form Exu Lucifer takes when he walks amongst men.

Sacred Items: musical instruments, skulls, chalices, red wine, absinthe, tridents.

Iconography: A handsome Exu with reddish hue and blue eyes, wearing a black suit and holding in his left hand roses and lilies, and in the right a harp shaped like a trident.

Ponto Cantado of Exu Sete Liras

Canta meu povo,	*Sing my people,*
Olha quem vem,	*Look who's coming,*
Seu Sete Liras ,	*Mr. Sete Liras,*
Trabalha na fé,	*Works in the faith,*
Todo seu povo vem pra dançá,	*All his people come to work,*
Seu Sete Liras,	*Mr. Sete Liras,*
No bem e no mal.	*In good and evil.*

Ponto Riscado of Exu Sete Liras

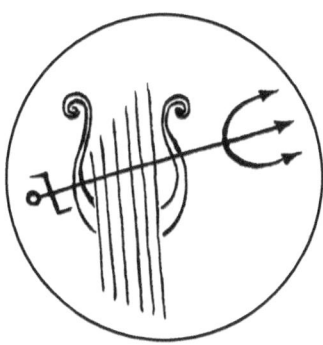

Exu Cigano
Gypsy Exu

Legends tell that Gypsy Exu was a captive by the name of Hassan Zingaro who was initiated into the Cult of Èsú, the Orisa. Upon gaining his freedom he became involved in macumba and created a fusion of native sorcery and gypsy magic. The magical knowledge of stars, ancestors and the power of nature coupled with the magical technology of Quimbanda ensured not only his freedom, but also an elevated position amongst his peers, which enabled him to return to his homeland. Upon his return to his people he was made King of the Gypsies, but he longed for beautiful Brazil and decided to bring his people to the land he missed so much, and so the gypsies came.

Exu Cigano walks with Exu Veludo and also has a relationship with the mixed line of Quimbanda. His influence in Brazilian spirituality is profound, which the vast amount of gypsy spirits in Brazil testifies to, though Pomba Gira Cigana is perhaps the most well known spirit of this pedigree. We also find these mysteries as unique cults worked independently of Quimbanda. The gypsy legacy of Quimbanda is strong and it is quite likely that the Queen of Quimbanda, Maria Padilha, was herself a gypsy.

Exu Cigano is a personification of the sorcerous mentality of the Roma people and he is prone to clairvoyance and any form of divination, but most of all works with cards. He is a tricky spirit that enjoys dance, song and hard liquor. When he is worked the atmosphere should be electric with joy.

Exu Cigano has a relationship with the saint of the Roma people known as St Sara Kali, a Black Virgin/Madonna commonly understood to be a black princess. She is also said to be the Three Marias, the stars in the belt of Orion. These stars, together with the constellation of the Southern Cross, are of tremendous importance for Brazil and are the luminaries that quicken the serpent powers in these lands.

Other legends tell us that Sara Kali was in truth Mary Magdalena. The bones of St Sara rest in the crypt of St Michael, she was canonized in 1712, with the 24th and 25th of May being her feast days. Even though she is not accepted by all Roma people, she is a maternal uniting force for the Roma people at large, and her relationship with Mary Magdalene, and by extension Pomba Gira Maria Padilha Cigana, adds to the mystery of Pomba Gira, the Queen.

Exu Cigano can be worked for good luck in business and travel and called upon as an aid in works of divination, in particular cards, be they playing cards, Lenormand or tarot.

Sacred Items: Decks of cards, fruits, wine, sweet liquor, daggers, silk, horses, veils, handkerchiefs.

Iconography: An Exu dressed in gypsy clothing.

Pontos Cantados of Exu Cigano

Cigano bate o pé, cigano bate o pé,	The gypsy stamps his foot, the gypsy stamps his foot,
Cigano entra na roda,	The gypsy enters the circle,
Pra salvar filhos de fé,	To save his sons of faith,
Quem vem de lá,	Who comes from there,
Quem vem de cá,	Who comes from here,
São ciganos que vem bailar,	They are the gypsies that come to dance,
Pisa firme Cigano,	Step firmly gypsy,
Quero ver o seu dançar,	I want to see your dance,
Pois na roda de Cigano,	Because in the circle of the gypsies,
Ninguém pode balançar.	Nobody can shake.
Por todos os caminhos,	By all the ways,
Que pisaram os meus pés,	Which my foot has set upon,
Por todas as estradas,	By all the roads,
Que pisaram os meus pés,	Which my foot has set upon,
Sou Cigano Rodrigo,	I am Cigano Rodrigo,
Guerreiro de todas armadas,	Warrior of all armies,
Com a força do sol e o brilho do luar,	With the strength of the Sun and the light of the Moon,
Cigano é guerreiro, Cigano vai lutar,	Cigano is warrior, Cigano will fight,

Povo Cigano faz sentir sua energia,	*Gypsy people make present its energy,*
Com sua magia e alegria de cantar,	*With it's magic and joy of singing,*
Com a força do sol	*With the strength of the sun*
e da lua,	*and the light of the moon,*
Eles sabem trabalhar,	*They know how to work,*
Povo Cigano sabe o segredo,	*Gypsy People know the secret,*
Pra ninguém nos derrubar.	*So no one will take us down.*
Cigano entra na roda,	*The gypsy enters the circle,*
Pra salvar filhos de fé,	*To save his sons of faith,*
Quem vem de lá,	*Who comes from there,*
Quem vem de cá,	*Who comes from here,*
São os ciganos que vem trabalhar,	*They are the gypsies that came to work,*
De longe eu vim,	*From far away I came,*
Caminhei sete pedreiras,	*I walked by seven quarries,*
Passei por cachoeiras,	*I passed by falls,*
Onde mora Aieiê,	*Where Aieié lives,*
Lá na campina onde	*There at the meadow where*
a lua está prateada,	*the moon is silver,*
Sou Cigano na alvorada,	*I am Gypsy at the dawn,*
Sou Cigano, eu sou mais eu,	*I am Gypsy, I am what I am,*
Cigano tem a força da lua,	*Gypsies hold the strength of the moon,*
De noite faz farra,	*At night they make parties,*
de dia ainda anda na rua,	*At day they walk the streets,*
Andar, andar, andar,	*To walk, walk, walk,*
Vendendo ilusões para algazu	*Selling illusions so someone*
comprar,	*buys it,*
Porque Cigano tem a força	*Because Gypsy holds the strength*
da lua,	*of the moon,*
Se você pediu, não devias prometer,	*If you asked, you should not promise,*
Se você prometeu, você tem que pagar,	*If you promised, you should pay,*
Se você não pagar, jamais vai andar.	*If you don't pay, you will never walk.*

Pontos Riscados of Exu Cigano

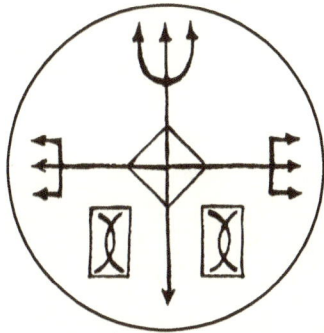
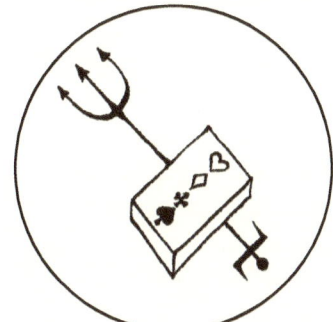

Exu Pagão (Bucon)
Exu Pagan

Pagan Exu is a spirit of doubt, separation and mistrust. To create hatred between friends and division between lovers is one of his fields of expertise. He is manifest in powerful emotions. This Exu obtains his energy from every situation where mistrust is encountered. He is found in desolate places, such as abandoned parks, houses and fields that have been left overgrown. Unlike other Exus, this Exu takes delight in offerings of milk mixed with whiskey, or any alcoholic beverage that contains milk. One should be careful in workings of this spirit. One needs to make a despacho before working with him, as his specific powers are all too easily drawn to the hearts of men and incite mistrust. This Exu is said to originate in a non-Christian country, according to some, he was an Arabian sorcerer, according to others African or Asian. This Exu possesses a vast range of knowledge that might seem alien when contrasted with the usual wealth of wisdom of the Exus. In spite of his mischievous nature, he can be a good ally and friend and usually comes with his Pomba Gira. He tends to work with great speed if he respects the Tatá or Yaya, but will bring confusion to those working him without due respect.

Sacred Items: Ruins, milk, whiskey, trident, tobacco, jewellery, dogs.
Iconography: A young, red-skinned Exu holding a trident, dressed in costly clothes and jewelry.

Ponto Cantado of Exu Pagão

Ele não foi batizado,	He was not baptized,
Não buscou a salvação, (bis)	He didn't seek salvation, (×2)
Mas é aquele quem vence demanda,	But he is the one that wins the magic combat,
Saravá Exu Pagão. (bis)	Saravá Exu Pagão. (×2)

Pontos Riscados of Exu Pagão

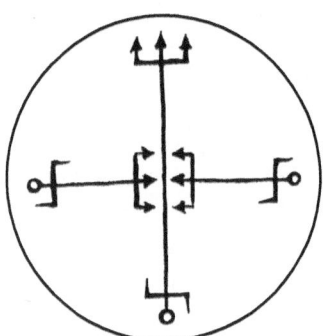

Ponto to inspire hatred and conflict between people.

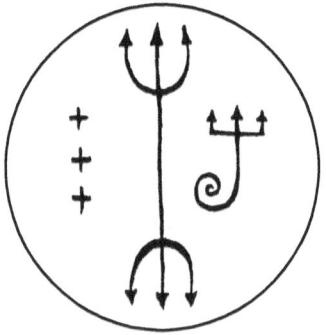

Ponto for unification and to end conflicts.

A Working to separate two or more people

This ritual will create great disturbance, rage and havoc amongst the people you want to attack. One can also use this working in order to separate good people from bad company.

The ritual is done on a Monday at midnight under a waning moon. Bring objects or photos of the people you want to separate, their names written on virgin paper, milk, Exu oil, black pemba, powdered charcoal, a lot of chili peppers and chili powders, Fight powder, War powder, three lemons, a lidded jar, seven black candles and seven red candles.
The first step of the ritual is best done in a basement where you take the jar and mark the ponto of Exu in its base with pemba. Place the volts over the ponto together with their names, cover this with the various powders and pour the juice of three lemons over it. Add the chili peppers and then the milk. Light the candles around the jar and sing the ponto of Exu Pagão. Burn either Exu oil or Exu incense and say: *Exu Pagão, I ask that you separate the persons NN and NN and ignite in their hearts hatred, wild and uncontrollable, to separate them forever.*

Close the jar and allow the candles to burn down. Every midnight for seven nights burn some incense or oil and say the same prayer while burning a black candle. The following Monday go to a crossroad and place the jar in the centre, asking the powers of the crossroad the license to work there. Recite the prayer seven times, lighting seven black candles around the jar. Take a stick and smash the vessel completely, scattering the remains all around. When the result has manifested, go back to the crossroads and give proper offerings to Exu Pagão.

It is important to note that whenever one is working this type of magic, one needs to take baths of herbs and salt every night after the prayers, so that the hostile energy will not remain attached to the ritualist.

Exu Zé Pelintra
Exu Joe Scoundrel

Zé pelintra is said to be both a *malandro* (scoundrel/hustler), a judge and a doctor. Many are the stories about his life and many are the myths. It is through this Exu that Quimbanda reveals its strongest connection with Catimbó. It is widely accepted that Zé Pelintra/José dos Anjos (Zé of the Angels) was born in the city of Bodocó in Pernambuco, a state steeped in the cult of Caboclos and encantados, and also Catimbó. The city of Bodocó later changed its name to Exu in honor of Exu Zé Pelintra.

It is said that already as a young man Zé was a street-smart boy with uncanny luck in gambling. Luck followed him and so did women as he pursued a tireless bohemian lifestyle in the city of Recife. He moved with his family further south, to Rio de Janeiro, where he almost immediately lost his parents to tuberculosis, leading him to a life in the slums. He didn't stay poor long and worked himself out of this situation, not only because of his luck, but because of his sharp mind and skill with knives.

Another legend tells how Zé, one drunken night, ended up in a fight with a handful of policemen after killing a fellow thief. They shot him, but no bullet would enter and thus he was reputed to have a 'closed body' because the devil himself protected him. After this incident Zé Pelintra gained notoriety and his rise to fame began, with this his bohemian lifestyle continued. It is said that towards the end of his life he had no less than 20 lovers, and one of them, the gypsy Zulmira, poisoned him in a fit of jealousy when he was in his early sixties.

Zé Pelintra was very fortunate in making contacts with powerful people, leading to his education in law and medicine. This has created quite a versatile spirit. He was a devotee of St Anthony and he never failed to partake of his procession on the 13th of June. Consequently, work with this Exu benefits from the simultaneous cultivation of St Anthony.

Exu Zé Pelintra is called upon to set things straight in houses that cultivate him, and he is noted to have quite a temper. He is used to release prisoners, to affect judicial matters, and most of all to be given a good gambling hand and to attract lovers. Some say he only attracts women to men, but this opinion is not universal. As for his gambling hand, he is reputed to give modest-to-good payouts. Zé Pelintra is concerned with fairness and the 'happy gift' that arrives in times of need.

Sacred Items: Dice, cards, canes, ties, perfume, grilled meat, hats, tridents, wine, whiskey, handcuffs.

Iconography: A handsome Exu dressed in a white suit and hat with a red shirt and white tie.

Pontos Cantados of Exu Zé Pelintra

Tranca Ruas e Zé Pelintra,
São dois grandes companheiros,
Tranca Ruas na Encruza,
E Zé Pelintra no Terreiro.

Tranca Ruas and Zé Pelintra,
Are two great companions,
Tranca Ruas at the Crossroad,
And Zé Pelintra at the Terreiro.

O Morro da Cruz está de luto,
Porque Zé Pelintra Morreu,
Zé Pelintra Malandro
   é Conquistador,
Ele Morreu Pela Mulher
   que mais Amou,
O Chora o Morro inteiro Chora,
Oh chora por causa do Zé,
Oh coitado Zé eu não sabia que
   tu amava esta mulher.

The Hill of the Cross is in mourning,
Because Zé Pelintra has died,
Zé Pelintra Malandro
   is a Conqueror,
He died by the Woman
   he most loved,
Cries the whole Hill, cries,
Oh, cries because of Zé,
Oh poor Zé I didn't know
   you loved this woman.

De terno branco,
   seu punhal de aço puro,
Seu ponto é seguro,
   quando vem pra trabalhar.
Segura o nego que esse nego
   é Zé Pelintra,

In a white suit,
   his dagger of pure steel,
His ponto is safe,
   when he comes to work.
Hold this blackness because this blackness
   is Zé Pelintra,

Na descida do morro,	As he is coming down the hill
ele vem pra trabalhar. (bis)	he comes to work. (×2)
Eu bem que disse a você, (bis)	I said this to you, (×2)
Mas parece que eu adivinho,	But it seems, I guess,
O feitiço que tu tinha, (bis)	The spell that you had, (×2)
Seu Zé Pelintra tirou,	Mr. Zé Pelintra took off,
Deu meia noite na lua, (bis)	It is midnight under the Moon, (×2)
Deu meio dia no sol,	It is midnight under the Sun,
Pois segura o ponto Seu Zé, (bis)	So hold the ponto Mr. Zé, (×2)
Que o ponto é de Catimbó,	'Cause the ponto is Catimbó.

Pontos Riscados of Exu Zé Pelintra

A Working to get rich

You will take a big jar and place it on his ponto. In this jar pour one litre of cachaça or rum. Light seven red candles and seven white candles around it and call Zé Pelintra. Then you will add to the alcohol fennel (*Fœniculum vulgare*), folha de fortuna (*Kalanchoe pinnata*) and a wide selection of different flowers; the more exquisite they are the better it is. You will add to this seven coins and honey. Macerate well while singing to Zé Pelintra. This will then be taken as a bath on Friday evening at twilight.

A Working to gain work

You will first give to him a rabbit, keeping the feet yourself. Sometime later, when the rabbit's feet are dried, you will give to Zé Pelintra one bottle of cognac and place within it star anis, a silver chain, a packet of needles, abre caminho (*Mentha vidris*) powder and one rabbit foot. One rabbit foot you will take for yourself as a good luck charm. Take the bottle to a crossroad in the woods and leave it there after calling Zé Pelintra.

Exu Ganga (Damoston)

Ganga is to be found mainly in the cemetery, where he can be evoked to create great disruption. He is good at doing any kind of work, but has a reputation for being especially capable of bringing about death. He is also a great healer and can be called upon to assist in the healing of terminal conditions. He dresses in black and grey and his manifestations are often accompanied by the smell of rotting meat. His name shows a clear connection to Kongolese practices. He is said to be a close ally of Maria Mulambo and resides within or close to garbage. He is in fact so close to Maria Mulambo that this Exu is at times called Exu Mulambo. In the kingdom of the Harp he is found at dumpsters, and especially those located in back alleys. He is an ambivalent spirit who partakes in art, dance and artistry, as well as in the trafficking of souls. He can be called upon to expel negativity and dross from workings and from complicated situations that need a solution.

Sacred Items: Rotten flesh, rags, musical instruments, trident, tobacco, cachaça.

Iconography: A red-hued Exu dressed in rags, holding a skull and a trident.

Ponto Cantado of Exu Ganga

Ganga lelê, Ganga lelê,	*Ganga lelê, Ganga lelê,*
Ele é Exu Ganga,	*He is Exu Ganga,*
Ganga lelê, Ganga lelê,	*Ganga lelê, Ganga lelê,*
Ele é Exu Ganga.	*He is Exu Ganga.*

Pontos Riscados of Exu Ganga

Ponto for protection.

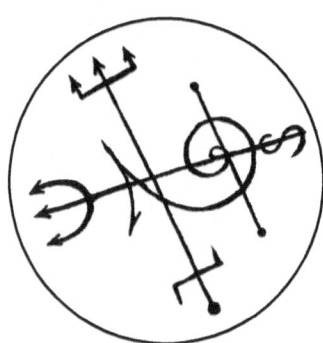

All-purpose ponto.

Ponto for attack, combat and defence.

Exu Malé (Sustugriel)

Exu Malé is said to be of a fluid constitution and manifests as a Preto Velho dressed in white, with a white beard. He is a true witch and knows how to work roots and conjure. In Exu Malé is found a great reservoir of African witchcraft and sorcery. He is good at dissolving spells and binding, and he is one of the most useful spirits for making despachos. He smokes a pipe and drinks cachaça and any type of wine. He is also deeply related to the powers of the moon and one would do well in observing her phases when working with him. He is also said to be an expert in constructing the Ngangas or spirit vessels of the Kongolese. In this he often calls upon the assistance of Exu Ganga. Exu Malé is himself a spirit of comfort in the kingdom of the Harp and is the confidant of Exu dos Infernos and Exu Sete Liras, serving as counseler to them both. Holding this function he also ensures the dynamic contrast in this kingdom is upheld and makes sure that although this is a turbulent and dangerous kingdom it is at all times kept in a kind of mysterious balance.

Sacred Items: Terracotta pots, pipe, trident, dry roots, cachaça.

Iconography: This Exu looks like a Preto Velho dressed in simple white clothes holding a trident and smoking a pipe.

Ponto Cantado of Exu Malé

Ai, ai, ai,	Ai, ai, ai,
Satanás já deu um berro,	Satan has already screamed,
Saravá Exú Malé, e gangá,	Saravá Exú Malé, e gangá,
Saravá Exú Malé,	Saravá Exú Malé,
Saravá seu obé de ferro.	Salutations to his iron knife.

Pontos Riscados of Exu Malé

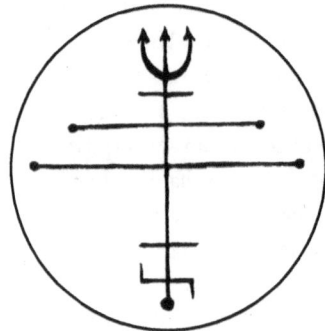

Ponto to manifest his powers.

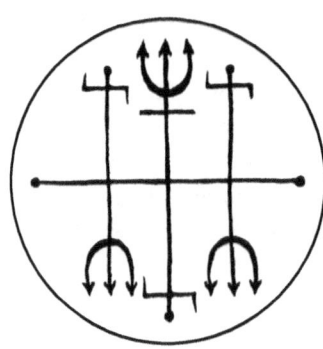

Ponto for works of attack and defence.

Exu Chama Dinheiro/Exu Pedra Negra
Exu Money Summoner/Exu of the Black Stone

Exu chama dinheiro and Exu Pedra Negra refer to the same Exu, under different names. His original title was Pedra Negra, but since he demonstrated remarkable powers to manifest money he gained his second title. The Exu of the Black Stone is deeply related to the earth and gives riches to those who call upon him. He holds maggots and centipedes as sacred. He is good to use when in financial hardship, and can solve problems with creditors. He can also be appealed to when a new business venture is planned.

He is an elegant spirit, richly adorned with expensive clothes and jewels, but at times he can also show himself as a cyclops. He enjoys sacrifices of red wine and honey, as well as sweet fruits. It should be mentioned that he can be rather unpredictable and there have been instances of communication failure with this Exu, so keep it clear and simple when working with him and pay attention to opportunities, because his treasures can surface in highly unexpected ways.

Sacred Items: Red wine, precious stones, fruits, honey, cigarillos, worms, coins, silver and gold.

Iconography: A naked Exu his private parts covered with a loincloth, carrying a trident.

Ponto Cantado of Exu Pedra Negra

Sala, salá mucalero,	Sala, salá mucalero,
Sala Lebará e sala,	Sala Lebará e sala,
Saravá Seu Pedra Negra,	Saravá Mr. Pedra Negra,
Sala munganga ê sala,	Sala munganga ê sala,
Não sei o que faço,	I don't know what to do,
Não sei o que resolver,	I don't know what to decide,
Estou para morrer,	I am about to die,
Exu Pedra Negra,	Exu Pedra Negra,
Vem me ajudar,	Come to help me,
Faz entrar dinheiro,	Make money manifest,
Para me salvar.	To save me.

Pontos Riscados of Exu Pedra Negra

Kabalistic ponto for work and petitions in business and to speed up transactions.

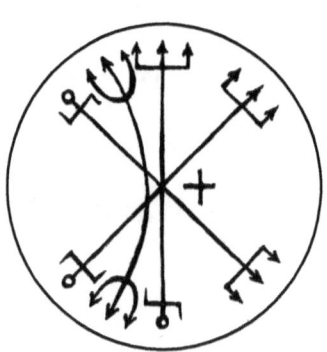

To fortify his power in workings.

The Kingdom of the Beach (Praia)

Exu Rei das Praias and Pomba Gira Rainha das Praias rule this kingdom. The king of this kingdom appears like a transparent marine creature or as a captain with a bloated body holding a pipe and a trident. Some say that he is the same as Exu Géreré. In this kingdom we find enigmatic phenomena of nature and the host of souls that were lost at sea. It is a kingdom that holds the secret of passions and memory. Natural catastrophes of wind or water have their origin in this kingdom. It is common to work in this kingdom for matters of love and purification. This kingdom can also enrage passions and the spirits here can bring insanity and depression, so naturally they also possess the cure for these afflictions.

The People of the Rivers · Exu dos Rios
The People of the Waterfalls · Exu Sete Cachoeiras
The People of the Stones · Exu Sete Pedras/Pedrinhas
The People of the Sailors · Exu Marinheiro
The People of the Ocean · Exu Maré
The People of the Mud · Exu do Lodo
The People of Bahia · Exu Bahiano
The People of the Wind · Exu dos Ventos
The People of the Islands · Exu do Côco

Exu dos Rios (Nebiros)
Exu of the Rivers

It is said that this Exu is particularly suitable for works aimed towards fame and success. This Exu lives in areas close to water, especially at the point where two streams meet and flow as one. This gives a lunar cast, and it is perhaps important to look at the energies present in this Exu from the perspective of moon and waters mixing. For Umbandistas this Exu is deeply connected with the river Orixa Oxum. But he is not only the sweet and calm waters of Oxum; he is also the rivers of maelstroms and counter currents. The river carries a power, lunar by nature, and therefore is unpredictable and changeable, and this temperament is reflected in this Exu. He is the King of the fresh waters and is as such related to emotions and communications, as well as to sudden devastation. With his fine manners this gentle spirit can remind one of Exu Veludo and Exu Marabô, but he can also suddenly change into a force of turbulence and terror. He is an expert in purifications using water, and knows the secrets of medicinal herbs and is therefore a good companion to Exu Curadôr and Exu Pimenta. He can be worked to sweeten or enrage people and also to bring good luck and unblock stagnant situations.

Sacred Items: Water, mud, pebbles, fresh water shells, water lilies, papyrus and all plants growing in water.

Iconography: He is in red and dark blue with duck feet. His figure is strong, but somewhat swollen. He carries a trident.

Pontos Cantados of Exu dos Rios

Meu senhor das almas,	*My lord of souls,*
Exu dos Rios vem aí, (bis)	*Exu dos Rios is arriving,* (×2)
Ele vem acompanhado,	*He comes together,*
De seu irmão Tiriri. (bis)	*With his brother Tiriri.* (×2)

O rio corre pro mar,	*The river runs to the sea,*
Rua corre pra encruza, (bis)	*Streets run to the crossroad,* (×2)
Louvado seja Exu dos Rios,	*Praise be to Exu dos Rios,*
Que demanda não recusa.(bis)	*Who does not refuse work.* (×2)
Quem me invoca nesta "Banda" é, é!	*Who invokes me in this "Banda" is, is!*
Só pode sê meu fio ê, ê ó	*Only can be my child é, é, ô,*
Gira ronda, gira ronda ê, ê, á,	*Spin around, spin around, ê, ê, á,*
Seu poder é sobre as águas ê, ê, ô!	*Its power is over the waters ê, ê, ô!*
Pra cruza fios de Umbanda,	*To cross the children of Umbanda,*
Já chegô Exu dos Rios ê, ê, á!	*Exu dos Rios already arrived ê, ê, ô!*

Ponto Riscado of Exu dos Rios
for bringing down his powers

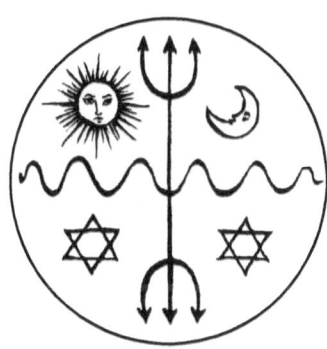

Exu Sete Cachoeiras (Khil)
Exu of the Seven Waterfalls

One of the caboclos quimbandeiros, he always carries an axe. Some say that it was this Exu that assisted Moses in parting the Red Sea. As with all Caboclos Quimbandeiros he is astute, serious, and demanding of the character of his votaries. His domain is the passions, and he can envigorate or calm them. Just like a waterfall can be deadly and majestic or serene and intoxicating, so too is the nature of this Exu. He is an Exu better worked by those who have already established a relationship with him, given that he is an Exu that has no problems in accepting an offering for a proposition he finds unworthy and then turning your life upside down. He is a chaotic force, so care should be taken.

Sacred Items: River stones, plants that grow close to waterfalls.

Iconography: A Caboclo with a proud posture, prominent horns and a red cape. He has a full beard and carries a trident.

Ponto Cantado of Exu Sete Cachoeiras

Treme terra,	*Tremble earth,*
Que Seu Sete Cachoeiras chegô,	*Because Mr. Sete Cachoeiras arrived,*
Treme mundo,	*Tremble everybody,*
Caia caia laroyé!	*Fall, fall, laroyê!*

Ponto Riscado of Exu Sete Cachoeiras

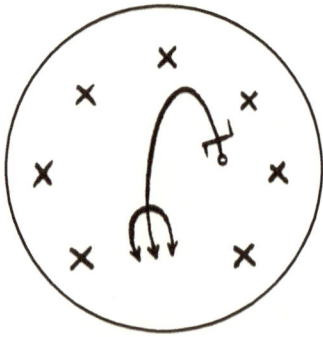

Exu Sete Pedras/Pedrinhas (Humots)
Exu of the Seven Pebbles

*S*ETE PEDRINHAS is related to all kinds of stones found in and at the ocean, both of the gross and precious kind. He is a great alchemist and can, like his twin in the woods (Humots), teach this science, but since the power of the Seven Stones is found at the ocean, his magic and alchemy will take on distinct marine qualities. Fluids and healing baths are essential in his domain. His knowledge of physics and chemistry makes him an expert in divination based on the tarot and is combined with astrological knowledge. We turn to this Exu to gain insight into problems and situations, and ask him for advice, especially when situations or people have drifted apart for no good reason. He is also said to be good at detecting secret manuscripts and occult texts. This Exu often shows himself as a caboclo of the ocean who some say rides on eagles and hawks at night. He is the power of obsidian and thunderstones and radically breaks down any obstruction. He is a serene Exu, bordering on the moral in terms of how we treat nature, so this must be part of our character when we work with this force. Some say that this Exu is capable of igniting such confidence in a man that he can accomplish the impossible. He is prone to give riches to those he favors and induces stability in any situation considered to be floating and moving out of control.

Sacred Items: Chemicals, stones, cowries, tarot cards.

Iconography: A well-dressed Exu surrounded by stones both precious and crude standing amidst the breaking waves.

Pontos Cantados of Exu Sete Pedras

Seu Sete Pedras,	Mr. Sete Pedras,
Livra os caminhos que passo,	Free the ways I pass by,
Seu Sete Pedras,	Mr. Sete Pedras,
Livra os caminhos que passo,	Free the ways I pass by,
Quando ando com Sete Pedras (bis)	When I walk with Sete Pedras (×2)
Meus caminhos não têm embaraço.	My ways have no obstacles.

La na pedreira ouvi gargalhá,	There at the quarry I heard laughing,
Seu Pedra Preta vem pra trabalhá,	Mr. Pedra Preta came to work,
Fica firmeza onde ele tá,	Where he is getting firm,
Seu Pedra Preta laroyê é saravá.	Mr. Pedra Pedra laroyê is sarava.

Pontos Riscados of Exu Sete Pedras/Pedrinhas

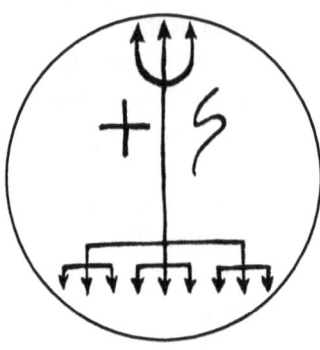

General ponto and to mark the despacho and ebo done with him.

Exu Marinheiro
Exu Sailor

MARINHEIRO is king of sailors and pirates and rules contraband, ports and marine life, especially fish and whales. He is seen as a captain dressed in red and black with a white captain's hat. He is a joyous Exu, easily given over to temptation and sweet words from seductive women. This Exu loves pipe tobacco, cachaça and white wine. He is the king of people who lost their lives at sea, but in particular those who lost their lives close to shore where they are referred to as *people of the sand*. He is a natural protector for anyone who works at sea and can be placated with champagne, white wine and padé made from seafood, peppers and cachaça.

Exu Marinheiro walks with Exu Gererê, a powerful sorcerer, who some say was either a Tatá Nganga or a Houngan. However, as Gererê is also spelled as Jeje, which is a Candomblé nation which cultivates Vodouns, it is probably from here that this Exu originates.

Exu Gererê

GERERÊ POSSESSES a wealth of knowledge and takes the form of a fisherman dressed in white and red. He holds the rulership of creatures of the Ocean such as catfish and octopus, but also undines and mermaids, often of a predatory nature. He is reputed to be a powerful sorcerer, a true Tatá who prefers the simple life of a fisherman. The magical workings of this Exu are considered extremely powerful and rapid, both for good and ill. Gererê in the Bantu language means network, and refers to his ability of spreading his magical powers like the fishermen's net. He should be worked at docks and piers. He is also the chief of a secret Nagô line that counts the following spirits which will attend him when he is in his kingdom: Exu Sete Cruzes, Exu Curadôr, Exu Capa Preta, Exu do Cemitério, Exu Ganga, Exu Gira Mundo, Exu Quebra Galho, and Pomba Gira Maria Padilha.

Pontos Cantados for Exu Marinheiro, Exu Gèrère
& the people of the Ocean shore and Sea

Se esse Exu é Marinheiro,	If this Exu is a Sailor,
Amarra ao tôco no Mar,	He binds the stump in the Sea,
Chove chuva,	Pour down rain,
Cai sereno,	Fall down dew,
Tôco no mesmo lugar.	Stump in the same place.
Morena da Praia,	Brunette from the Beach,
Atira seus olhos pro Mar,	Sets her eyes to the Sea,
Morena da Praia,	Brunette from the Beach,
Que seu amor vai chegar	That your love will arrive.
Ele foi pra muito longe,	He went to far far way,
Foi a navegar,	He went sailing,
Morena da Praia,	Brunette from the Beach,
Ele esta para voltar...	He is about to come...
Trabalhava no Cais do Porto,	He worked at the Port,
Levando saveiros pro Mar,	Bringing boats to the Sea,
Ele é Seu Marinheiro,	He is Mr. Marinheiro,
Pescador das Almas do Mar.	Fisher of the Souls of the Sea.
Ai vem Exu Marineiro	Here comes Exu Sailor,
do Fundo do Mar,	from the depths of the Sea,
Para trabalhar	To work,
Ele se leva todas palavras,	He brings all the words,
Mas as verdades ficam no Ar.	But the truths stay in the Air.

Ponto Riscado of Exu Marinheiro

General purpose ponto.

Ponto Riscado of Exu Gererê

Ponto for calling this Exu.

Exu Maré (Pentagony)

a name which is a fusion between the Orixa Osumaré, the rainbow serpent that is said to be the tracks of Olodumare (God) in the heavens, and Maré, the ocean tides. This Exu is called upon whenever we feel the need to do our works in secret, such as in clandestine affairs of love and business. He is a marvelous healer and seawater collected in a conch bearing his ponto serves as an immediate dispeller of negativity. He loves champagne and beer, and these can be offered at the ocean shore over his ponto. He is said to be the totality of the movements of the ocean and lives in the waves, the starfish, the volcanic eruptions in the ocean and is a caretaker and protector of all Pomba Giras living at the ocean shore. This Exu is also known as the Exu of the Muddy Beach, which is a more proper designation for this Exu. His expertise is related to the art of hiding treasures and belongings, and he can be used in order to create favourable alliances. He can also teach the art of astral travel. Contrary to Exu Pemba and John Skull, he is often used in despachos on the beach at night. He can effectively release spells, especially love-bindings. He is quite a generous Exu who takes delight in presents and enjoys cachaça mixed with honey or coconut water and sweet red wine, champagne and beer are also to his liking. He walks in the company of Exu do Lodo, Exu of the Mud, and when they work together they make wonderful purifications, especially for expelling sadness and depression.

Sacred Items: Honey, wine, sea sand, mud, charcoal, tridents.

Iconography: A slender young Exu red of hue holding a trident and a skull.

Pontos Cantados of Exu Maré

Tava na beira da Praia,	I was at the shore of the beach,
Todo filho a saravá,	All the children were saluting,
Eu chôro de alegria,	I cry with joy,
Quando tudo é alegria,	When all is happiness,
Eu chôro de tristeza,	I cry with sadness,
Quando vou pra lá pro Mar,	When I go there to the sea,

Nganga é é é...	*Nganga é é é...*
Ele chora na Aruanda,	*He cries in Aruanda,*
Nganga é, é, é,	*Nganga é, é, é,*
Ele é Exu Maré.	*He is Exu Maré.*
Calunguinha do Mar,	*Little Calunga from the Ocean,*
Calunguinha do Mar,	*Little Calunga from the Ocean,*
ôi Calunga!	*oh Calunga!*
Calunguinha do Mar,	*Little Calunga from the Ocean,*
Leva as kizilias pro Mar.	*Take the evil energies to the Ocean.*

Pontos Riscados of Exu Maré

Ponto of protection to be used in whatever situation.

Ponto for calling up this Exu.

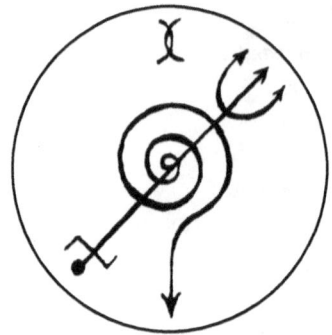
Ponto for domination.

A Working to put an end to alcoholism

This working should be done on a Friday under a waning moon at midnight. Go to the ocean shore and ask permission of the guardians of the Ocean using three black candles, three white candles and three red candles. Bring with you a bottle of cachaça and the name of the person you want to cure written on seven pieces of paper. On a black cloth mark with white pemba the ponto for domination and place the candles around it. Sing the ponto and state your request. Place the paper strips inside the cachaça and pour the contents on the ponto in seven glugs. Each time, say: *Oh Exu Maré, help NN to stop drinking. As the moon wanes, so will his drinking cease.*

Leave the place taking seven steps backwards before turning around. Leave the place and return to offer champagne and cigars when the work is completed.

Exu do Lodo
Exu of the Mud

Exu do Lodo is a companion of the Preto Velhos and of those in particular Pai Congo (Father Congo) and Pai Arruda (Father Rue), and is an extraordinary power to resort to when situations become stagnant. When he is called upon he shows himself as a dark-hued Exu dressed in simple clothes, carrying a medicine bag and a cane. He manifests in seaweed and is an Exu that gives nutrition to the roots of the plants at the ocean shore. Some describe him as a Preto Velho covered in seaweed. He can be called upon side by side with Pomba Gira das Praias in workings that demand a softening of hard hearts. He also takes special care of those souls lost in the ocean, which gives him the position as Omolu's hand stretching from the Calunga to the ocean shore. Any cemetery close to the ocean is under his rule. He is an enigmatic and scary force. He never speaks, just grunts, but even not being able to speak he understands all and is very compassionate.

Sacred Items: Sea sand, white wine, octopus, seaweed, rue, tobacco.

Iconography: A dark-hued Exu that rises from the mud, holding a cane or a mound of seaweed.

Pontos Cantados of Exu do Lodo

Na praia deserta eu vi Exu,	At the desert beach I saw Exu,
Então o meu corpo tremeu todo, (bis)	Then my whole body trembled, (×2)
Acendi minha vela e o meu charuto,	I lit my candle and my cigar,
Arrie minha marafo,	I placed down my marafo,
Saravei Exu do Lodo. (bis)	Saluted Exu do Lodo. (×2)

Se pó na pedra rebentou,	If powder at the Stone broke,
Exu do Lodo chegou,	Exu do Lodo arrived,
Exu do Lodo gargalhou,	Exu do Lodo laughed,
Exu do Lodo que linda garoa,	Exu do Lodo, how beautiful his drizzle,
Esta caindo lá no cemitério,	Is falling there at the cemetery,
Chuva grossa e chuva miúda,	Heavy rain and day dew rain,
Que esta molhando sua catacumba.	That is pouring over your catacomb.

Quando pega a madrugada,	When the dawn catches,
Exu do Lodo na Quimbanda chega,	Exu do Lodo in Quimbanda arrives,
Ele vem do cemitério,	He comes from the cemetery,
Vem sair a lua cheia.	He comes to see the full moon.
Exu do Lodo é,	Exu do Lodo is,
Meu compadre na Kimbanda,	My friend in Kimbanda,
Exu do Lodo é,	Exu do Lodo is,
Vem saravar a	Who comes to salute and work
nossa banda.	our banda.
Tomou dendê a meia noite,	He took palm oil at midnight,
eu quero ver,	I want to see it,
Quem é que diz que Do Lodo	Who is the one that says the
nao faz nada,	Muddy One does nothing,
Eu caminhava nas portas	I was walking at the doors
da Calunga,	of the Calunga,
Quando a nuvems cobriam	When the clouds covered
todo o céu,	all the sky,
Estava troando nas portas	I was roaring at the gates
da Aruanda,	of Aruanda,
Eu vi a chuva romper	I saw the rain breaking
a madrugada,	the dawn,
Eu vi um homem parado numa tumba,	I saw a man standing at a tomb,
Caveira em mão,	Skull in one hand,
lá na outra seu chapéu,	and in the other, his hat,
Exu do Lodo é meu Pai,	Exu do Lodo is my father,
Trabalha na Lei de Exu,	He works by the Law of Exu,
Lá na Calunga onde	There at the Calunga where
vive Omolu,	Omolu lives,
Na beira da praia escutei	At the shore of the beach I heard
um grito de guerra.	a scream of war.

Exu que está na terra,	*Exu was in the land,*
* quem é, quem é,*	* Who is, who is,*
É o povo Quimbandeiro que vem	*And people of Quimbanda that come*
* Do Lodo,*	* from Do Lodo,*
Exu Marê com Exu do Lodo,	*Exu Marê with Exu do Lodo.*

Pontos Riscados of Exu do Lodo

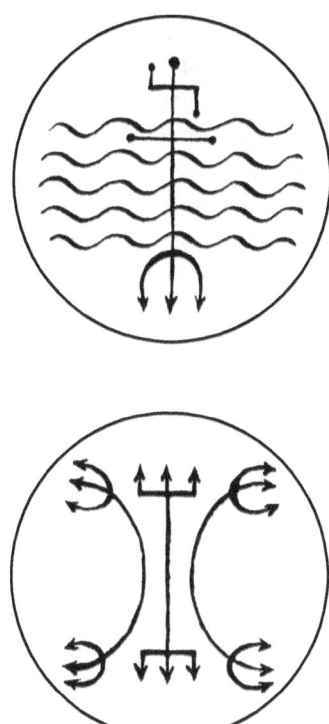

Exu Bahiano
Bahia Exu

BAHIA IS THE STATE IN BRAZIL where a great influx of Africans arrived, primarily to the city of Salvador, called the City of All Saints, given the enormous melting-pot of West African traditions that came here. As such this Exu typifies a particular memory, legacy and mentality. He is an easygoing Exu, cheerful and laidback. If there is an Exu in Quimbanda that is a feel-good Exu, it is this one. He is rarely used for sorcerous workings, but rather he is appealed to when situations are stuck, when money is not flowing properly and in all forms of complicated social situations. He is commonly approached by simple people with real and material problems that are searching for social advancement and contentment. He likes the beach, and crossroads close to the ocean are preferred places to leave offerings to him. He likes typical Bahia food, heavily spiced with chili and coriander. He loves cachaça, beer and cigarettes.

Sacred Items: Cachaça, meat, coriander, peppers of all kind, beer.

Iconography: A black-hued Exu dressed in black pants and a red t-shirt holding a trident.

Pontos Cantados of Exu Bahiano

Cadê do Mato,	*Who by the Woods,*
Cadê pro Bará,	*Who by the Bará.*
Povo da Bahia,	*People of Bahia,*
Que vem trabaiá.	*That came to work.*
Firma Bahiano,	*Get strength Bahiano,*
Agora que eu quero ver,	*Now I want to see,*
Com seu cachimbo,	*With his pipe,*
Com azeite de dendê,	*With palm oil,*
Eu quero ver os Bahianos de Aruanda,	*I want to see the Bahianos of Aruanda,*
Trabalhando na Umbanda.	*Working in Umbanda.*

Ponto Riscado of Exu Bahiano

Exu dos Ventos (Bechard)
Exu of the Winds

HE COMES AS THE WIND when called upon. Frenetic dances and flappings of the cape are often witnessed when this Exu enters the terreiro. Mountaintops and windy places are domains especially suitable for working with him. Wherever we find natural disasters caused by wind, he is present. His form is that of a black spirit appearing to move even when he stands still. His magic is in the realm of reptiles, especially toads and vipers, but he is also a great exorcist and purifier. He represents climatic changes and all types of wind, from gentle breezes to tornados. This Exu loves to purify malignant atmospheres and has important connections to Omolu and Calunga. He is often referred to as Tatá Ventaniana, in honour of his Kongo origin. He has another path, referred to as Corta Vento, which is an aspect often used to soften the devastating powers of the wind and to bring order to a confused mind.

Sacred Items: Dust, bark from trees destroyed by wind and lightning, moss and stones taken from windy mountains, tobacco, cachaça.

Iconography: A firm spirit with thick horns a full beard and fangs. He is holding a trident and has a pile of dust in his hands.

Pontos Cantados of Exu dos Ventos

Venta toda noite,	The wind blows all night,
Sopra todo dia,	It blows all day,
Ele é Exu do Vento,	He is Exu do Vento
Tatá Sete Ventanias	Tatá Seven Winds.

Exu do Vento, do Vento, do Vento...	Exu do Vento, of the Wind, of the Wind...
Do Fundo do Mar,	From the bottom of the sea,
Se leva todas as palavras,	He brings all the words,
Mas as verdades ficam no Ar.	But the truths stays in the Air.

Ele tinha uma casa e agora não tem,	He had a house and He hasn't now,
Porque o Vento levou...	Because the Wind took it...
Ele tinha dinheiro e agora não tem,	He had Money and He hasn't now.
Porque o Vento levou...	Because the Wind took it...
Ai Exu dos Ventos,	Ah Exu dos Ventos,
Meu grande camarada,	My great comrade,
Ele quer que você,	He wants you,
Arrume a sua morada.	To find a dwelling place.

Quem trabalha com fumaça,	Who works with smoke,
Quem trabalha no Ar,	Who works with air,
Só é Exu, só ele é...	It is just Exu, It is just him...
Quem sabe trabalhar,	Who knows how to work,
Chegou Exu do Ar,	Exu of the Winds arrived,
Para todo mal levar. (bis)	To cast out all evil (×2)

Ponto Riscado of Exu dos Ventos

Exu do Coco
Exu of the Coconut

Living in palm trees he is the king of any island-dweller in the Ocean. He is an Exu mainly used in works of protection and to bring peace to situations. Some say that he holds the power to manipulate people's minds and has a deadly hand, if that is necessary. He is an Exu with philosophical inclinations, who loves to speak about the creation of the world and matters pertaining to theology. We might see him as the voice of reason in Quimbanda, and thus he can be called upon to sort out difficulties and conflicts between two or more people. This is because, like the coconut itself, Exu sees both sides, both the light and the dark and focuses on uniting them. As such he is a great force to call upon to gain insight into conflicts, internal as well as external.

Sacred Items: Palm trees, beach sand, coconuts, basil, ferns.

Iconography: A black Exu carrying a white veil, with a stout palm-like posture carrying a coconut and a candle along with a trident.

Ponto Cantado of Exu do Coco

Na praia tem um coco,	There is a coconut at the beach,
Tem um coco, ai um côco,	There is a coconut, ah a coconut,
ai um coco, (bis)	ah a coconut, (×2)
Ele é Exu do Coco que trabalha	He is Exu do Coco that works there at
lá na ilha,	the island,
Ele é Exu do Coco o que vem	He is Exu do Coco that comes
pra trabalhá. (bis)	to work. (×2)

Pontos Riscados of Exu do Coco

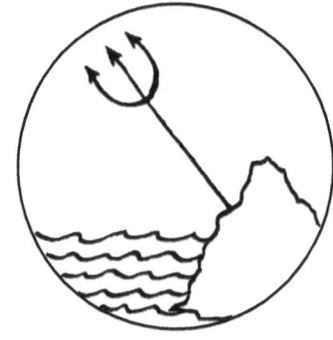

Despacho

THIS BOOK WAS WRITTEN, as any magical work should be, with the spirits sat on my shoulders. I went to my temple and I started the work with offerings to Exu Mor, Exu Dragão and Pomba Gira Rainha da Figueira do Inferno. Throughout this work these loyal friends and fiends have inspired me and opened avenues of new insight, both within me and within the world at large. I feel I have gained a renewed sense of perspective and this renewed perspective is this gift, this text given from us to you.

I am quite aware that some will find this book gives away too much, and question what happened to my vow of secrecy. I understand this, but at the same time I also understand that a secret can never be told, it must be experienced to be grasped. So, yes, this book does disclose too much, but only to the faithful ones, those who with an open heart and honest soul are able to truly see beneath.

This book is the product of magical writing as befits a talismanic publisher like Scarlet Imprint. The book was started with ceremonies, petitions and offerings to Exu Mor, and throughout the gestation of this text the spirits have been called upon to monitor, inspire, close and reveal, leaving me solely as their scribe in this revelation of grammar and gospel.

The most profound perspectives in this journey of text and thought have been the constant attention spirit has ignited in me about masculinity, what is a man, a true man, this construct molded by Mars, Mercury and Saturn with sickles of fire? I have gone through stages that have matured my understanding about this complex issue, so often said to be simple. The male essence has a rich colouration, a hot blade of fumes and fire, an axis of embers the world can turn upon. I have come to realize the great variety of masculinity amongst my companions. I have found that male perfection is in many ways Stoic, it is about honour and chivalry. These traits I have found in the most diverse men across cultures, social status, temperaments and Fate. I have found lack of honour to be detrimental to the cultivation of a healthy soul and to be the gateway of misery and self-hatred.

This book is not only a book dedicated to Exu and Quimbanda, but it is a testament celebrating the aspects of creation we understand to be masculine. There is a certain bravery to the accomplished male. This bravery can take the form of the mandrake, holly or oak, it can be the comfort of the walnut tree or the shades of the yew. It can be the upright and erect pride of the palm tree and the majestic tenderness of the mango tree, or the venomous beauty of the aconite. I see the knight as the fulfillment of male potential. If we look at one typical oath a knight was to swear this becomes evident:

To ever be a good knight and true
Reverent and generous
Champion of the right and the good

A knight was deemed to be worthy of this station when he had performed acts of selfless love, to have fought the good fight and denied lies and deception. It was demanded that the knight demonstrate strength of character and a generous readiness to be polite with all, disregarding rank and status. It was only natural that from this knighthood chivalric love took form in the Middle Ages. It was about choosing well at the crossroad and being motivated by love in harmony with the crown of the world tree.

I can't help seeing this being the mystery at the heart of Quimbanda. Pomba Gira Rainha da Figueira do Inferno is woman of seven husbands, these husbands are the knightly court of perfected males. They are the protectors of the wisdom of the world, which resides in woman, and in this lies the secret aspiration and grail of the knight, the accomplished male.

As such I feel this book disclosing the mystery of Exu, in the form of keys and directions, is also disclosing the mystery of manhood. So with this the book is at its end, a gift to the host of Exu and a celebration of good men constantly perfecting their nature.

Glossary

Alguidar: terracotta bowl.

Amací: herbal bath, but originally this was a beer-based fermented herbal brew that made part of one's baptism/initiation in the cult.

Amarrar: to bind, most usually used to refer to love spells aiming towards binding one person to another.

Arruanda: an alternative spelling of Luanda in Congo where many slaves were shipped out to the New World. The term is used in reverence of this memory.

Assentamento: The spirit vessel, usually made from a terracotta jar.

Buraco: literally *hole*, but also a term used for people that are in a state of disgrace and poverty, a bad stage in their life.

Caboclo: Native Indian, indigenous to Brazil, but also more generally used in reference to the spirits of knowledge found in the wilderness.

Cafuzo: People of Indian and Black blood.

Cachaça: Sugar cane alcohol.

Cambono/a: An initiated person who assists the medium and directs the spirit during possession.

Campo Santo: The Graveyard.

Catiço: Literally *charmed one* in reference to people suddenly disappearing in nature, as with the European *fairy taken*. Sometimes it is also used to define the spiritual calibre of Exus and Pomba Giras as *spirits of enchantment*.

Charuto: Cigar.

Demanda: To demand, in the sense of a forceful request made of the spirit. A working, a spell.

Dendé: Palm oil.

Despacho: A magical working, often involving padê, which aims to send spirits on a mission and also to cleanse someone of impurities.

Ebó: A Yorubá term signifying *sacrifice*, in Quimbanda used interchangeably with *mironga*, (see MIRONGA and DESPACHO).

Egun: Departed soul.

Feitiçaria: Sorcery.

Fundanga/Fula/Polvora: Gunpowder.

GIRA: Ritual celebration in honour of the spirits.

KIUMBA: Similar to larvae. A spirit of the dead with a fragmented personality and memory, hence no direction. Originally from the Kikongo/Kimbundu word for skull.

LAROYÊ: A salutation of the spirits of Quimbanda, an elision of the Yoruba Iya Ile Ayé, meaning *I give reverence to the mothers of the earth*.

LOMBA: The grave, sepulchre, specifically the gravemound.

LUANDA: Alternative spelling of Arruanda, (see ARRUANDA).

MACUMBA: A common phrase referring to any form of spellwork and demanda, often used in reference to Quimbanda workings.

MALANDRO: Typified by Zé Pelintra it refers to the people of the streets and the kingdom of the Harp that are related to bars, taverns, gambling and bordellos. They are commonly seen as trickster spirits related to chance and opportunity.

MARAFO: Any high-proof alcoholic distillate.

MIRONGA: Generic term for spellcraft, from the most simple to the most elaborate.

NKULU: Used in reference to one's spirit guides/Exu Tatá. Originally a kikongo term referring to ancestry.

PADÊ: A dish made from manioc flour or corn flour and peppers as basic ingredients that serves as a food-offering when making ebó and despacho in Quimbanda.

PATACO: Money.

PEMBA: Sacred chalk used to draw pontos riscados, (see PONTOS RISCADOS). Can also be used as a component of magical powders.

PITÚ: Cigarette.

PONTOS CANTADOS: Songs designed to praise or manifest spirits.

PONTOS RISCADOS: The spirit signatures or designs replicating the spirits' nature used to call them into manifestation.

PRETO VELHO: Literally *Old Blacks*, the category of spirits that preserved the African wisdom.

TABAQUE: A ritual session involving the calling upon of spirits with drums.

TATÁ: Priest in the double sense of being the one that possesses the secrets of his Exu and/or Pomba Gira in the form of the spirit vessel. It is also used as a reference to one's mentor both mundane and spiritual, as well as the director of a Quimbanda temple.

Terreiro/Tenda: Space set aside for the cultivation of the spirits of Quimbanda.

Tostão: Coins, also shorthand for the herb tostão de Oxum, which is used to secure abundance and better cash flow.

Tronco: The trunk, the foundation of a terreiro. It can also signify the terreiro or temple of Exu and Pomba Gira itself, as well as the first assentamento that was made for the new house, as well as referring to the main spirit giving support to the Tatá.

Yayá: Female variant of Tatá, (see tatá).

Selected Bibliography

AGRIPPA, HENRY CORNELIUS, *Three Books of Occult Philosophy*. Llewellyn, US 1995.
—— *Declamation on the Nobility and Preeminence of the Female Sex*. University of Chicago Press, US 1996.
ALVA, ANTONIO,*Como desmanchar trabalhos de Quimbanda (Magia Negra)*. Editora Eco, Brazil 1974.
—— *Trabalhos práticos de Magia Negra*. Editora Pallas, Brazil 1985.
ATHANÁSIO, *O Livro do Feiticeiro*. Editora Eco, Brazil (n/d).
BAILY, CYRIL, *The Religion of Ancient Rome*. Archibald Constable & Co., UK 1907.
BRAGA, LOURENÇO, *Trabalhos de Umbanda ou Magia Pratica*. Bibiloteca Espiritualista, Brazil 1956.
—— *Umbanda e Magia Branca/Quimbanda Magia Negra* (2 volumes). Editora Borsoi, Brazil, 1951.
BASTIDE, ROGER, *African Civilisations in the New World*. C. Hurst & Co., London 1971.
—— *The African Religions of Brazil*. Johns Hopkins University Press, US 1978.
BROWN, DIANA DEG, *Umbanda*. Columbia University Press, US 1986.
BRUNO, GIORDANO, *Cause, Principle and Unity*. Cambridge University Press, UK 1998.
BURCKHARDT, TITUS, *Alchemy*.Penguin, US 1971.
CÂMARA CASCUDO, L., *Dicionário do Folklore Brasileiro*. Ediouro, Brazil 1998.
CAPONE, STEFANIA, *A Busca da Àfrica no Candomblé*. Editora Pallas, Brazil 2004.
CAVALCANTE, SEVERINO, *Feitiços do Catimbó*. Editora Eco, Brazil (n/d).
EUFRAZIO, POMPILIO POSSERA,*Catecismo do Umbandista*. Editora Eco, Brazil 1964.
FONTENELLE, ALUIZIO, *Exu*. Editora Aurora, Brazil 1954.
FREYRE, GILBERTO, *Casa Grande é Senzala*. Editora Record, Brazil 1933/88.
FRISVOLD, NICHOLAJ, DE MATTOS, *Kiumbanda*. Chadezoad, Brazil 2006.
—— *Palo Mayombe – The Garden of Blood & Bones*. Scarlet Imprint, UK 2010.
—— *Pomba Gira & the Quimbanda of Mbumba Nzila*. Scarlet Imprint, UK 2011.
GREY, PETER, *The Red Goddess*. Scarlet Imprint, UK 2007.
LECOUTEUX, CLAUDE, *The Return of the Dead*. Inner Traditions, US 2009.
—— *Phantom Armies of the Nights*. Inner Traditions, US 2011.
LIEBLING, ROBERT, *Legends of the Fire Spirits*.I.B. Tauris, UK 2010.
LIGIÉRO, ZECA, *Malandró Divino*. Nova Era, Brazil 2002.
MCGREGOR, PEDRO, *The Moon and Two Mountains*.Souvenir Press, UK 1966.
MOLINA, N.A., *Antigo Livro de São Cipriano: O Gigante e verdadeiro capa de aço*. Editora Espiritualista, Brazil (n/d).
—— *Feitiços de um Preto Velho Quimbandeiro*. Editora Espiritualists, Brazil (n/d).
—— *Na Gira dos Exu*. Editora Espirtualista, Brazil (n/d).

———*Saravá Exu*. Editora Espiritualista, Brazil (n/d).
———*Saravá Maria Padilha*. Editora Espiritualista, Brazil (n/d).
———*Saravá Pomba Gira*. Editora Espiritualista, Brazil (n/d).
MOREIRA, ALDEMAR, *Formas populares da Religião*. Editora Iresi, Brazil (n/d).
PHAF-RHEINBERGER, I & PINTO, T, *AfricAmericas*. Iberoamericana, Brazil 2008.
SOUZA, LAURA DE MELLO, *O Diabo e a terra de Santa Cruz*. Compania das Letras, Brazil 1987.
ST. CLAIR, DAVID, *Drum and Candle*. MacDonald & Co., UK 1971.
STRATTON-KENT, JAKE, *The True Grimoire*. Scarlet Imprint, UK 2009.
SUSSOL, MAX, *O Livro dos Feitiços Brasileiros*. DCL, Brazil 1995.
TEIXEIRA, ANTÔNIO ALVES, *A Magia e os Encantos da Pomba-Gira*. Editora Eco, Brazil 1970.

Index of Exus

A

Exu das Almas 76, 132, 161, **172**, **173**
Exu Arranca Toco 57, 131, 133, 224, **237–239**
Exu Asa Negra 8, 25, 78, 94, 200, **265–267**
(see also Sete Lombas)

B

Exu Bahiano 135, 305, **320**, **321**
Exu Brasa 57, 71, 131, 133, 240, **246**, **247**

C

Exu do Cabaré 76, 134, 285, **287**, **288**
Exu Calunga 17, 20, 59, 77, 129, 130, 131, 133, 134, 136, 195, **221–213**, 222, 223, 274
Exu das Campinas 52, 60, 131, 133, 224, **230**, **231**
Exu Capa Preta da Encruzilhada 258
Exu Capa Preta 8, 42, 58, 83, 118, 130, 134, 191, 240, **258–263**, 311
Exu Carangola 54, 57, **62**, 131
Exu Caveira 8, 54, 57, 62, 76, 130, 131, 134, 190, 191, 236, 240, 241, **248–253**, 262
  Exu João Caveira **248**, **252**, **253**, 273
Exu do Cemitério 58, 130, **253**, **254**, 311
Exu Chama Dinheiro 135, 285, **303**, **304**
(see also Pedra Negra)
Exu do Cheiro 59, 76, 131, 133, 224, **236**, 237
Exu Cigano 135, 285, **290–293**

Exu do Coco 135, 305, **323**, **324**
Exu Corcunda 134, 240, **255**, **256**
Exu Curadôr 53, 58, 63, 131, 134, 216, 264, **271–273**, 306, 311

D

Exu das Duas Cabeças 6, **153**, **154**, 155, 161, 246

G

Exu Ganga 56, 58, 131, 135, 206, 285, **299**, **300**, 301, 311
  Exu Mulambo 206, 299
Exu Gererê 57, 58, 131, **311–313**
Exu Gira Mundo 58, 75, 79, 130, 134, 264, **274–276**, 311

I

Exu dos Infernos 77, 134, 285, **286**, 301

K

Exu Kaminaloá 52, 56, 58, 76, 131, 133, 195, **206–208**, 270

L

Exu do Lodo 57, 71, 135, 305, 314, **317–319**
Exu Lucifer 8, 89, 118, 134, 136, 139, 151, 152, 227, 284, 285, 289

M

Maioral 8, 8, 9, 10, 17, 77, 79, 101, 129, **136–145**, 151, 159, 195, 236, 237

Exu Malé 122, 131, 135, 285, **301**, **302**
Exu Mangueira 42, 56, 81, 129, 133, 195, **202–205**, 206
Exu Marabá 59, 130, 134, 264, **270**, **271**
Exu Marabô 42, 56, 65, 83, 129, 132, 161, **173–177**, 202, 305, 306
Exu Maré 131, 135, 305, **314–316**, 319
Exu Marinheiro 135, 305, **311–313**
Exu das Matas 53, 130, 133, 224, **228–230**
Exu Meia Noite 8, 6, 42, 61, 81, 121, 127, 130, 131, 133, 195, **215–220**, 233, 248, 272, 273
Exu Mirim 56, 131, 132, 161, **190–194**
Exu Morcego 8, 25, 53, 58, 59, 78, 81, 83, 94, 130, 132, 161, **185–188**, 200, 225, 252, 253
Exu Mor i, 5, 6, 73, 80, 81, 83, 89, 129, 136, 142, **146–152**, 155, 195, 326

N

Exu Nove Luzes 134, 264, **276**, **277**

O

Exu Omolu 131, **157–160**

P

Exu Pagão 57, 131, 135, 225, 285, **293–295**
Exu Pantera Negra 59, **65**, **66**, 74, 79, 131, 224
Exu Pedra Negra 59, 65, 130, **303**, **304** (see also Chama Dinheiro)
Exu Pemba 57, 131, 134, 264, **268**, **269**, 314
Exu Pimenta 53, 56, **63**, 131, 306
Exu Pinga Fogo **64**, **65**
Exu Pomba Gira 130, **155**, **156**, 163, 212
Exu Porteira 76, 117, 133, 164, 240, **241**, **242**

Q

Exu Quebra Galho 58, 75, 76, 130, 133, 224, **225**, **226**, 311
Exu Quirombô 57, 131, 133, 195, **198–200**

R

Exu Rei das Sete Encruzilhadas 56, 89, 129, 130, 132, 136, **162–165**
Exu dos Rios 42, 56, 60, 129, 130, 135, 305, **306**, **307**

S

Exu Serra Negra 73, 133, 224, **231**, **232**
Exu Sete Cachoeiras 59, 130, 135, 305, **308**
Exu Sete Catacumbas 133, 240, **244–246**
Exu Sete Cobras 133, 224, **234**, **235**
Exu Sete Covas 134, 240, **256**, **257**
Exu Sete Cruzeiros 133, 195, **200**, **201**
Exu das Sete Cruzes 58, 78, 82, 121, 130, 133, 195, **209–214**, 311
Exu Sete Encruzilhadas 76, 132, 161, 164
Exu Sete Estrelhas 188 (see also Exu das Sete Gargalhadas)
Exu das Sete Gargalhadas 132, 161, **188–190**, 214, 241
Exu Sete Liras 135, 285, 288, **289**, **289**, 301
Exu Sete Lombas 134, 264, **265–267** (see also Asa Negra)
Exu das Sete Montanhas 56, 131, 134, 264, **278**
Exu das Sete Pedras 59, 130, 133, 224, **233**, **234**
Exu Sete Pedras/Pedrinhas 135, 305, **309**, **310**
Exu Sete Poeiras 59, 130, 134, 264, **283**, **284**

Exu Sete Portas 59, 75, 130, 133, 195,
    214, 215
Exu Sete Sombras 59, 130, 133, 224, **227,
    228**, 230
Exu Sete Tumbas 133, 240, **243, 244**

T

Exu Tatá Caveira 57, 117, 131, 134, 264,
    279–282
Exu Tiriri 56, 129, 130, 132, 161, **178–181**,
    252, 253
Exu Tranca Ruas 8, 54, 56, 78, 119, 129,
    132, 161, **165–171**, 178, 258
Exu Tranca Tudo 59, 130, 133, 195,
    196–198, 230
Exu Tronqueira 59, 130

V

Exu Veludo 8, 56, 74, 76, 79, 129, 132, 161,
    181–185, 195, 200, 289, 290, 306
Exu dos Ventos 59, 130, 135, 305, **321–323**
  Tatá Ventaniana 321

Y

Exu Yangi 153
  (see Exu das Duas Cabeças)

Z

Exu Zé Pelintra 135, 285, **296–299**